'Eight left-of-centre historians have been expeditiously brought together to provide what the subtitle claims is "A New History of Britain Since 1939". All write clearly and sensibly, most with alert wit ... the political history which dominates this valuable book is important'

Scotland on Sunday

'[A] feisty and digestible collection of essays by leading academic historians ... It's all a good read and a happy breath of fresh air'   *The Scotsman*

'Stimulating ... these essays will provide useful pegs for the discussion of many recent historiographical debates and ... can point up the difficulties both in establishing "historical truth" and the importance of maintaining that, though there may be many versions of a historical event, not all interpretations are equally valid'

Times Educational Supplement

'In *From Blitz to Blair,* Nick Tiratsoo and his impressive cast of contributors seek to redress the imbalance in histories of Britain in the 20th century ... illuminating'   *The Tribune*

'Excellent history ... a compelling read'   *New Statesman*

'*From Blitz to Blair* performs two important functions. It takes the fight to those crude partisans of the New Right who would revise the history of the past sixty years to suit their current ideological purposes. While doing so it provides a bouncy introduction for those coming to the study of mid- to late-twentieth-century Britain for the first time'

Peter Hennessy

'An engaging ... survey of the postwar ...

... Supplement

From Blitz to Blair

A New History of Britain Since 1939

Edited by
NICK TIRATSOO

PHŒNIX

A PHOENIX PAPERBACK

First published in Great Britain
by Weidenfeld & Nicolson in 1997
This paperback edition published in 1998 by Phoenix,
a division of Orion Books Ltd,
Orion House, 5 Upper St Martin's Lane,
London WC2H 9EA

A CIP catalogue record for this book
is available from the British Library

ISBN: 0 75380 504 9

Printed and bound in Great Britain by
The Guernsey Press Co. Ltd, Guernsey,
Channel Islands

ACKNOWLEDGEMENTS

This book is in large part a collaborative enterprise. The editor would like to thank all the contributors for their interest and co-operation. He also wishes to gratefully acknowledge help and advice from Sandra Baum, Mark Clapson, Terence R. Gourvish, James Obelkevich, his parents Eric and Sylvia Tiratsoo, and the editorial team at Weidenfeld, especially Rebecca Wilson.

CONTENTS

Preface   ix

I   'Hunger ... is a Very Good Thing': Britain in the   1
     1930s
     Tony Mason

II   The Good War: 1939–1945   25
     Steven Fielding

III Churchill and the Price of Victory: 1939–1945   53
     Paul Addison

IV   Reconstructing Britain: Labour in Power 1945–1951   77
     Jim Tomlinson

V   'Never-Never Land': Britain under the   102
     Conservatives 1951–1964
     Dilwyn Porter

VI   The Wilson Years: 1964–1970   132
     Kenneth O. Morgan

VII 'You've Never Had It So Bad': Britain in the 1970s   163
     Nick Tiratsoo

VIII Miracle or Mirage?: The Thatcher Years 1979–1997   191
     Paul Hirst

     Notes   218
     Further Reading   224
     Contributors   228
     Index   231

PREFACE

In the past ten years or so, there has been a remarkable growth of interest in Britain's recent past. As the nation faces important choices about its future, a cacophony of voices have sought to explain the successes and failures of the post-war period. Much of the running in this debate has been made by historians and political commentators who identify with Thatcherism. They have created what amounts a new consensus, a version of events which has percolated into the media and the classroom. This book is a direct reply to these right-wing evangelists. Its aims to strip away the 'ideological distortion distilled from prejudice and hindsight'[1] that mars so much recent comment and to reinstate a view of British history which is both realistic and balanced.

The Thatcherite analysis begins with a characterization of the 1930s. It is argued that Britain at that time was largely a happy place, a land of social stability and entrepreneurial vigour which sat at the heart of a well-ordered empire. Some were undoubtedly poor but hard work and thrift offered the real possibility of advancement. Then came the war and four decades of catastrophic decline. A great superpower ended up as a bit-player in someone else's drama. What makes this collapse so regrettable, in the Thatcherites' view, is that it was entirely avoidable. Mistakes were made at every level. Governments created and then clung to an expensive welfare system which sapped economic vitality. Too much power was ceded to the trade unions. Successive Foreign

Secretaries allowed themselves to be pushed around by the Americans, and, worse still, by every tinpot dictator who wanted to tweak the lion's tail. Ultimately, the politicians of both main political parties were to blame. Tories like Macmillan and Heath lacked resolve and were unwilling to stand up for traditional principles. Labour simply taxed and spent, aiming only to aggrandize its working-class supporters. Fortunately, just as the country reached rock-bottom in the 1970s, a saviour came to the rescue. Mrs Thatcher was a different type of leader, who saw through the conceits and self-deception of the past. Thatcherism rescued Britain from the miasma and set it on the road to prosperity. Even New Labour has had to accept the decisive change of direction. The contrast is between the dark days of the past and the bright Thatcherite future.

Most of these points have been repeated so many times in the last few years that they seem self-evidently true. Nevertheless, each is deeply flawed, as the following chapters will show. Indeed, terms like decline and revival are themselves highly questionable. Ordinary Britons have seen their standards of living increase enormously in the post-war period. Britain has continued to excel in many fields, for example the arts and science. The country might have lost an empire but there are many who would ask whether this was a morally defensible or economically advantageous arrangement anyway. Nor are the achievements of the Thatcher governments as significant as some assert. Modest economic gains in the 1980s were obtained at extraordinary social cost, and in a way that squandered the once-and-for-all benefits of North Sea oil. The complexity of the recent past is such that it cannot possibly be crammed into a simple story of collapse and renewal.

What can be suggested with some confidence, surveying these years, is that the British have rarely agreed about how their country should be. Conservatives and their allies in the middle classes have continually sought to minimize change. The dream has been of warm beer and village cricket, the kind of landscape that is glimpsed in Thomas the Tank Engine stories. By contrast,

Labour has always had an urban edge, and to some extent embraced the technocratic and the liberal. At its best, the party has been both rational and compassionate, the proponent of industrial modernization and the creator of the welfare state, a party that is in step with the modern world. Put in these terms, the interesting question is why so much of Britain has remained impervious to Labour's charms.

It should be said at once that Labour governments have never has an easy time in office. Attlee and Wilson both took over at times of acute crisis. Each faced a hostile press and vested interests that were determined to prevent reform. On the other hand, it is clear that Labour has, to a certain extent, been the architect of its own misfortunes. Leadership problems sometimes limited effectiveness, as in the late 1960s. Moreover, the party has long countenanced practices and attitudes which have proved unacceptable to the ordinary voter. An organization that spoke of democracy did not practise what it preached. Generosity of spirit and a championing of the underdog could be replaced by a kind of Victorian fascination with improving the unwashed. The party used a tone that was overly masculine, subverting its relatively enlightened record on women's issues. Labour, in short, did not always speak either for or to the people.

Tony Blair's election in 1997 gives hope that some of these problems are being surmounted. Labour is now a much more open party than it has ever been before. An explicit commitment to work in partnership with others promises progress in many different directions. The politicians' reflex to control and manipulate may be a thing of the past. Traditional values, above all an emphasis on fairness, have not been jettisoned, though they are to be pursued with a greater degree of realism. Above all, Labour appears to have learned the essential lesson that a government cannot stand remote from the electorate. Dialogue is always preferable to diktat.

Nick Tiratsoo
May 1997

CHAPTER I

'HUNGER ... IS A VERY GOOD THING': BRITAIN IN THE 1930S

TONY MASON

There used to be no two ways of thinking about the 1930s. They were 'hungry' or 'frightened', the 'Devil's Decade' or, in the words of the poet W. H. Auden, that 'low, dishonest decade'. They were marked by the scar of economic depression and unemployment and further disfigured by the growing threat of war. Even Norman Tebbit, in his own eyes the epitome of upward mobility, recalled the hard times after his father, an assistant manager of a jewellers and pawnbrokers, owning a motorbike and sidecar, buying his own house and employing domestic help, lost his job in 1931 soon after Norman was born, and quickly lost in addition the house, motorbike and most of the family's possessions. There followed a series of moves down the housing market, including living in the top half of a small three-bedroom house in Edmonton, north London. Mr Tebbit senior cycled around looking for work – an image which his son would put to political use fifty years later in another depression – and eventually obtained casual work as a house painter. It was barely a living and needed to be supplemented by the bit of money Mrs Tebbit brought in by cleaning for a local schoolteacher. Norman recalls shopping late on a Saturday night in Edmonton market in order to pick up the cheap perishable food that stall-holders could not keep over a weekend. Rearmament orders at the Royal Small Arms factory in Enfield eventually led to regular work for his father from the mid 1930s.[1]

Norman Tebbit's father was one of the lucky ones. Unemployment was never less than 10 per cent of the insured population in the 1930s, at a time when some important groups such as agricultural workers, women and the self-employed were not included in the statistics. In a Britain in which three-quarters of the occupied population were manual workers, one in seven was out of work on an average working day, one in five in the worst years of 1931, 1932 and 1933. Unemployment tended to be concentrated in particular industries, coalmining, iron and steel, shipbuilding and textiles, for example, which themselves were located in particular geographical areas, mainly central Scotland, Northern Ireland, South Wales and the North-East and North-West of England. These became the so-called distressed areas and, later, special areas, subject to several government inquiries and legislation. In 1939, when unemployment had fallen to single figures in London and the South-East, the Midlands and the South-West, it remained 12 per cent in the North-East, 15 per cent in the North-West, 16 per cent in Scotland, 22 per cent in Wales and 26 per cent in Northern Ireland. Specific industries reflect a similar pattern, with 24 per cent of dockworkers and fishermen without jobs, 22 per cent of workers in linen textiles and pottery, 21 per cent in shipbuilding and 13 per cent in coalmining. Some of these were among the long-term workless who had had no jobs for over two years. In some mining towns like Crook in County Durham, three-quarters of the unemployed had been without a job for over five years.

But if unemployment was at its worst in particular industries and particular places, nowhere escaped its chill presence and few workers the anxiety and feelings of insecurity which accompanied it. In January 1939 the national weekly *Picture Post* featured one of the unemployed, selected from a group waiting outside the labour exchange in Peckham, south London. He was thirty-five and married with four children. He looked older, partly because he had no teeth. Bad teeth was a characteristic shared by many working-class people because of poor diets and an inability to afford dental treatment. When the young writer Christopher Isherwood wanted to identify with the workers he took up chocolate- and sweet-eating and stopped cleaning his teeth. The unemployed man outside the Peckham labour exchange had lost his teeth for other reasons. Although without a regular job for three years he had previously earned good money as a spray enamel maker. After nine years the chemical processes used in the work had rotted his teeth, which had all been extracted. This operation made him ill and cost him both five weeks off work and his job. Without work he could not afford dentures. His four children were aged between three and a half and nine, and three others had died in infancy. The family rented two rooms plus a kitchen and had £2 7s 6d a week on which to live. He visited the employment exchange on three days a week, on the last of which, Friday, he was paid his benefit. All of it was handed over to his wife except for a shilling or so which he spent on fares, cigarettes and newspapers. The family had applied for a council house but had been told that they would not become sufficiently overcrowded until one boy and one girl had reached the age of ten. His wife was characterized as a good manager who could make a little go a long way, as she needed to.

Their food was very basic. Breakfast was usually tea, bread and margarine with a little bacon on Sunday, a rare luxury. Dinner, the midday meal, was either a stew or boiled fish, with potatoes, bread and tea. On Sunday, it might be the cheapest broken meat plus potatoes. At night, the usual fare was cocoa, bread and margarine. Fresh fruit or fresh vegetables rarely entered the diet. This was poverty at its starkest, and it was not restricted to the families of the unemployed. Low wages, the poor health of the main breadwinner, old age or large families, singly or together dragged people below the poverty line, as social investigators like Booth and Rowntree found they had done at the end of the nineteenth century. In York 44 per cent of the families living in poverty in 1899 were still stricken by it in the 1930s. Even the old-style primary poverty still existed, making miserable the lives of 10 per cent of all Bristol families in 1937. Bristol was one of the most prosperous of British cities, yet 19 per cent of its families had insufficient income for a minimal level of decency.[2]

But over the last forty years or so this grim view of the 1930s has been increasingly challenged by a more optimistic account. Yes, say the revisionists, the old staple industries which had made Britain the nineteenth-century workshop of the world were in decline: but their decline was accompanied by the growth of newer industries such as motor manufacturing, electrical engineering, man-made fibres and chemicals. As the old staples had been spatially concentrated in the North of England, Scotland and South Wales, so these new sectors had their headquarters in the South, and particularly along an axis from the East Midlands to London, taking in the growing towns and cities of Leicester, Coventry, Birmingham and Oxford and the string of suburbs stretched across Western Avenue as it rushed towards London. The building trades had never been so busy and more new houses were going up in the 1930s than at any time before. Indeed, the 365,000 new houses built in 1936 was a number not to be exceeded until 1964. They were built largely for the growing numbers of white-collar and managerial staff and prosperous workers of the new industries, realizing their dream of home ownership and a better standard of living in the suburbs. Economic growth was about as fast as it had been at any time since the mid-nineteenth century and not much below what it would be in the 1950s and 1960s. Those in work had never had it so good. Real wages rose as prices fell, indeed real money wages increased faster than salaries. Increases in income tax and transfer payments to the poor via state welfare benefits meant significant improvements for many of the less well off. Family incomes were also affected by the gradual decline in family size, which spread to many working-class families between the wars.

All this resulted in a growth in consumption of a wide variety of products, from new furnishings to more sugar and tobacco. By 1939 most families had access to a radio – nearly 9,000,000

4

licences were issued – and many bought records to play on their gramophones. Sales of electricity had multiplied at least twenty times since the 1920s. Two million cars were on the roads, small by American standards but numbers that would not be surpassed in Britain until 1949. Half a million motorbikes and countless bicycles, many bought on hire-purchase for a few shillings a week, gave new meaning to the idea of individual mobility.

More people had more to spend on entertainment and leisure than ever before. By 1939 eleven million workers were entitled to one week's paid holiday, and twenty million visitors went to the English seaside in that year. Dance-halls were one of the crazes of the 1930s, public houses continued to do good business in spite of a decline in the per-capita consumption of drink, and the cinema finally emerged as the mass entertainment industry *par excellence*, helped by the spread of sound and the development of Technicolor. Twenty million tickets a week were sold in 1939; in Liverpool, 40 per cent of the population went once a week and 25 per cent twice or more. More people were buying daily and Sunday newspapers, and savings banks deposits had doubled since 1920. The verdict of the new historiography has been unequivocal: qualitatively and quantitatively things were much better than before. Epithets like 'hungry' just don't fit the reality of most people's lives. But it was a fragile prosperity, which in one of the world's richest countries, backed by its largest empire, was still barely skin-deep, leaving large numbers of the population deprived, especially in important areas of life such as health, housing and education.

There was, of course, no comprehensive national health service. National health insurance covered only 42 per cent of the population in 1938. Friendly societies provided health insurance for only about a quarter of the population. Many working-class households contributed small regular sums to support their local hospitals – 62 per cent in Bristol in 1937, for example – but many others could not afford even that. In fact, despite statutory scales and departmental standards, there was a great diversity in the health care available from one place to another, with the areas of high unemployment unable to generate sufficient resources from local rates to provide the necessary services. Prosperous and progressive local authorities were building new health centres with modern facilities, but things were nothing like so good in the distressed areas. Unemployment caused ill health and revealed it. The longer a man was without a job the more difficult it was to maintain social contacts and living standards. Not only were the diet and physical health of the poor and the unemployed worse, those out of work complained of feeling unwell more than those with jobs. Unemployment in the 1930s was a very stressful condition.

Women's health suffered more than men's. Women ate less and in general had less money to spend on themselves. Married women suffered all the physical stresses and strains of childbearing and rearing and having to make ends meet, and a growing proportion had to combine these domestic burdens with paid work outside the home. Among the poor, and particularly in areas like County Durham and South Wales, there was a slow deterioration in the health of younger women. Maternal mortality rates only began to fall in the late 1930s, and improvements in the figures for infant mortality slowed down in that decade and were declining more slowly than in other comparable countries. Liverpool's infant mortality rate was two and a half times that of Rotterdam in 1936, Birmingham's twice as much, and the infant death rate in Glasgow in 1937 higher than Tokyo's. And rates varied between poor districts and prosperous ones even across the same city. In Plymouth in 1938 the infant mortality rate ranged from 16 per 1,000 live births to 109 per 1,000. Nor was there always the sympathy from the professional health workers that the sick had a right to expect. A punitive attitude persisted towards the poor. The Medical Officer of Health for Liverpool believed that dental care was not required in Maternity and Child Welfare Centres because few teeth were required for mastication and women were only pressing for dental services for 'cosmetic' reasons.[3]

Not that eating was all it was cracked up to be. As the Conservative MP Sir F. Fremantle noted in the House of Commons in November 1936, 'Hunger, to a certain extent, is a very good thing.' He was expressing some doubt about the benefits of school milk and school dinners, which would merely encourage less to be provided by 'bad or careless parents at home'. Only 2 per cent of the school population were enjoying free school meals in 1939. By 1936 it was clear that many working-class families were on diets which fell well below the scales recommended by the British Medical Association. Classic contemporary studies by Dr G. C. M. McGonigle, the Medical Officer of Health for Stockton-on-Tees, *Poverty and Public Health*, written with J. Kirby (1937), and by J. Boyd Orr, *Food, Health and Income* (1936), an examination of over a thousand family budgets, clearly established the links between poverty, inadequate diet and poor housing, with Boyd Orr finding that over 50 per cent of the population had diets inadequate for good health. Of course, such conclusions were challenged by the Conservative-dominated national government, but, prompted by a combination of poverty studies, even the members of that administration felt something had to be done to improve the physical fitness of the nation. In 1935, for example, 35 per cent of applicants for the armed forces were declared unfit, and there was a growing awareness of Germany's and Italy's concentration on health and physical fitness. A government-sponsored fitness campaign in 1937–8 based around the Physical Training and Recreation Act was the feeble response.

To sum up, improvements had been made in the people's health, but far too many had not benefited from them. The quality of life and the chances of death still depended on where a person was born and brought up: 30,000 people died in Northumberland and Durham, Lancashire and Cheshire and South Wales each year due to 'local conditions'. Even in booming London there were boroughs which recorded consistently higher death rates than elsewhere, and they were the predominantly working-class areas of Bermondsey, Finsbury, Poplar and South-wark. Death rates in most industrial areas were at least one-quarter and sometimes half as much again as the average for England and Wales. Class differences in mortality rates were increasing between the wars, when standards of health ought to have been much higher as spending on health services as a proportion of gross national product had risen from 1 per cent in 1921 to 2 per cent in 1937. The new facilities were unevenly spread and led to glaring disparities within and between families, classes and regions.

Much the same pattern can be seen in that other crucial area for social well-being, housing. By September 1939, over 40 per cent of British families were living in houses built since 1911. Many of these were in the expanding suburbs, features found throughout Britain but especially marked in the more prosperous Midlands and South. The number of people living in the suburbs of the thirteen great conurbations of Southern England rose by half between the wars, so that by 1938 they contained 13 per cent of the total population of Great Britain, more than all of Tyneside, South Wales and Clydeside put together. But the majority of the British population had not graduated to the fresh air and extra space of the suburbs in 1939. Nearly 8 per cent of the family population of Great Britain remained overcrowded in 1939, with more than two people sharing each room. Five per cent of the older houses were in such poor condition that they were scheduled for slum-clearance. In 1939 over a million families were still too poor to pay rent for decent housing on the open market. Facilities remained primitive for many families. Only 10 per cent of working-class houses in Middlesbrough had a bath. Few working-class houses had access to piped hot water, lavatories were usually outside and, apart from the kitchen and living room, rooms would rarely, if ever, be heated. Britain was largely a coal-fire society with the open grate the focus of most households. Cheap coal meant a fire could be kept going all day from first thing in the morning to last thing at night. Cosy it could be, but sooty and dirty it also was. Research by the Carnegie Trust in Cardiff, Glasgow and Liverpool at the end of the 1930s suggested that one-quarter of all homes were dirty and untidy, 50 per cent fairly clean and tidy and only one-third very clean and tidy. Some 8.7 million households were wired for electricity in 1939, 65 per cent of the total, but that left 35 per cent lacking the most attractive source of power of the twentieth century. Not only were a third of all houses not wired up; many of those working-class homes which had electricity had been fitted with only the basic lighting circuit or a single plug socket, so that the growth in consumption of electricity in these years was concentrated among the better-off in the prosperous South-East.[4]

Life chances, health and housing all left much to be desired in the Britain of 1939, and education was another area of exclusion for large numbers of young Britons. Although the school-leaving age had been raised to fourteen, and although the half-time system (whereby children employed in textile mills spent half their time in work and half in the classroom) had been abolished, few working-class children were able to continue their education beyond fourteen. This was partly because so many families still needed the wages, however small, that their children could earn, and partly because of the costs of secondary schooling. Most grammar or technical schools were fee-paying, with only a very few free scholarships offered. The parents of about 5 per cent of children paid £250 a year to send their children to grammar schools. This ensured that 60 per cent of grammar-school places went to these middle-class fee payers whether their children were suitable for an academic education or not. Less than 10 per cent of working-class boys reaching the age of eleven in the 1930s entered selective secondary schools. It was a long-remembered disappointment, and many former working-class boys and girls felt with some bitterness that though they had the ability to cope with a grammar-school education, they had been denied the opportunity. Jane Taverner was looking back to her schooling in the 1920s but her recollections can stand for many in the following decade:

I was put in for the scholarship. I remember the rating I got because I didn't pass, but I didn't try because I knew that if I passed, I couldn't go. I wanted to pass, but you see it was no use, because although there was help, it wouldn't have been enough for our family. Actually, I didn't try and I was hauled over the coals. Headmistress had me in didn't she? 'Why didn't you pass? What did you do?' And suppose I didn't answer. 'I don't know,' I said … To this day I see her. We have a chatter and she'll tell me at times, 'And I'll never know why you didn't pass that scholarship,' and I've never told her…[5]

The pseudo-scientific belief that there existed three types of mind was used by authority figures inside and outside government to justify the unjustifiable. The three types of mind were the abstract, the mechanical and the concrete (this latter term, presumably, because holders of this type were difficult to penetrate). Those with abstract casts of mine were fitted for grammar schools and professional jobs; those with mechanical minds were technical-school material and suitable for craftsman's jobs; and those with concrete minds were destined for modern schools and unskilled work. This was to be at the core of the later 1944 Education Act. All this meant that only 4 per cent of seventeen-year-olds were receiving full-time education in Britain at the end of the 1930s. Only 1 per cent of school-leavers had any paper qualifications, and only one in sixteen finished up in skilled employment. It seems entirely appropriate that the investigation into British young people sponsored by the Carnegie Trust carried out between 1937 and 1939 (but not published until 1943) should have been called 'Disinherited Youth'.

It is important to underline how many people had their lives blighted by poor health, little or inadequate health care, bad housing and minimal education. But these were symptoms of the problem rather than the problem itself. Why did so few people have money to spare after they had met the costs of the minimum necessary for basic food, clothes, shelter, warmth and light? Britain was a rich country, but most of the privately owned wealth was in a very few hands. John Hilton calculated in 1938 that the 1.5 per cent of the British people worth £10,000 or more owned 56 per cent of personally ownable wealth and the half per cent of the population with £100,000 or more owned 18 per cent of total wealth. The same pattern emerged from an investigation of incomes. Those receiving over £10,000 a year were only one-half of 1 per cent of all income receivers but got 6 per cent of the total aggregate income, while the eleven and a half million with incomes of less than £2 10s a week, comprising two-thirds of all income recipients, got only one-third of the total. A further five million people received between £2 10s and £5 a week. Three out of every four adults in 1938 possessed less than £100. Most of the additional purchasing power which had come into the hands of workers and their families via falling prices and rising real wages had been spent on 'better feeding and clothing and housing and furnishing and holidaying and quite right too'. But it had also gone on 'pools, perms and pints; on cigarettes, cinemas and singles-and-splashes; on turnstiles, totalizators, and twiddlems' and all manner 'of two pennyworths of this and that', and also, it should be said, on buying bicycles or gramophones on hire-purchase and the weekly burial insurance premiums. What was difficult was putting a worthwhile sum by for that inclement weather which would certainly affect most families.[6]

Small savers were remarkably numerous, as the eleven million with deposits in the Post Office Savings Bank at the end of the 1930s demonstrate. Even over half of the very poorest families saved something weekly, usually amounting to a few pence for boots or clothes, and money went into Hospital Saturday Funds and the ubiquitous burial insurance. But all of this, including most of the money in the Post Office, was in very small amounts. Saving up the small fortune, getting together a decent lump sum, was exceptional, a fact underlined by John Hilton's story about the clerk who had never earned more than £4 10s a week but was retiring at sixty-five because he had £5,000 put by. At his farewell dinner, he told his fellow clerks how he had been able to do it: first, by his own abstemious and thrifty habits; even more, thanks to the carefulness and good management of his wife; but still more he owed his good fortune to the fact than an aunt had recently died and left him £4,957. To save large sums you must handle large sums, and most people never would. The only way for the vast majority to get together that lump sum which would provide some security to fight off the assassins of sickness and unemployment was to win it on the football pools. Gambling was Britain's second biggest industry in 1939, with a turnover in excess of £200 million a year. Ten million people filled in the pools every week, all no doubt hoping to win the £350,000 one lucky winner received, about £4 million at 1997 prices. Most would probably have been satisfied to have three, or perhaps four, figures in some cosy bank account. The pools were the National Lottery of their day. John Hilton was advocating something like one in 1938, to be run by the state rather than by a profit-making company. A shilling in the pound of all income would go into a pool, 'out of which lovely damsels in smart uniforms shall draw blindfold, once a week ... so many names of so many Toms, Dicks and Harrys ... Peggies, Joans and Kates, each one of whom shall thereupon get ... a thousand pounds'.

In 1939 one out of five families had no possessions but pawn tickets and debts with incomes barely enough to keep body and soul together. These families often lacked food, certainly lacked fortune and opportunity and frequently enough probably lacked joy. 'Another three out of ten families have only just enough coming in to make ends meet. Their children are not going to have much of a chance in life.' A few would go up in the world: the vast majority would follow in father's footsteps, to the dead-end jobs, low wages and hand-to-mouth life. Most of the rest lived in an insecure world 'suspended between the heaven of relative affluence and the hell of gnawing want', and all this at the centre of the world's richest and most powerful empire.

The contrast between the lifestyles of the many and those of the well-off minority was stark and never more visible than during each May to July when the aristocratic and fashionable descended on London for a round of visits, parties, balls and sporting events and when the young daughters of the rich came out as debutantes into the marriage market of the London Season, culminating in their presentation at court. Rhoda Walker-Heneage-Vivian was the daughter of an admiral and lived in a castle in Wales as well as a large town house in London where the Season was spent. A typical day in July 1939 saw her rise at 10.00 a.m., enjoy a leisurely breakfast and then go window-shopping around Oxford Street and Bond Street. A lunch party with other 'debs' was followed by a visit to the cinema and then, in the evening, dinner and dancing until the early hours. Her monthly allowance of £20 to 'buy accessories' was more than most families earned in the same period. The food which was thrown away after the lavish dinners and suppers would have been very welcome in many poor households.

The middle classes too had bags of disposable income, which enabled the higher-income groups to sit down to elaborate meals in large, well-equipped houses. They bought private health care, insurance and pensions and private education for their children, especially the boys. They also had a choice of a growing range of consumer goods, from clothes to motorcars, from tennis racquets to telephones. The telephone became an important part of middle-class daily life, especially for ringing up local shopkeepers and tradesmen and for arranging social events. Possession of a telephone was a 1930s status symbol. At the beginning of the decade both Bournemouth and Epsom had one telephone for every 3.5 households; Barnsley had one for every 17 and Merthyr Tydfil one for every 47.[7]

The middle class and their children had more leisure time than the majority, which was translated into more excursions to entertainments and sporting events and, in London and the South-East especially, trips to 'town'. All sections of the middle class could be found taking tea and almost rubbing shoulders in Lyons Corner Houses. Their prosperity was also translated into more and longer holidays. Both the middle classes and the aristocracy maintained their comfortable lifestyles by the employment of a large number of mainly female servants, who did all the fetching, carrying, cleaning and cooking for wages which, even accounting for the fact that board, lodging and working clothes were often found, were scandalously low. Even many lower-middle-class households had one maid of all work, often sadly known as the 'slavey'. Never had so much been done for so few. Could different government economic policies have improved the lot of more of the people? Perhaps the government could have managed the economy with a more imaginative touch?

Apart from three years of minority Labour administrations, the Conservative Party dominated the whole of the 1920s and 1930s, and its remedy for restructuring the economy, which the persistent unemployment in the old staple industries reflected, was deflation. The interests of the City, the banks and financial institutions in general were placed ahead of the priorities of manufacturing industry. Successive Tory governments were happy to live with long-term regional unemployment as part of the price which had to be paid for the adjustments that the economy required. In fact, many industrialists failed to oppose the policy in part because, like many Conservatives, they were obsessed with the idea that labour was at the root of the problems of British industry, not management. Perhaps a less extreme deflationary policy would have improved many individual lives. There were alternatives to British-style deflation practised in several European countries, but British governments were cautious and reluctant to innovate. There was little chance of a British New Deal. Lloyd George, Oswald Mosley and J. M. Keynes, all in favour of more government intervention, had only limited support in economics and political high places.[8]

When the Great Depression of 1929–32 added cyclical to the already existing structural unemployment, it might have provided the opportunity for government to try something new. But very little changed. True, two sacred cows were slaughtered. In 1931 Britain came off the gold standard and the pound was allowed to depreciate with the aim of helping exports by cutting their price. Bank rate remained at 2 per cent in the years 1932 to 1939, though how far lower interest rates actually helped economic recovery is still open to argument. Certainly bank lending does not seem to have grown very much in the 1930s.

The other sacred cow to be abandoned was free trade. The Import Duties Act of 1932 brought in a general tariff of 20 per cent, exempting some foods and raw materials and Empire products. Again, it is not clear what impact this had on economic activity, though it may have helped business confidence and some industries may have benefited, but it seems unlikely that the project of industrial rationalization was furthered very much. It might have created a platform for more government intervention and expansionist policies, but they did not come.

As for the unemployed, they required more rapid economic growth or a public works programme, which would have lifted morale even if its economic effect in the depressed areas might have been limited. The Treasury had always opposed public works and did not really change its attitude from Churchill's statement in 1929 that 'very little additional employment and no permanent employment could ... be created by State borrowing and State expenditure'. There was a great reluctance to unbalance the budget, particularly in the context of the high cost of servicing the national debt and the adverse trade balance of the 1930s. Nonetheless, political considerations did produce the Special Areas Act of 1934, but the government's heart was hardly in it, as is demonstrated by the fact that two of the worst-hit areas, Lancashire and Northern Ireland, were mysteriously excluded. Two Commissioners were given one million pounds a year each to spend, but few genuine jobs were created. Indeed some of the money was spent eccentrically, sums going for example to local Women's Institutes in Durham to organize cookery classes while repeated requests to provide funds for boots and clothing for the poor in South Wales were refused. Further legislation in 1936–7 augmented the powers of the Commissioners and some trading estates were built in areas of high unemployment, such as the Team Valley in County Durham.

Rearmament began in 1935 and was deficit-financed from 1937. By 1938 it had created a million jobs in iron and steel, coal and engineering, reviving the old staples in some of the most depressed regions. Placing some rearmament contracts in the North-East or Scotland was the nearest the government came to economic planning and reflation. And if rearmament *did* reduce unemployment, more could have been done earlier. But the Conservative governments of the 1930s were in no mood to experiment, anxious not to destroy a fragile business confidence which might seriously upset the economy, provoke political repercussions at home and undermine Britain's world-power status. But one should always be suspicious of Conservatives who say 'there is no alternative'.

Britain's persistent economic problems were one of the main factors which produced a tentative attitude by government to the rise of Fascism in Europe. Britain's Empire conferred world-power status on its small offshore island but with an economy which could not deliver the resources to meet the responsibilities. Foreign and military policymakers suffered nightmares about a war on three fronts against Germany in the west, Italy in the Mediterranean and Japan in the Far East. The British did not want a war, certainly not in Europe, but British policy had long aimed to prevent domination of the continent by any single power. Soon after 1933, Germany seemed to be a problem again. There were other anxieties. With the next war in mind Stanley Baldwin told the House of Commons in 1932:

> I think it is well also for the man in the street to realise that there is no power on earth that can protect him from being bombed. Whatever people may tell him the bomber will always get through, and it is very

easy to understand that, if you realise the area of space. The only defence is offence, which means that you have to kill more women and children more quickly than the enemy...[9]

The related anxiety was that the working class would let the side down and be unable to stand the strain. There would be panic in the streets.

Britain may have wanted peace and the British Empire may have needed it, but the omens were not good even before Hitler grasped power in Germany in 1933. The talks and conferences on disarmament had made little progress. And there was a growing feeling among the public which mattered – politicians, civil servants, journalists – that Germany had been too harshly punished after the 1914–18 war and that the Versailles Treaty had been too punitive. Germany had lost its colonial empire as well as territory in Europe to the new states of Poland and Czechoslovakia. The Rhineland was occupied and demilitarized. Perhaps Germany's grievances against the peace treaty were genuine. If all those Germans scattered about Central and Eastern Europe merely wanted to live together under the same government, what could be wrong with that? It was common sense and fair play to make judicious concessions. It was out of such attitudes that the policy was born which became known as appeasement: identify the real grievances of a major player and respond sensibly before they led to war. Again there were policy alternatives, such as an alliance with Germany's enemies, the USSR for example, but since the Russian Revolution of 1917 most British politicians had been anti-Communist, and anyway alliances seemed to be a throwback to the bad old days before 1914 when they were supposed to keep the peace via the balance of power but had clearly failed. There was the League of Nations, but it was only as effective as the big powers wanted it to be, and although there was much support for it among the British it could neither inhibit Japanese aggression in Manchuria in 1931 nor prevent the cheap victory of Italian forces in Abyssinia in 1935.

Appeasement could look like weakness. While Italy and Germany helped Franco's rebels in the Spanish Civil War, the British stood firm on the policy of non-intervention. Twelve months earlier Britain and Germany had signed a naval agreement accepting the fact of German rearmament and the breach of the Versailles Treaty which it entailed. Nineteen-thirty-six saw German troops march into the previously demilitarized Rhineland; it was, after all, their own backyard, as many apologists were quick to point out. Doing nothing was sending the wrong messages to Hitler. But if he simply wanted all Germans in a single state, then surely that could and ought to be done without war. But appeasement ignored the persecution of the Jews and other ethnic minorities in Germany, along with dissenters and members of the labour movement, many of whom were shut up in concentration camps.

The Anschluss with Austria was no problem – Austrians were Germans anyway – but the next phase focused on the trickier issue of those Germans living inside the borders of Czechoslovakia in the Sudetenland. For one thing, the French had a treaty with the Czechs, each promising help if the other was attacked. But in 1938, with Hitler threatening to liberate the Sudenten Germans by force, the British Prime Minister, Neville Chamberlain, nearly seventy and never having travelled by plane before, flew to Germany three times in order to ensure the peaceful detachment of the Sudetenland. If at first you don't succeed, fly, fly and fly again . . . It was peace with honour but, more important to most of the British, peace in our time. There was widespread relief when the Munich agreement was signed. Nobody in Britain wanted war, but after the relief was the nagging question, where was all this going to stop? *Punch* published a famous cartoon showing a grave and a headstone on which was written 'Adolf Hitler. This is my last territorial claim in Europe.' Should we have helped a faraway country of which we knew nothing? In March 1939, Germany invaded Prague, showing that Nazi ambitions were not limited to Germans and provoking the British government to give its guarantee to Poland. Controversy still surrounds the failure of the British government to forge an agreement with the Soviet Union, which could have prevented the Nazi–Soviet pact that, along with the introduction of conscription, spoilt the end of the holiday season in August 1939. Would a different foreign policy have avoided war?

Britain was a major player in Europe, but its Empire ensured that its interests were worldwide. Yet it was no more able to act independently, without alliances, outside Europe than inside it. In the second half of the 1930s the nightmare of a war on three fronts seemed likely to become reality. Indeed Britain was so anxious to remain on good terms with Japan that the Foreign Office secretly told the British Olympic Committee to support Tokyo as the site of the 1940 Olympic Games at a meeting of the IOC in the face of widespread feelings that the Games could not be held in a country at war with China, a fellow member of the Olympic movement. The Empire was vulnerable, particularly in the East, Singapore, Hong Kong, maybe even India and Australia. But a major war in the Far East could hardly be successfully prosecuted by Britain alone, either economically or militarily, and it was very late in the day before the Dominions realized this. Even British rearmament, it could be argued, came reluctantly and therefore late. The point was that British warships could go to the Pacific only if Europe was peaceful. A similar balancing act was performed with the Royal Air Force. Was its role to defend France if invaded, fulfilling Baldwin's assurance that the British frontier was on the Rhine, or merely to defend the British Isles? Expanding the Army so that it could intervene meaningfully in Europe was thought ruinously expensive, and one of the several reasons for the Munich agreement was that the British Chiefs of Staff did not think the forces ready to fight in 1938.

It was a good thing that the 'White Dominions', by 1939 autonomous communities within the Empire and equal in status to Britain, agreed to ensure that the British were not standing alone in 1940. But if the Empire was still ready to answer the call of the Crown it was also part of the problem. Britain no longer had the power and the resources to play the old world role and, as the Government of India Act of 1935 implied, it no longer had the will to prevent determined nationalists from moving down the highway towards the city called independence. Yet imperial attitudes and pretensions remained. Egypt had been officially 'independent' since 1936 but, as has been often pointed out, British troops were stationed there to protect the imperial artery of Suez as if Egypt was a more arid version of Hertfordshire. The old British Empire ended with the Statute of Westminster in 1931, but Churchill would still be telling Eden in 1944 that the maintenance of the Empire was one of the things the British had been fighting for and which would not be given up.

The shadow of war was never clearer than over the Britain of 1939, yet it had been a factor in the lives of many of the people for most of the 1930s. Britain could neither go it alone nor construct a worthwhile series of alliances that might not have prevented war but would certainly have given the people at home and in the Empire more confidence about its outcome. Peace at Munich had been received with widespread gratitude, but with the passing of time the Munich agreement had come to look shabby, just one more piece of short-termism. And if war was to come, and the air attacks which British policymakers had so long feared, where was the protection for the people? The first letter to the editor in *The Times* on 2 January 1939 dealt with the need for deep bomb-proof shelters in Britain. It pointed to the lessons which ought to be learned from the air raids currently going on in Barcelona. Deep shelters were better than evacuation of populations because evacuation damaged family life and morale. There was no sign, in 1939, that Britain was building them.

What was it like to live in the 1930s? Of course it depended on a lot of things: whether you were male or female, where you were born, who your parents were, how old you were, how fit or how ill, how large a family you were part of, what sort of education you had had, whether you were working or not, and if you were what sort of job with what rate of pay, what kind of house in what kind of neighbourhood. The impact of the Great Depression was very different for very different people. To a considerable extent unemployment was concentrated, and for those with jobs, especially in the new industries in the Midlands and the South-East, wages were improving: fitters in engineering were earning more than coalminers, and real earnings improved for many workers as prices came down. The unemployed carried much of the burden as the painful market-driven restructuring of the economy began, and little was done to remedy the structural causes of poverty. If increased means and increased leisure are what civilizes man, and presumably woman, the unemployed had neither, certainly not the former, and having no job did not make them a leisured class. Yes, they could fall back on the safety net of unemployment insurance or the dole, but like most state benefits these were not designed to secure longer-term subsistence and often fell below the minimum scales recommended by the medical profession and other experts. One-tenth of the population, including one-quarter of all children, were living either on such benefits or on their low-wage equivalents. Many of the poor were unaware of their rights and it was in informing the jobless about theirs that the National Unemployed Workers' Movement (NUWM) attracted most of the support it did.

Old ideas that the poor were divided between the deserving and the undeserving resurfaced in the form of a belief that the working class were responsible for their own misfortunes and that any significant relief of them would not be in the public interest. But, as we have seen, it was not just the unemployed and the very poor, together with their families, who were troubled by this state of affairs. Much of the population lived insecure lives not knowing when it might be their turn to join the dole queue, with all which that might mean for both them and their families, and many others lived a hand-to-mouth existence or made ends meet only after great struggles and personal sacrifices. Almost three-quarters of the total population of Britain were ordinary working people and few can have escaped the feelings of anxiety and insecurity which inevitably accompanied widespread unemployment. Life was hard for most, as the class-specific average infant mortality figures clearly reveal: Social Class I, thirty-three deaths per 1,000 live births; Social Class III, skilled manual workers, fifty-eight deaths per 1,000 live births; and Social Class V, unskilled manual workers, seventy-seven deaths per 1,000 live births.

That so many were in the same boat was probably one of the reasons for the lack of a real political challenge to the Tories. Political extremism got nowhere. The Facists collapsed after violence at a rally at Olympia in 1934 and their anti-Semitism had little appeal outside London. Communist Party membership went up from 2,000 in 1930 to 18,000 on the eve of the war, and the party and individual members were undoubtedly influential in trade unions and among the unemployed via the NUWM, but they were never a political force. In the 1935 general election they managed to contest only two seats of the 615 in the Commons (thought they did win one). The 1930s was the Tory decade, as an anxious electorate turned to the Conservative-dominated national government after the economic crisis and the collapse of the minority Labour government in 1931. Conservative Party candidates polled 53.7 per cent of the vote in 1935 and were never under any pressure from the Opposition. Although their rhetoric was the language of class harmony their predominance was based on the creation of an anti-labour coalition against the political idea of the working class. Many frightened, ignorant, pessimistic and, it has to be said, convinced workers voted for them in the two general elections of the decade.

The Conservative Party had money, organization and members, whereas the Labour Party was badly damaged by the débâcle of 1931 and, though it made something of a recovery later, it remained a trade union party dependent on the old industrial areas of the North and Celtic fringe. In the general election of 1935, in the whole of Southern and South-East England, from Lincolnshire to Cornwall, but excluding London, the Conservatives and their allies won 156 seats, whereas Labour won only 15. The government faced no effective challenge from that source and indeed its power reflected the cautious traditionalism still dominant in most sectors of society. The gross inequalities that have been emphasized in this chapter did not produce much social conflict. There was a general acceptance of the structure of authority and the values of King and Empire. And when Edward VII stepped out of line in 1936 with the divorced Mrs Simpson, he had little alternative to abdication. The poor may have been bottom dogs at home but they could console themselves that the British were top dogs in the colonies. Employers were even more powerful than usual with unemployment so high. Crime grew at the modest rate of only 6 per cent per annum and most of that was for fairly minor property offences. The annual average number of persons committed for trial on a charge of murder was smaller in the 1930s than in both the decade before 1914 and the one after 1945. A shared national culture of newspapers and radio, a consumption and leisure boom for those fortunate enough to stay in work and a better welfare system than many had experienced before, although you had to watch your Ps and Qs to take advantage, all contributed to a shared reluctance to change. Getting by was hard for most folk and probably as much as they could manage. Narrow horizons and introversion was widespread as people got on with their own lives with little interest in the outside world. This was the poverty of desire which John Burns had identified and about which Ernest Bevin would later complain. Examples of it abounded. Mass-Observation analysed 15,000 conversations recorded in Bolton and discovered that on a normal day less than 1 per cent were about politics.[10] Only half the population regularly turned out to vote in local elections. Most people accepted their lot, made the best of it and a virtue out of doing without.

Ignorance, indifference and lack of leadership came from a government grown smug after long years in power without effective challenge. But they were presiding over an unequal and unfair society, going nowhere, and for many of whose members surviving was enough. Britain was a very traditional society of Gentlemen and Players, where there was little room for social mobility. Most people were locked into the family they were born into and would almost certainly follow in father's or mother's footsteps. Such modernizing and progressive spirits as there were were easily frustrated. Optimistic interpretations of such a society seem a clear case of defending the bad against the worst. And at the end of a decade of unemployment and insecurity came a war for which an overstretched Britain was hardly well prepared and in which it was only saved from defeat by first the Empire, then America and finally the German obsession with Lebensraum in the east. Britain was still one of the richest countries in the world in the 1930s, yet far too many were excluded from its benefits. It was a decade of missed chances and wasted opportunities. Britain ought to have been a better place to live.

CHAPTER II

THE GOOD WAR:
1939–1945

STEVEN FIELDING

For many Britons born after 1945, perhaps even some reading this book, the Second World War is as distant as the Battle of Waterloo.[1] Their understanding of the conflict has been obtained through watching black-and-white films such as *The Dam Busters*, *The Wooden Horse* or *The Colditz Story* on Sunday-afternoon television which, to say the least, present a very peculiar view of the period. Perhaps there are those with an active interest in the war, but most of these enjoy a rather unhealthy obsession with military uniforms, tanks and guns. Thus, for most in their early forties or younger, the war is a confused jumble of images: weary soldiers retreating from Dunkirk; Winston Churchill making his Victory sign; St Paul's Cathedral majestic during the Blitz; cheery Cockneys singing as bombs fell overhead; and Churchill, once more, on the balcony of Buckingham Palace waving to crowds cheering the news of Hitler's defeat.

So far as professional historians are concerned, there is, of course, a more sophisticated and informed appreciation of the war and its impact on British society and politics. The classic accounts of this period are Paul Addison's *The Road to 1945* (1975) and Angus Calder's *The People's War* (1969). Reading these works it is clear that for many of the generation which lived through it, either as adults or as children, the Second World War was more than Vera Lynn singing 'We'll meet again': it was the most significant – and benevolent – of events. This is because it was thought to have promoted social solidarity and the belief that government could pursue policies which avoided mass unemployment and gave citizens protection from the worst effects of illness and old age through a welfare state. According to this view, wartime egalitarianism reached its consummation at the 1945 general election. This was when both manual workers and members of the middle class joined together in unprecedented numbers to vote for the Labour Party so that it could build a 'New Jerusalem'. As the radical historian A. J. P. Taylor wrote in the 1960s, for these and other reasons 1939–45 had been a 'good war'.

᾿ This perception of the war was especially popular on the left and centre-left. For Michael Foot, Labour leader between 1980 and 1983, and for many others, invoking the 'spirit of 1945' conjured up the hope that the party could revive this lost wartime idealism amid the dark, divisive days of Thatcherism. Perhaps one reason why Labour suffered such a crushing defeat in 1983 was that those who had no direct experience of the war failed to understand what Foot was going on about. For many of them, if the war had been responsible for the policies of the subsequent thirty years, it had little to recommend it. This was what 1970s punk rockers had, almost literally, spat their venom against: post-war boredom, apathy, national decline and economic failure – England could not even qualify for World Cups any more. Whatever might be said of the Conservative leader Margaret Thatcher, at least she was against all that.

It was hardly a coincidence, then, that the Conservative victory in 1979 uncovered another view of the war which took its cue from those who saw government intervention in economy and society as evil. Some historians, particularly Corelli Barnett in *The Audit of War* (1986), suggested that the conflict had accellerated or even initiated national decline. According to this interpretation, one endorsed in Thatcher's memoirs, the left had set the political agenda during the war. While Churchill was preoccupied with defeating Hitler, Labour members of his coalition government fostered what she describes as an 'essentially socialist mentality' in the British people. This was underpinned by the mixing of men and women from different backgrounds in the services which aroused, in the better-off, an 'acute twinge of social conscience and a demand for the state to step in and ameliorate social conditions'. Thus many members of the wartime generation wanted the state to 'take the foremost position in our national life and summon up a spirit of collective endeavour in peace as in war'. This was a dangerous illusion. Quoting the contemporary right-wing journalist Colm Brogan, Thatcher considered that in 1945 the country had 'voted to eat their cake and have it ... for high wages and low production and a world of plenty'. To make matters worse, this soft-headed collectivism had gone on to 'distort' society until it inevitably collapsed in the late 1970s, to be finally disposed of by Thatcher's own governments.[2]

There are, then, two quite distinct views of the war. This chapter is an attempt to make sense of them, to try to answer the question: was the Britain which emerged in July 1945 any better than the one that went to war in September 1939? Was the idealism so praised in earlier accounts of the conflict as misplaced as later critics suggest? In other words, did Britain have a 'good' or 'bad' war?

When Britain went to war with Germany on Sunday, 3 September 1939, the country had been governed by a Conservative-dominated 'national' coalition for eight years. Neville Chamberlain, Prime Minister since 1937, had used his office to appease Hitler's territorial demands. This he did with the eager support of an overwhelming majority of Conservative MPs. Chamberlain promoted appeasement for a number of reasons, a few worthy, most base. First, like many others, he believed that Germany had a just case, given the vindictive nature of the 1919 Versailles Treaty. Second, he was genuinely horrified by the prospect of the death and destruction which would result from another world war.

Third, he saw conflict with Germany as strengthening what he considered to be the real threat to 'civilization' – Soviet Communism. Fourth, the Prime Minister considered that war would ruin Britain economically and lead to the loss of the Empire, already policed by insufficient military personnel. Finally, and perhaps decisively, he feared the domestic repercussions of a major war. Chamberlain would have endorsed the view of the Conservative MP Robert Boothby, who wrote in November 1939 that: 'You cannot go through a world convulsion of this magnitude without fundamental changes in the social as well as the economic structure. It is inconceivable to me that our present hereditary system ... can survive the struggle without drastic alteration.'[3] For these reasons, Chamberlain did his best to avoid war, even sacrificing Czechoslovakia in 1938 to prevent such an outcome. Unfortunately, Hitler could not be satisfied: his invasion of Poland left Chamberlain with no option but to declare war. This was a deeply felt, personal defeat for the Premier: his radio speech which announced the outbreak of hostilities was desperately low-key; fellow appeasers thought it 'pathetically moving'.

Despite the rapid fall of Poland, Chamberlain and his cohorts still hoped to bring Hitler to the negotiating table through a Royal Navy blockade of German ports while the French Maginot Line frustrated any advance westwards. A major land conflict was, from this perspective, unnecessary. It was also undesirable: to mobilize and arm millions of British troops, rather than sustain an extant and relatively cheap navy, threatened to disrupt the economy and initiate potentially dangerous social change. Even those measures, such as food rationing, which many experts considered necessary to the competent and equitable management of resources, were implemented belatedly and reluctantly. This was a government that wanted to minimize the consequences of war just as much as it had earlier tried to evade conflict itself. It took the phrase 'Business as usual' as its watchword. The result, critics complained, was that, just as in peacetime, policy produced inefficient and unfair outcomes – bad enough in any situation but inexcusable during a period of war.

Six months after the invasion of Poland, little of military consequence had happened. According to Chamberlain, at least, everything was going to plan; indeed, on 4 April 1940 he declared that Hitler had now 'missed the bus'. Unfortunately for the Prime Minister, within four days German forces had invaded Denmark and Norway; the Allied response proved to be totally inept. The swift fall of these two countries led to a Commons debate which revealed the existence of a previously muted hostility to Chamberlain from within his own ranks. Wishing to see a more active war policy, Labour turned the debate into a vote of confidence. Despite enduring severe attacks, even from the Conservative benches, Chamberlain won a majority. Yet this formal victory was a moral defeat, as one-fifth of all national coalition MPs had either voted against or failed to support their leader. In peacetime, Chamberlain might have shrugged this off; in the face of the Norwegian disaster, he was forced to seek an accommodation with his enemies. Through gritted teeth, he asked Labour, a party whose members he was once accused of treating like dirt, to join the government. Clement Attlee, the Labour leader, made it clear that this was impossible while he remained in office. This refusal reflected a widespread mistrust of Chamberlain's domestic and foreign policies within the labour movement. If Labour's leaders were to enter government, those most responsible for mass unemployment and appeasement had to go.

Attlee's rejection of Chamberlain's overtures meant that a new premier had to be found from within Conservative ranks. Chamberlain called Lord Halifax and Winston Churchill to a meeting. Although he enjoyed the support of the Prime Minister, most Conservative MPs and King George VI, Halifax was hampered by the fact that as Foreign Secretary he had supported appeasement. Churchill, on the other hand, had consistently warned against the German threat while on the backbenches. Since becoming First Lord of the Admiralty in 1939 he had made speeches which, in contrast to those of other ministers, sounded as if he actually wanted to win the war. As a result, Churchill enjoyed popular approval. In the end, however, it was Halifax's reluctance to lead rather than Churchill's support in the country which proved decisive. Thus, to the chagrin of Conservative Members and the delight of the country, Churchill became Prime Minister on 10 May 1940. He quickly formed a government which, as it enjoyed Labour's full participation and active support, could truly be described as national. Perhaps the greatest sign that things had changed was the appointment of Ernest Bevin, General Secretary of the Transport and General Workers' Union, as Minister of Labour.

Within hours of Churchill's government being formed, Hitler's armies had invaded the Low Countries. After British and French forces responded by advancing into Belgium, German tanks to their south broke through the Ardennes forest, 'blitzkrieged' north to the English Channel and had cut them off by 20 May. The trapped Allied forces retreated to the coast, hoping to find an unoccupied port from where they could evacuate. The 'miracle of Dunkirk' was that they did: that, despite intense German bombardment, as many as 350,000 troops, by various gimcrack ways, evaded capture, crossed the Channel and arrived safely in Britain. Less miraculous, however, was the fact that they had been forced to leave most of their hardware on the beaches, and that Holland and Belgium were under German occupation.

After the French and Germans agreed an armistice on 22 June, Britain stood alone. Had the Germans been able to launch an immediate amphibious invasion, there is little doubt that Britain would also have capitulated. The country's best troops were either prisoners of war or in a state of shock. But the Germans needed time to assemble their ships. They also required control of the air, so Hitler gave his Luftwaffe the task of destroying the Royal Air Force. Thus began the Battle of Britain, during which the 'few' in their Hurricanes and Spitfires, as much through luck as judgement, held on to air superiority over Southern England. With the coming of inclement weather in the early autumn the threat of invasion had passed. It did not return until the following spring, by which time Hitler had turned east to deal with the Soviet Union.

The summer of 1940 was more than the country's most desperate military crisis. George Orwell, for one, viewed Dunkirk as the most important turning point in British history. According to him, in that spectacular disaster both the working and middle classes for the first time saw the 'utter rottenness' of the status quo.[4] Others on the left also hoped the crisis would force Britons to repudiate the old world of waste, misery and exclusion. The idea seemed to be that things were so bad, some good *had* to come of it. Evan Durbin, who entered Parliament as part of Labour's post-war intake, wrote in 1942:

> War is a fearful thing, destructive and bestial, but it does free men's minds. The only barriers to our swifter emancipation are the shackles of habitual thought and the darkness of the inward eye. War tears the familiar fabric of life to pieces, it kills and it tortures, but it breaks chains as well as homes and opens doors as well as graves ... Now is the time, when men's minds are free, to build our life anew.
>
> Let us then embrace this unwelcome opportunity and gather an unexpected harvest from the blood-drenched field. Then the dead will not have died in vain.[5]

Orwell and Durbin went further than most, but various opinion surveys showed that the public had become extremely critical of their leaders. They looked, in particular, at the inter-war governing elite, the likes of Chamberlain and his predecessor Stanley Baldwin, in a new and negative light. The polemical pamphlet *Guilty Men*, written four days after Dunkirk by three journalists, including Michael Foot, argued that, if it had been a military disaster, it was one caused by the political failures of the Conservative-led national governments. Appeasement abroad and non-interventionism at home had been the preconditions for calamity. This was, of course, a highly partisan view; however, it contained more than a few grains of truth. *Guilty Men* helped give coherence to popular thinking, selling more than 200,000 copies, despite being banned by major distributors. Although the authors merely called for the 'guilty men' to resign from office, others went further. When a candidate at a subsequent by-election was asked to ensure that Baldwin and 'the other guilty men' were 'impeached and hanged', the questioner was widely applauded.

While formally presiding over the crisis, Churchill's coalition was generally excepted from criticism. As a former backbench critic of his own party, Churchill was one of the few 'innocent' Conservatives. Labour, of course, had been in opposition since 1931 and its flirtation with pacifism in the early part of the decade was long forgotten. In the later 1930s, Attlee had denounced Chamberlain's home and foreign policies. Yet Churchill was unable fully to dissociate himself from the 'guilty men'. Chamberlain continued in the Cabinet and remained party leader until terminal cancer forced his retirement late in 1940. Many of the former Premier's old associates also clung to office well into the war. Most Conservative MPs regretted Chamberlain's departure and were at best lukewarm about the new leader. Their faith in appeasement might have diminished, but they remained committed to the party's established domestic priorities. Although there were fewer 'guilty men' in government after 1940, as late as 1945 the Conservative Party in Parliament was still jam-packed with them.

If some of the 'guilty men' remained in office, they were forced to accept the fact that the Dunkirk shambles meant that government had to transform the conflict into a 'total war' or face defeat. This was the kind of all-embracing, state-led operation which Chamberlain had done his best to avoid but which now public opinion and military necessity demanded. The crisis did not stop Conservatives wondering what the point of defeating Germany was if it caused a social revolution at home. However, in the shadow of a Nazi invasion, even they appreciated the need temporarily to put that consideration to one side. So, while still perceiving it as a threat to individual liberty, most Conservatives agreed that massive state intervention in society and economy was now the only means by which the country's freedom could be preserved. Churchill argued in public and private that government had to take whatever measures were necessary to meet the demands of the emergency, even if these promoted unwelcome social change. He taxed (and borrowed) and spent to an unprecedented degree not because he wanted to, but because there was no alternative if the country was to survive.

In pursuit of total war, therefore, the coalition mobilized Britain's resources, human and otherwise. Millions of men and women from diverse backgrounds were needed by the armed services, as well as by the factories which supplied them with ships, planes, tanks, guns and uniforms. In return for this compulsion, the state distributed scarce resources as equitably as possible to maximize efficiency and maintain morale: a vast range of consumer goods were rationed and their prices controlled. These measures inevitably led to long queues, tedious form-filling and the creation of a black market. The better-off grumbled, but a majority accepted higher taxes and the restriction of choice as necessary inconveniences. In contrast, many in the working class, especially those who had endured the worst of the inter-war depression, gladly welcomed government intervention. Unlike in the 1930s, such people were guaranteed access to a basic minimum of specified foodstuffs at a cost they could afford: their quality of life improved. This was a cause of perhaps one of the war's most ironic achievements: side by side with mass death and destruction, infant mortality rates fell faster than in peacetime.

As a result, total-war measures appeared to 'level' society by reducing various inequalities. The very rhetoric of total war, which stressed that the people were, whatever their differences, 'all in it together', also promoted egalitarian attitudes. This made a number of established injustices, especially those which impeded the war effort, harder to justify. Those on the left welcomed these developments, seeing them as harbingers of a New Jerusalem;

from the right came only expressions of horror at the destruction of the established order. Yet, if some of the grossest of inter-war inequalities were abolished by changes in policy, the more egalitarian spirit was much less in evidence: social tension and bigotry remained a feature of wartime life. For many, even total war proved little more than the truth of the adage that my enemy's enemy is my friend. As will be seen from closer examination, if total war improved many people's lives it did not erode all those prejudices, deriving from differences of class, gender and ethnicity, which legitimized the denial of social justice before 1939.

Even under Chamberlain's wartime regime, certain measures had been taken, albeit diffidently, that were thought to have promoted a greater sense of community between the classes. Within days of the outbreak of war, just over 1.5 million children and mothers were evacuated from bomb-threatened urban centres to the safety of rural and semi-rural districts. The vast majority of these evacuees were working class; many bore the marks of long-term poverty. Seventy per cent of children from Liverpool's infamous Scotland Road district billeted in one Shropshire village were verminous. More typically, nearly half of all two-year-old evacuees were infested with lice; bed-wetting and inadequate clothes and shoes were also common. Optimistic contemporaries hoped that bringing inner-city children face to face with people untouched by the depression would have significant repercussions. By seeing the desperate state of many innocent children for themselves, members of the comfortable middle class might begin to question the morality of mass unemployment. Chamberlain's own reaction is instructive. He wrote to his sister: 'I never knew that such conditions existed, and I feel ashamed of having been so ignorant of my neighbours. For the rest of my life I will try to make amends by helping such people to live cleaner and healthier lives.'[6]

Evacuation did not necessarily promote egalitarianism: responses were mixed to say the least. In the eyes of some, working class mothers appeared to be negligent sluts; their children, wild animals. In Berkshire, members of a Congregational church opposed evacuation, asking whether there was 'any necessity for the spoilation of decent homes and furniture [or] the corruption of speech and moral standards of our own children'. When youngsters were discovered to be lice-ridden, some observers blamed this on their social environment; others looked to their parents' moral failings. The values which sustained many middle-class folk through the inter-war years, which allowed them to accept unemployment as something rather unfortunate that others had to suffer for the good of the nation – and their savings – remained inviolate. According to this point of view, the evacuees' difficulties would not be solved by official meddling, especially if financed by their taxes. Instead, they wanted working-class girls to be taught to be good mothers at school: instruction, not intervention, was their remedy. Thus, although Chamberlain wanted to 'help' the poor, he did not think a welfare state the appropriate remedy.

Commentators at the time thought that the Blitz, which began in the autumn of 1940, would be another way of drawing the country together. After all, German bombs fell on everybody, even the Royal Family in Buckingham Palace. The Blitz was not, however, a universal experience, nor was its impact equitably shared, being concentrated in London and other large towns and cities. Moreover, in such places, those living closest to manu-facturing districts or dockyards were the worst affected: simply by virtue of residence, therefore, the Luftwaffe hit the workers hardest. Those members of the middle class unfortunate enough to live close to strategic targets were often able to move to relatives or friends. If forced to endure the bombing, the better-off also had access to superior facilities. At one extreme, guests in London's Dorchester Hotel had shelters equipped with fluffy eiderdown cots and silk sheets. At the other end of the spectrum, residents in the capital's East End enjoyed more primitive arrangements. Railway arches were used as a refuge by as many as 15,000 people on bad nights: these, of course, had no sanitation and were often infested with rats.

If the Blitz created a spirit of comradeship, it was more within working-class communities, rather than between the classes. Indeed, some East Enders were so disgusted with their lot that they booed the King and Queen on at least one visit intended to boost morale. Still, even class solidarity was circumscribed by ethnic prejudice. In 1943, 173 people were crushed to death after panic gripped a crowd entering an East End tube station at the start of a raid. Many blamed this tragedy on the district's long-established Jewish population. One resident explained: 'They lost their nerve . . . They haven't got steadiness like we have. We may be slow but we are sure. But the Jews are different.'

It was in the services that wartime changes were most directly experienced, but even here there were limits. The future left-wing Labour MP Eric Heffer was a carpenter until called up to join the RAF in late 1940. As he recalled:

> We recruits came from all walks of life. This was evident when we went to bed. Some had no pyjamas and slept in their shirts, some slept in their underwear, and some, like myself, had good striped flannel Co-op pyjamas. The posher ones had poplin and one or two actually had silk pyjamas. They had their legs pulled unmercifully but everyone recognized that we were all in the same boat and we had to get on together. We did – very quickly.[7]

The prospect of shared danger drew those in the ranks together, despite their different backgrounds. However, this sentiment did not necessarily extend to their superiors, middle and upper-middle class almost to a man. Heffer reported that, on his post, officers automatically sat in the front rows during film shows which meant that other ranks could not always see the screen. Such minor irritations – others included having to salute officers' cars even when unoccupied – did not enamour established authority to conscripts.

At the peak of the war effort, there were three and a half

million men and women in uniform. Millions more stayed on the Home Front; many of them laboured, either voluntarily or under compulsion, on the factory floor. At the workplace they experienced the various beneficial changes initiated by total war. Bevin had entered the Ministry of Labour promising unions unprecedented fairness; this promoted the expectation that class acrimony would be absent from the workplace, at least for the duration. In an attempt to cut across traditional cleavages and give priority to the national interest, many factories formed joint production committees. These were composed of an equal number of managers and workers who were charged with resolving problems and increasing efficiency through discussion. They enjoyed some success. More enlightened managers came to appreciate that workers could be encouraged to greater efforts if treated like human beings. A number took the almost revolutionary step of providing employees with toilets and canteens. Even so, as the war came to an end, accustomed suspicions resumed: in 1944 days lost through strikes amounted to four times the 1940 total. Such feelings had not, in truth, ever gone away. During 1940 the Labour activist Jennie Lee came across a group of mechanics working in a Lancashire aircraft factory:

> I thought they were singing 'There will always be an England'. But when I listened more carefully I found that to the same tune they had invented words of their own. Instead of 'there will always be an England' they sang 'Will there always be an England – with a job in it for me?'[8]

Men and women who had endured years without work or had lived under the permanent threat of unemployment obviously welcomed the favourable wartime conditions. By June 1944 the unemployed numbered only 54,000 or 0.7 per cent of the employable population. The war not only guaranteed work for all fit enough to do it but also provided plenty of overtime to those in vital industries. As a consequence, average earnings increased by 80 per cent, whereas prices only rose 60 per cent between 1939 and 1945. Many, however, saw war work as little more than a brief respite from poverty. As they believed mass unemployment would return with the peace, workers struck for higher wages while they could. Similarly, managers used to a cowed workforce did not always respond well when expected to treat union officials with something other than contempt. The result, especially in those industries such as coalmining and shipbuilding which had the worst industrial relations before the war, was at times explosive.

Total war necessitated measures which improved the lives of manual workers and aroused the resentment of some members of the middle class. In a similar way, the conflict also elevated women's status – contemporaries spoke of a 'revolution' in gender relations – at the cost of some male rancour. The acute labour shortage forced government first to encourage and then conscript women into the uniformed services and war work. Indeed, Britain mobilized a far greater proportion of its female population than any other combatant nation. By 1943, the peak of the war effort, seven and a half million women were in paid employment; many found themselves in formerly men-only occupations. Thus, while before the war women had constituted only one in ten of those employed in engineering, by 1943 the proportion had risen to just over one-third. The traditional sexual division of labour seemed to be breaking down under the pressure of total war.

The government introduced compulsion with great regret, and the first Act of Parliament came as late as December 1941. Indeed, it was not until January 1943 that all women between nineteen and forty could be directed to part-time work if they had domestic responsibilities, or to full-time employment if they did not. Churchill and Bevin both feared that state interference in domestic affairs would undermine men's morale. As one male in his thirties declared in 1941 when asked about the matter: 'If married women are called up home life will vanish ... Men coming home on leave will find that they can only see their wives for an hour or two a day. Men in reserved occupations will come back to cold, untidy houses with no meal ready.' It was only because an insufficient number of women had volunteered that conscription had been introduced. Many females saw factory work as dull and dirty; others also believed the Victorian stereotype that factory workers were unladylike, lewd and uncouth. Most, however, were reluctant to take up the double burden of domestic and workplace responsibilities. As one woman stated: 'I've got enough to do at home.' For, while women were expected to perform previously male tasks, and for less pay, they were also required to uphold traditional expressions of femininity. Cosmetic adverts emphasized the continued importance of female display, even presenting close attention to make-up as a duty given its role in sustaining male morale.

The equivocal nature of women's wartime role was expressed in a feature film *The Gentle Sex* (1943), which followed the fortunes of seven women drafted into the Army Territorial Service. They eventually became, among other things, lorry and ambulance drivers as well as mechanics. The film tried to convince its audience that, as the opening commentary stated, 'without the women we couldn't carry on at all'. However, it also wanted to reassure men especially that women in uniform did not cease to be, well, women – they remained 'strange, incalculable creatures'. At the end of the film, the audience was told that, when peace came, the women would marry, make homes and have babies. This, in fact, was what most females wanted to do. In a 1943 survey, only 25 per cent expressed a desire to remain in factory work after the war. One young woman said: 'You can't look on anything you do during the war as what you really mean to do; it's just filling in the time till you can live your own life again.'

A few observers also noted that the war had produced some modest improvements in race relations. Britain's black population was no more than 10,000 strong in 1939. Generations of imperialist propaganda, which found its way into children's comics and popular novels, had imbued most white Britons with an innate sense of superiority over blacks. Some thought the conflict had tempered this outlook. Certainly, the war exposed various examples of discrimination which clashed with wartime needs. Thus, when a young black girl raised in Stepney was refused entry into the Women's Land Army because local farmers did not want to billet her in their homes, press and Parliament ridiculed them. Such furores were used by interested parties as platforms to preach racial tolerance. A number of skilled West Indian workers were also allowed to enter the country to fill job vacancies. Employers were initially reluctant to give them work, but the need for their skills was the best argument against this attitude. Although admired for their abilities and their contribution to the war effort, black workers were never fully accepted. They were expected to return home as soon as peace had resumed.

The extent of the British people's cultural conservatism, evident from the above episodes, is further illustrated by the popularity of a certain type of feature film during the war. By 1945 cinema attendances had reached thirty million per week: one study revealed that 70 per cent of adults 'sometimes' went, while 30 per cent attended at least once a week. The films most appreciated were crude comedies and, more significantly, productions with melodramatic plots and gentleman heroes. Probably the most celebrated British film of the war was Noël Coward's *In Which We Serve* (1943), a superior version of the latter genre.

'This is the story of a ship,' the narrator declared at the start of the film. The ship was HMS *Torrin*, a battle cruiser. The story took the audience through its service in Atlantic convoys, the Dunkirk evacuation and, finally, action in the Mediterranean. The film's main characters represented society's three social classes. Coward was the captain, a restrained, stiff-upper-lipped patrician. Bernard Miles played the petty officer as quintessentially lower-middle class: pompous, awkward but good natured. John Mills took the role of an ordinary seaman, a cheery Cockney working man always ready to crack a joke. The ship was clearly a metaphor for Britain at war, one representing the country as a society in which all knew their place but were united against the 'Hun'. Indeed, Coward's captain was like a lord of the manor, and the crew his loyal villagers: the *Torrin* is a floating country house.

In the film, tradition and continuity are the key themes. The Royal Navy was the least modern of all the services, being the fighting force of Raleigh and Nelson. As the commentary concludes: 'We are an island race, the sea has ruled our destiny,' and the Navy has valiantly defended Britain 'in spite of changing values in a changing world'. The naval setting also allowed Coward virtually to ignore the Home Front: the women in the film do little more than wait for news of their men. *In Which We Serve* depicts a 'traditional' sort of war – not a total war, the one that was actually being fought. Despite, or because of, this emphasis the film resonated in the nation's imagination like no other.

Coward was a sentimental traditionalist, so it is no surprise that he produced a film like *In Which We Serve*. Perhaps more revealing is the way even films with pretensions to more liberal social attitudes remained trapped in class assumptions. The subjects of *Journey Together* (1945) were two RAF pilot trainees. One was working class, had left school at fourteen but had studied hard in his spare time to obtain the qualifications necessary to train as a pilot. The other was a nice but shockingly dim Cambridge undergraduate. At one stage, the latter declared to the former: 'you make me feel like a bloated plutocrat ... anyway we're both in the same boat now'. Yet it is the Cambridge man who becomes the pilot and the elementary-school boy who is forced to become the less glamorous and subordinate navigator.

British wartime culture still had a place for those who rejected each and every social change provoked by total war. Evelyn Waugh, a snob's snob, wrote his novel *Brideshead Revisited* during 1944 while recovering from injuries sustained in conflict. It was, he later wrote, 'a souvenir of the Second World War', of a time when the English country house seemed doomed and the aristocracy appeared in danger of losing its identity. In the novel, Brideshead, a symbol of the ease and elegance of the upper-class style of life, is commandeered by the army. One of the young officers billeted there is Hooper, described as a sallow, lower-middle-class youth with a flat Midlands accent, someone who looks scarcely human. Hooper is guilty of many things: he is ill at ease with servants and calls his men by their first names. He is unromantic, unheroic and obsessed with efficiency. So far as Waugh is concerned, Hooper represented the future rulers of Britain. To him, the war had brought the enemy to the gates – and that enemy was not Adolf Hitler.

Nineteen-forty-two was a turning point in the war. Not only had the United States become involved but, by the end of the year, the Soviets had stalled the last major German offensive at Stalingrad, while British forces repulsed Rommel at El Alamein. Most Britons recognized that, although great sacrifices were still in order, victory was now assured. As Churchill put it, this was the end of the beginning, if not the beginning of the end. People began to anticipate the peace. Assuming that, after a brief boom, mass unemployment would quickly return, many ordinary people did not relish the prospect. Yet, while before 1939 even many of the unemployed had thought their plight unavoidable, wartime experience had indicated otherwise. Not only had the 1940 crisis discredited those politicians who had allowed mass unemployment to persist, it had also forced government to abandon non-interventionism. The result was increased production, full employment and an unprecedented – if imperfect – sense of national unity. It was one thing to accept economic depression as inevitable when nothing else seemed credible; it was quite another to do so when a viable alternative was shown to exist.

Before 1942 Churchill refused to think about post-war Britain, arguing that the country had to focus on winning the war. In truth, he saw little wrong with inter-war society and looked on promises of change as irrelevant. Labour ministers were frustrated by this, but their place in the coalition forced them to remain quiet. In the public domain, however, in popular weeklies like *Picture Post*, left-thinking writers were given a platform on which to make their speculations. After 1942, an increasing number of people wanted Churchill to spell out what peacetime Britain would look like. That pressure gained enormous force with the publication of Sir William Beveridge's report *Social Insurance and Allied Services* in December 1942. This proved to be the most significant political event of the war, establishing the parameters of the debate on post-war Britain and placing party differences in stark relief. Beveridge had been a leading civil servant, Director of the London School of Economics and, at the outbreak of war, Master of University College, Oxford. Despite early social work in London's slums, he was no wet egalitarian, once declaring that the 'well-to-do represent on the whole a higher level of character and ability than the working classes ... the upper classes are on the whole the better classes'. A Liberal, Beveridge was a long-standing advocate of social reform because he believed it would increase economic efficiency. That it might be seen to be morally right as well was, in some ways, simply a bonus.

In June 1941 Beveridge was asked by the Labour Minister of Health to chair a committee charged with surveying existing social insurance provision. He was expected to make proposals to rationalize the supply of state old-age pensions, unemployment benefit and health cover. The existing arrangements were, according to many accounts, uncoordinated, inadequate and confusing. They also left millions without protection: about half the population was excluded from public national health insurance. Potentially, this was a worthy but dull commission: in the hands of someone other than an egomaniac it would have remained so. Beveridge, however, had grander ideas and was determined to make his mark on wartime thinking. Even before his committee sat, he had decided its conclusions and went on to dominate proceedings to ensure they were accepted. As publication date neared, Beveridge also trailed his views in the press and obtained widespread publicity.

In his report, Beveridge proposed one unified scheme to cover old age, unemployment and illness and so give every citizen 'cradle to the grave' security. This would be financed by compulsory contributions from employee, employer and the state. Each person would make the same flat-rate contribution and receive the same benefits. These payments were set at a higher level than before the war but could not be described as generous, since they were designed to allow subsistence only. Beveridge expected that individuals would continue to make their own private provision, if they so desired, to supplement such benefits. Moreover, while requiring increased contributions from individual, employer and the state, Beveridge took into account the country's parlous wartime economic condition. The question was, could the country afford not to adopt his measures?

Beveridge prefaced his report with the statement that a 'revolutionary moment in the world's history is a time for revolution, not patching'. His scheme, however, hardly proposed turning society upside down. Indeed, in her memoirs, Margaret Thatcher, who in the early 1960s served in the Ministry of Pensions, indicated her strong approval of Beveridge's main proposals. She even detected a 'Thatcherite' ring in the report's rhetoric, particularly the part which stated that the 'State in organizing security should not stifle incentive, opportunity [or] responsibility'. She also responded warmly to Beveridge's warning that the unemployed should 'not feel that income for idleness, however caused, can come from a bottomless purse'.

The report's spectacular impact was mainly due to what Beveridge referred to as his 'assumptions', without which a social security system could not function effectively. These included the avoidance of mass unemployment and the creation of a national health service. To the public, it appeared that a government official was finally articulating what they had been thinking for some time. Opinion polls showed that 86 per cent wanted the proposals adopted. As one middle-aged male manual worker said, 'it will make the ordinary man think that the country at last has some regard for him as he is supposed to have regard for the country'. Yet many also feared that the government would not live up to the report's promise, a reaction confirmed by the response of prominent industrialists and leading Conservatives.

Although some business people favoured modifying inter-war government economic and social policy, their representatives certainly did not. The President of the Federation of British Industries warned against change for its own sake, stating that it was 'vitally necessary . . . that we should avoid debasing our desire for a better world into a mere wish for less work and more pay'. At the British Employers' Confederation, his counterpart pointed out that Britain had not gone to war to improve its social services. Summing up opinion from this quarter, the *Daily Telegraph* described the report as 'half way to Moscow'. Others considered it even closer to Communist principles than that. It was no surprise, therefore, that Beveridge was not welcomed with open arms by Conservatives in the Cabinet. The Chancellor of the Exchequer, Sir Kingsley Wood, one of Chamberlain's old colleagues, considered it too costly. Churchill was at one with the 'guilty men' on this issue, thinking the report fostered a 'dangerous optimism' out of step with the 'hard facts of life'. Most Conservative MPs also dissented from much of the report, believing that, in particular, unemployment benefits should be set below subsistence levels so they did not undermine the incentive to work. Indeed, because they had accurately anticipated the nature of Beveridge's proposals, Conservatives had sought their suppression. However, once word got out this proved impossible, placing Churchill in an awkward position. Such a well-supported document could not be openly disavowed without damaging morale and so the war effort. He attempted a none too convincing balancing act, accepting the report in principle but avoiding specific commitments. The public was not satisfied. Labour fully supported the Beveridge report, which in many ways reflected the party's established policy. Having to maintain outward unity, Labour's representatives in the coalition were careful not to criticize Churchill in public. Behind the scenes, however, they fought hard but mostly unsuccessfully to persuade him to accept the report and other proposals which diverged from inter-war think-ing. In contrast to their leaders' caution, backbench Labour MPs in February 1943 voted for the full and immediate implementation of Beveridge. By this point, the public were in no doubt about which party best reflected their hopes for peacetime.

Labour's wider response to post-war policy was most clearly expressed by Herbert Morrison in speeches and articles delivered in the last two years of war. Morrison was one of Labour's most experienced leaders, having held office in the 1929–31 government before leading the London County Council for most of the 1930s. During the war he became Home Secretary and, in effect, Attlee's deputy and closest rival. He was also an important influence on Labour's attitude to the nationalization of industry. Despite all his electoral and programmatic pragmatism, he was also a determined socialist, who wanted to transform the nature of society. Morrison did not, however, allow his ultimate ends to determine his immediate outlook: he was a hard-headed radical. Summing up the Labour leadership's approach to policy, he told one party gathering:

> It's not enough to get up and thump the table and talk about the Socialisation of All the Means of Production, Distribution and Exchange. I've done my share of that in my time; you would always count on a cheer of some sort. But it doesn't begin to get near the real problems of how to act.[9]

'The tasks of government', he reminded Labour party members, 'are complex and difficult' and had to be informed by 'good sense' rather than 'emotionalism'. 'Paradise', he noted with accustomed bluntness, 'will not be handed to you on a plate.' It was a message many of the party's leaders of the time repeated on platforms across the country.

Of course, Morrison welcomed Beveridge. However, he did not lose sight of the fact that its 'essential basis' was full employment. 'It would be a mockery', he warned, 'if we allowed the phrase social security to mean no more than bigger and better doles. Real social security means work – secure, productive and happy jobs.' While post-war policy should aim to prevent extreme want and hardship, he cautioned that 'if the total national income is itself less than it should be, everybody will suffer, the workers particularly'. Thus the 'battle of the next few years is the battle for production – to see that we produce the right goods in ample quantities and in the most efficient way'. Labour, then, stood for 'a rising standard of production coupled with a rising standard of life and security for our people'. Within this environment, workers were free to improve their wages and working conditions. However, they should never lose sight of the fact that the 'paramount' concern was the promotion of 'an over-all increase in general productivity and industrial efficiency'. There were, then, few illusions among the Labour leadership that Britain faced a long hard slog in order to sustain post-war social security. That this would be difficult was widely appreciated, even before the full scale of the economic damage caused by the war was discovered.

Labour's key assumption was that the public ownership of certain industries and the increased regulation of those remaining in the private sector would be economically beneficial. The belief that the state could be a benevolent force was best expressed in Douglas Jay's maxim that 'the man in Whitehall knows best'. By no means all economists shared this faith. Some continued to believe that only markets, unrestricted by government interference, would provide material plenty. Indeed, it was in 1944 that F. A. Hayek published *The Road to Serfdom*, which exerted such a profound influence over the Thatcherites of the 1980s. However, Hayek wrote at a time when the failure of free markets seemed palpable, and not just to members of the Labour party. Hayek's was a doctrine which appeared to have been disproved by experience: it had only promoted collective misery in the 1930s and national disaster in 1940.

Following the opinions of many other economists, Morrison argued that, in any case, the free market had ceased to exist, at least as the Victorians would have had understood the term.

Government intervention was required to overcome the dominance of private monopolies which had formed in a number of key industries. Before the war these combines had restricted output to maximize profits and so condemned millions of workers to unemployment in order to keep their few shareholders happy. Indeed, the 'restrictive practices' of the cartels were believed to have discouraged initiative and the development of new forms of organization and technology. According to Morrison, only when government took direct control of such industries would managers and workers be free of the shareholders' dead hand. This newfound liberty would allow them to serve the public interest. While favouring intervention, Morrison was not, then, hostile to the notion of competition or to the development of individual talents. As he stated: 'I want the free enterprise of the efficient managements, the technicians, the scientists, the foremen and the workmen.' He also conceded that not all industries were controlled by monopolies and proposed legislation to ensure the continuation of competition outside the state sector. Indeed, he explained that government had to 'develop a positive, helpful and constructive attitude towards industry; it has got to share with industry the problems of being enterprising'.

It was a tired electorate that went to the polls in July 1945 to choose a government for the first time in ten years. Wartime exertions had taken their toll and, for those in uniform, the job remained to be done: the Japanese had yet to put down their arms. Labour's manifesto, *Let Us Face the Future*, stated that it was a 'Socialist Party, and proud of it', which aimed to establish the 'Socialist Commonwealth of Great Britain'. This, however, was its 'ultimate purpose'. As Labour Party members were 'practical-minded men and women' they appreciated that socialism would not 'come overnight, as the product of a weekend revolution'. So the rest of the document went on to list Labour's 'practical' policies. The manifesto was the work of many hands, but it bore the mark of Morrison. It also reflected Labour's brand of practical idealism and its message was echoed in countless campaign speeches delivered by hundreds of candidates.

During the campaign, Labour portrayed itself as the party most interested in discovering practical solutions to everyday problems. Candidates stressed their empathy with the hopes and fears of the millions who looked uneasily into the future. Even those on the Labour left followed this prosaic emphasis. To the electorate of bomb-damaged Plymouth Devonport, Michael Foot wrote:

> Home is the best word in the English language. We shall not have won the peace until every citizen in Devonport and every citizen of England has a good roof over his head, the chance to marry and bring up his children, safe from the fears of unemployment, sickness and war.[10]

As James Callaghan, the future Labour Prime Minister, declared in South Cardiff: 'We built the Spitfires. Now we can build the houses.' Labour also argued that the state had to concern itself directly with the nation's numerous problems because 1940 proved that private enterprise, left to its own devices, was unable to cope. What would once have appeared Labour's most ideological proposition – nationalization – seemed, in this context at least, eminently sensible.

Labour's approach was successful. The issue which most pre-occupied the country was how to end the acute housing shortage: German bombers had compounded a problem caused by inter-war neglect. Twice as many voters thought Labour best able to solve this than the Conservatives. While Labour appeared pragmatic, the Conservatives now looked dogmatic, clinging to an outmoded faith in the market and unaccountably hostile to the state. This impression was reinforced by Churchill's radio address at the start of the campaign. In this he warned that Attlee, with whom he had governed the country for five years, would eventually require 'some form of Gestapo' to implement his programme. Although this prediction might have been applauded by Professor Hayek, many others shook their heads in total disbelief.

The scale of Labour's landslide victory shocked everybody, including the party's own leaders. The general view had been that Churchill's wartime leadership guaranteed the Conservatives power with, at worst, a reduced Commons majority. Instead, Labour made 203 gains over its 1935 position, finishing with 393 MPs to the Conservatives' 213. The party's share of votes cast was less impressive than indicated by its Parliamentary majority: even so, at 47.8 per cent, this was Labour's best showing to date. Party leaders now claimed that Labour was the 'people's party', having drawn support from across the social spectrum. Indeed it had, but it was far from evenly spread. At the extremes, although just over three-quarters of those employed in industrial occupations supported Labour, barely 10 per cent of top business people did. Even so, Labour did benefit from unprecedentedly high middle-class support, although this was concentrated in the lower-middle class, about one-third of whom voted for the party.

Labour's remarkable support, wherever it came from, was not due to starry-eyed idealism. As some commentators noted, many new Labour voters switched their allegiance because they detested the Conservatives so much. Others had supported Attlee in the belief that while Labour would not win the election, he deserved more MPs. Labour voters were also not, for the most part, ideologically committed socialists: they were not even unqualified advocates of nationalization. However, they did hope – manual working class and lower-middle class alike – that a greater role for the state in both the economy and welfare provision meant they all stood a better chance of avoiding inter-war insecurities. In contrast, the Conservatives, a few reforms aside, promised a return to that world.

On the surface at least, the Britain which celebrated the Japanese surrender in August 1945 was not so very different from the one that had heard Chamberlain announcing the outbreak of war nearly six years before. Despite the war, this was still a hierarchical society: class still mattered; men still treated women in a most peculiar way; colour and ethnic differences still aroused hostile responses. In politics, however, the war had made its mark. The inter-war political elite saw its credibility left marooned on the beaches of Dunkirk. This military crisis caused a significant number of people to question many of their accustomed rulers' policy assumptions. They began to appreciate that the inter-war period's misfortunes had not, after all, been inevitable. They started to think it possible to arrange society in such a way as to minimize its worst insecurities. This was not caused by liberal guilt – although some of the comfortable did now feel uneasy – or by the sudden revelation that poverty was immoral, even if some did think that. The depression had not just hurt the unemployed of Northern England; by promoting a wider sense of uncertainty, it had even affected those with jobs in the prosperous South. The prospect of guaranteed protection, against the worst that life could throw at you, was something which appealed more to those who suffered inter-war poverty, unemployment or short-time work; it also had its charms for the fully employed bank clerk, teacher and shop assistant. The war had not eradicated social differences and prejudices, but it had given people a sense that they shared a common interest, both in fighting Hitler and in voting Labour. If this led to popular support for what would later be called state collectivism, it was underpinned by individual self-interest. If the war was not the moral adventure some on the left thought it had been, it also did not create the self-deluded naivety imagined by those on the right.

Labour, which gained most from these wartime developments, had been preaching in the wilderness for some time before 1939. The events of 1940 made its case better than any party propagandist could have hoped. In talking about building a 'New Jerusalem' – and some also referred to a 'revolution' – Labour leaders meant reforming society as it was. This meant taking into account the realities of an economy already in relative decline, battered by a depression and hammered by the war. It also meant learning from wartime experience which showed that economic progress could be achieved by treating people like human beings, rather than as factors of production to be dispensed with when and if market forces dictated. There may have been some voters who thought that a Labour government would give them a secure income for no work. If so, they had not been listening to the party whose rhetoric overran with references to the need for 'hard work'. Labour promised to be the party of the 'useful people', those who made an active contribution to the economy – not parasites who lived off the work of others, be they lumpen scroungers or upper-class drones.

CHAPTER III

CHURCHILL AND THE PRICE OF VICTORY: 1939–1945

PAUL ADDISON

For twenty years after the end of the Second World War, Winston Churchill was a living legend. With the passing of time his mighty reputation as a war leader seemed to increase rather than diminish, magnified by his own six-volume history of the war, and the almost deliberate construction of a Churchill myth by admirers on both sides of the Atlantic. In 1965, the year of his death, the former Labour Prime Minister Clement Attlee described him as 'the greatest citizen of the world of our time', while the historian A. J. P. Taylor referred to him, in a famous footnote, as 'the saviour of his country'.[1]

Neither Attlee nor Taylor regarded Churchill as infallible. Both were critical of particular episodes in his conduct of the war. But, as they saw it, his errors paled into insignificance by comparison with the colossal achievement of leading Britain to victory against Nazi Germany. Altogether different is the portrait of Churchill now presented to us by revisionist historians. Far from being the 'saviour of his country', Churchill is alleged to have led Britain into a calamitous war that destroyed its independence and brought about the collapse of the British Empire. Churchill is also accused of opening the door to socialism in 1945, thereby ushering in an era of social and economic malaise that was only terminated by the 'Thatcherite revolution' of 1979–90.

In a broad sense, the attack on Churchill is part of a wider revision of the history of Britain in the Second World War. Ever since the 1960s, historians have been trying to disentangle the truth as they see it from the myths of wartime propaganda and the self-interested accounts of politicians and others. The patriotic interpretation of the British at war as a united people, ennobled by the struggle against an evil dictatorship, has been replaced by a more streetwise account in which the divisive and discreditable aspects of wartime society are well to the fore. Once full of neighbourly Cockneys defying the Blitz, the home front has been repopulated with factious politicians, incompetent managers, malingering workers, unfaithful husbands and wives, racists, looters, black marketeers and other prototypes of Essex Man.

It was never likely that Churchill would escape the deflationary effects of revisionism, but the attack when it came had an unexpected twist. At the zenith of his post-war reputation such mutterings as there were against the 'Churchill myth' usually came from the left. Many Labour supporters had never forgiven him for the General Strike or his 'Gestapo' speech of 1945. The Conservative nation, meanwhile, seemed to idolize him. In the pages of the *Daily Mail* and the *Daily Telegraph* his name was sacrosanct, and any substantial criticism of him was regarded as bordering on the treasonable. Even today most Conservatives hold Churchill in high esteem – but in recent years the most radical assaults on his reputation have come from the right.

On further reflection the source of the attack can be more readily understood. Between 1900, when he was first elected to the House of Commons, and 1940, when he succeeded Neville Chamberlain as Prime Minister, there were many bitter quarrels between Churchill and the Conservatives. He changed parties twice – from Conservative to Liberal in 1904, and back to the Conservatives in 1924. True Conservatives never forgot that he had 'ratted' on them at the start of his career, and were not deceived when he returned to the party fold. They knew him to be a great adventurer whose highly egocentric statesmanship frequently overrode the claims of party loyalty. Their mistrust was confirmed by the events of the 1930s, when Churchill rebelled against two successive leaders of the party, Stanley Baldwin and Neville Chamberlain. At last mistrust blazed into hostility when Churchill denounced Chamberlain over the Munich agreement of September 1938.

During the Second World War Churchill and the Conservatives staged a great reconciliation when he assumed the leadership of the party in succession to Chamberlain. But it was a shotgun marriage and a very difficult one in the early stages. By the end of the war Churchill's position as party leader was impregnable. But, just as some Conservatives have never forgiven Michael Heseltine for his part in the overthrow of Margaret Thatcher in 1990, so the 'men of Munich' never entirely forgave Churchill for his attacks on Chamberlain and the policy of appeasement. Today's right-wing revisionists are the spiritual heirs and descendants of the *Munichois*, but with a difference: they believe that Chamberlain should have taken the appeasement of Nazi Germany to even greater lengths.

The policy of appeasement had been based in part on the fear that a prolonged war with Germany would have damaging consequences for the British Empire, the economy and the social order at home. Even after the outbreak of hostilities in September 1939 Chamberlain clung to the hope that such consequences might be avoided if the 'phoney war' ended in a stalemate and the negotiation of a compromise peace. But on 10 May 1940 the German assault on France and the Low Countries, coinciding with the appointment of Churchill as Prime Minister, marked the beginning of a more pugnacious regime. Addressing the House of Commons on 13 May Churchill said: 'You ask what is our aim? I can answer in one word: it is victory, victory in spite of all costs, victory in spite of all terror, victory, however long and hard the road may be; for without victory, there is no survival.'

In party political terms the cost of victory was to fall mainly on the Conservatives. They were never in danger of experiencing a catastrophe of the kind which had overtaken the Liberals in the

First World War. The unity of the party was maintained and so too was the social bedrock on which Toryism was founded. The upper and middle classes, for the most part, together with a substantial minority of manual workers, remained true blue. Even in the general election of 1945, which is often regarded as a disaster for the party, the Conservatives obtained 10 million votes and 40 per cent of all votes cast.

The war years, nevertheless, proved to be difficult or hostile terrain for the Conservatives. In order to win the war, they were compelled to ally with forces inimical to their own interests and values. The most spectacular example of this was the Anglo-Soviet alliance which followed Hitler's invasion of Russia in June 1941. Conservatives who had so often denounced Soviet Communism had to purse their lips as the popularity of the Red Army soared and with it the legend of 'Uncle Joe'. They watched the victorious advance of Soviet troops into Central and Eastern Europe with foreboding, and the appeasement of Stalin by Churchill with uneasy consciences. Some twenty-five Conservative MPs, including Alec Dunglass, the future Sir Alec Douglas-Home, voted against the Yalta agreement in February 1945.

For some Tories the terms of the Anglo-American alliance were also a cause for concern. They were angered by persistent demands by the United States for the dismantling of imperial preference and the liquidation of the Empire east of Suez. Churchill, for whom the maintenance of good relations with Roosevelt was an absolute priority, tended to stifle Tory dissent on such questions. As a devout believer in the common interests of the 'English-speaking peoples', he was reluctant to admit that Britain and the United States were rivals as well as allies. But he was in fact well aware of this. There came a point where he was so offended by criticisms of the British Empire in the American press that even he spoke out. 'We mean to hold our own,' he declared on 10 November 1942. 'I have not become the King's first minister in order to preside over the liquidation of the British Empire.'

Conservative anxieties were also fuelled by conditions at home. In the House of Commons the Conservatives still commanded – except for a handful of seats lost at by-elections – the enormous majority they had obtained in the general election of 1935. But in May 1940 they were compelled, for the sake of national unity, to invite Labour to share office in a coalition government. It was Labour's refusal to serve under Chamberlain that sealed his fate, and gave Churchill the opportunity of the premiership. After this, the Conservatives began to find themselves under siege and on the defensive. As the war economy was fully mobilized under state direction and control, conditions on the home front began to resemble those of a society halfway to socialism. Property rights and the liberty of the individual were overridden by administrative decree. The differential between salaries and wages, an approximate measure of the gap between the middle classes and the working classes, narrowed sharply. Employers and managers were confronted by full employment and a labour force with much greater bargaining power. The higher rates of income tax were raised to levels which led Churchill himself to protest. Though their effects were very uneven, rationing and austerity also tended to produce a levelling down of the middle classes.

Broadly speaking, Conservatives accepted that 'war socialism' was a patriotic necessity which had to be tolerated for the duration of the war. They were also aware that the Labour Party and the radical intelligentsia regarded the war as an opportunity for converting wartime conditions into the basis of a new social order. As the Tory MP Sir Tufton Beamish noted in October 1940: 'Every trade union and the co-operative movement and the rather cowardly ... pseudo-intelligent left movements are using every minute to promote their pestilential views.'[2] After the British victory over Rommel at Alamein, in November 1942, this perception of the danger was somewhat obscured by the belief that Churchill would be re-elected at the end of the war on a tide of popular gratitude. Whether he would lead a Conservative government, or a revived coalition, was a matter for speculation, but a straight Labour victory appeared unlikely.

How significant *was* the damage inflicted on the Conservatives by the Second World War? The most obvious cost was the electoral defeat of 1945 and the subsequent exclusion of the party from office for a period of six years. In the sense that the electoral pendulum soon swung back to the Conservatives, who then enjoyed a period of thirteen years in office, 1945 may appear to be no more than a temporary setback. But the injuries done to the Tory nation were deeper and more long-lasting than appeared on the surface. The world for which the Tory had stood in 1939 – the British Empire abroad and the social hierarchy at home – had been undermined by the war and the 'Attlee settlement' of 1945 to 1951. Furthermore the legacy of the war was a more equally balanced two-party system in which the enhanced power and popularity of Labour were factors that could never be safely ignored by Conservative party managers. In the five general elections between 1922 and 1935, Labour never obtained more than 37.1 per cent of the national vote. In the eight general elections between 1945 and 1970, Labour never obtained less than 43 per cent of the national vote. A further consequence was the ascendancy within the Tory Party after 1945 of an assortment of Whigs, Grandees and One-Nation Tories whose strategy was to steer the party towards the middle ground in politics.

In the past Conservative historians have tended to regard the political consequences of the war as inevitable. The revisionists of the right disagree. The pioneer in this respect was the Peterhouse historian Maurice Cowling, whose book *The Impact of Hitler* (1975) put the case for peace with Germany in such veiled scholarly language that only a handful of academics understood him. He spoke more plainly in a newspaper article of 1989 commemorating the fiftieth anniversary of the outbreak of war. Britain, he argued, should never have gone to war with Hitler. Though the balance was a fine one, Britain had no more to fear from the domination of Europe by Nazi Germany than it had from the domination of Europe by the United States and the Soviet Union. The victory of 1945 was Russo-American while the British were in effect one of the defeated powers. By staying out, Britain would have avoided 'the disestablishment of the Empire and the establishment of socialism'.[3]

In Cowling's view the responsibility for war lay partly with Neville Chamberlain for declaring it, and partly with Winston Churchill. Others laid the blame exclusively on Churchill. This was one of the themes of David Irving's *Churchill's War*, a two-volume work of which only the first volume has yet been published in Britain. With the aid of prodigious research into the archives, Irving sought to present his subject as an evil genius. Always a controversial historian, and frequently accused of Nazi sympathies, Irving was notorious for the claim that Hitler had played no part in the Holocaust, which (Irving claimed) had been masterminded by Himmler and deliberately kept secret from the Führer. Many publishers turned down both volumes of Irving's book before the first volume saw the light of day in Australia in 1987.

Irving hated Churchill so much that he flung all manner of personal as well as political allegations against him. The Churchill of his book was a callous, bloodthirsty careerist, who squandered the lives of thousands of British and Commonwealth troops in the quest for fame and power. Irving also claimed that Churchill's wartime decisions led to the virtual extinction of the Empire, which could have been saved had Churchill been prepared to make peace with Hitler in 1940. The 'Irving thesis', which attracted much attention and controversy in the Australian press, was best summed up by the headline in the *Sydney Morning Herald*: ' "Drunk" who cost Britain its Empire'.[4]

When the first volume of *Churchill's War* was published in Britain in 1989 the press paid little attention. Whatever his merits as a researcher, Irving was regarded as too sympathetic to Hitler for his judgements to be taken seriously. The way was therefore open for a debunking of Churchill by right-wing historians who enjoyed a greater respectability than Irving.

On 2 January 1993 the historian and politician Alan Clark published in *The Times* an article in which he hailed a new biography of Churchill by John Charmley as 'probably the most important revisionist text to be published since the war'. Clark argued that Churchill needed the crisis of 1940 more than the crisis needed him. It was only by imposing on the British the goal of victory at all costs over Germany that Churchill could retain the position he had so recently won as Prime Minister. But the pursuit of victory meant the abandonment of the Conservative aim of preserving the status quo: hence it would have been in the national interest to make peace. 'There were several occasions', wrote Clark, 'when a rational leader could have got, first reasonable, then excellent terms from Hitler.' But Churchill pressed on regardless.[5]

In the heated controversy which followed, the 'Charmley thesis' was treated as startlingly original: few seemed to have heard of Cowling or Irving. At the same time the arguments put forward by Charmley in his book were muddled up with other claims made by him in articles and interviews, and for good measure confused with the more cavalier judgements of Clark. This made Charmley's book appear more sensational than it was. A witty and perceptive biography of Churchill, it was fairly orthodox in its treatment of him up to 1940. Nor in the subsequent wartime chapters did Charmley explicitly state that Churchill could or should have entered into negotiations with Hitler. In the conclusion, however, he asserted that Churchill, through his conduct of the war, had betrayed the causes he had once championed: 'Churchill stood for the British Empire, for British independence and for an "anti-Socialist" vision of Britain. By July 1945 the first of these was on the skids, the second was dependent solely on America and the third had just vanished in a Labour election victory.'[6]

What are we to make of the Cowling–Irving–Clark–Charmley

thesis? It is by no means a fantasy. The British probably did have the opportunity of obtaining a compromise peace in the summer of 1940. Though Churchill suppressed the facts in his war memoirs, we know now that the issue was discussed by the five members of the War Cabinet – Churchill, Chamberlain, Halifax, Attlee and Greenwood – between 26 and 28 May 1940. The military position of both France and Britain was desperate, with the French Army disintegrating and the British Expeditionary Force fighting its way towards Dunkirk. Mussolini, who had yet to enter the war, offered to act as a mediator between Germany and the Allies in the negotiation of a general European settlement. The French government, led by Pierre Reynaud, was eager to pursue this escape-route and pressed the British to co-operate. The war Cabinet discussions were dominated by Halifax, who argued that if the British could obtain terms 'which did not postulate the destruction of our independence we should be foolish if we did not accept them'. According to Chamberlain's diary, Churchill appeared at one point to agree, remarking on 26 May that 'if we could get out of this jam by giving up Malta and Gibraltar and some African colonies, he would jump at it'.

Churchill at this point had yet to establish his authority as Prime Minister. He was not yet in a position to override a combination of Chamberlain and Halifax, should they choose to stand together. In all probability the views he expressed on compromise peace reflected a position he was tactically compelled to adopt, rather than his own preferred war aim of outright victory. There was also a crucial difference between Halifax's position and his own, which led Halifax to threaten resignation. While Halifax wanted to steer the War Cabinet towards immediate negotiations, Churchill argued for a delay of two or three months on the grounds that Britain might obtain better terms later on. In the end it was he who prevailed at a critical meeting of the War Cabinet at 4 p.m. on 28 May.

When the question of a compromise peace arose again after the French armistice in June 1940, Halifax's deputy, R. A. Butler, invited Bjorn Prytz, the Swedish minister in London, to the Foreign Office and gave him an oral message from Halifax that 'common sense and not bravado would dictate the British Government's policy'. This may have been an attempt to bypass Churchill and elicit Germany's peace terms, but if so it was quickly stifled by the Prime Minister himself. After this he rested on the argument that Britain was more likely to obtain an acceptable peace offer by fighting on – thus postponing the question indefinitely.

The peace-with-Hitler thesis assumes that the British had the option of sitting out the war in splendid isolation, with the Empire safe and sound, and the social fabric intact. This is surely an illusion. German peace terms would almost certainly have included the restoration of some or all of the former German colonies, plus the satisfaction of Mussolini's claims to Malta and other Mediterranean strongholds. So much for the idea that a compromise peace would have ensured the integrity of the Empire.

The assertion that it would have guaranteed the survival of Britain as a great power is equally implausible. Ever since the late seventeenth century Britain had played a leading role in continental diplomacy. Successive governments had recognized that, since Britain was geographically a part of Europe, the Empire could be defended only through the maintenance of a European balance of power. A compromise peace that left Hitler in effective control of the whole of the continent, while Mussolini monopolized the Mediterranean, would have marked the end of Britain as a great power.

The British, presumably, could have negotiated a peace which left Britain itself – with the possible exception of the Channel Islands – free of occupying forces. The monarchy, Big Ben and the Mother of Parliaments would have carried on as though nothing unusual had happened. But on the periphery of a Nazified Europe a vanquished Britain would gradually have become a satellite state whose domestic politics were overshadowed by the triumph of Fascism and the fear of offending Germany. Sir Oswald Mosley and his supporters would have become for the first time a force to be reckoned with, and Fascism a creed with a magnetic attraction for the rising young men of the right. How long would it have been before Hitler called for the suppression of anti-German elements in British politics? How long would it have been before he demanded British co-operation in a European programme to 'resolve the Jewish problem'?

The British Empire in India and the Far East would probably have been granted a temporary respite by a compromise peace. As Clark argues, the British would have been free to move forces to the Far East in order to deter or repulse a Japanese assault. The successful defence of Malaya and Singapore would have given British authority in India an extra lease of life, and convinced Australia and New Zealand that Britain was still capable of protecting them. Yet this whole position east of Suez would have depended on the readiness of Hitler and Mussolini to behave as trustworthy neighbours to a Britain already defeated and stripped of some of its possessions. As long as Britain was vulnerable to blackmail in Europe, the Empire would have been in long-term jeopardy. Churchill's own judgement, delivered to a meeting of ministers outside the War Cabinet on 28 May 1940, was as follows:

> He declared his own decision – despite the current tragedy – to continue the war against Germany without any thought of a negotiated peace. He observed that Hitler would probably be ready to make such a peace, since he was now about to gain all that he wanted in Europe, for the time being at least, and had no particular ambition to conquer Britain. But the Prime Minister added that in his judgment the prospect of Nazi rule throughout the Continent was intolerable, and that its protracted existence would become a steadily increasing threat to Britain itself and to British imperial rule overseas.[7]

The British Empire had been in long-term decline since the turn of the century. Where the Boers and the Irish had led, Gandhi and the Indian Congress party had followed. The best hope of preserving the Empire for another generation lay in the revival of Britain as a European power through the liberation of France, the Low Countries and Scandinavia, and the overthrow of the Nazi regime itself. The alternative to dependence on Nazi Germany was, perhaps, dependence on the United States, a nation hostile to imperialism. But dependence on Nazi Germany would only have been the first step into a nightmare future in which slavery or genocide would have awaited the subject peoples over whom the British ruled. Dependence on the United States was the civilized route to the end of Empire.

It is one of the curiosities of the revisionist case that Churchill alone is held responsible for the British commitment to a total war, while the Conservatives are presented as potential appeasers thrust beneath the wheels of his chariot. The Conservatives had been the party of total war between 1914 and 1918. It was a role which many of them who had previously supported appeasement were eager to repeat after the German occupation of Prague in March 1939. Hitherto obscure Tory backbenchers demanded conscription and a more robust foreign policy. During the two-day pause which followed the German invasion of Poland on 1 September 1939, Conservative MPs were prominent in the clamour for Chamberlain to declare war. It was Conservatives again who rebelled against him in May 1940 for failing to prosecute the war with sufficient vigour. But as yet no evidence has come to light of a movement in favour of a compromise peace on the Conservative backbenches in the summer of 1940. Even Chamberlain seems to have concluded by the end of May 1940 that appeasement was a lost cause. If Halifax and Butler wanted to keep the door to negotiations open, this was probably because they were at the Foreign Office, which existed for the purpose of negotiating. The revisionists seem to be postulating the existence in the summer of 1940 of a party of ultra-appeasers which may never have existed at all.

The debate over peace with Hitler distracts attention from other aspects of Churchill's war leadership. If he is to be charged with waging war at too high a cost in blood and treasure, there are other grounds on which a prosecution might be based. It could be argued, for example, that the war was prolonged unnecessarily by his persistent refusal to acknowledge the German opposition to Hitler, or to set out peace terms intended to divide the regime from its opponents. But this is a matter for counterfactual speculation. The quality of Churchill's judgement as a military leader is a matter on which there is a wealth of hard evidence dating back to Gallipoli. Some military historians, like Ronald Lewin and John Keegan, have taken a broadly favourable view of Churchill's conduct of grand strategy. Others, like Basil Liddell Hart, Stephen Roskill or Tuvia Ben-Moshe, have been strongly critical. Churchill's main contribution to the decline of the British Empire may well have been the failure of his military judgement in the Far East. Though he is careful to acknowledge the drive and inspiration Churchill imparted to the war effort, Roskill writes:

> As regards the Far East, he took decisions which destroyed not only Britain's position in the entire area but that of other European powers as well; while the attempt to defend Greece probably delayed the clearance of the Axis armies from North Africa by some two years, and brought many trials and disappointments in its train. His dedication to the bombing of Germany instead of first securing the safety of our sea communications ... must also be classed as a major strategic error ... Last among his major mistakes and misjudgments may be placed his acceptance at Casablanca early in 1943 of the 'Unconditional Surrender' dogma.[8]

The other main revisionist charge against Churchill – that he opened the door to a Labour victory 1945 – has first of all to be separated from the Thatcherite reading of post-war British history that so often accompanies it. Labour's victory, the argument runs, was a disaster from which Britain was unable to recover until the worst of its effects were reversed by the Thatcher governments of 1979 to 1990. This self-serving view of the past is about three parts propaganda to one part history. The idea that the British economy was fatally damaged by the establishment of the post-war welfare state, or by the nationalization of coal and the railways, has received little support from economic historians. It also seems unlikely that Thatcherite economic policies were ever a viable alternative in the 1940s, 1950s or 1960s: organized labour was too powerful for any government to have 'smashed the unions', privatized the coalmines and so on.

That said, it is clear that a Churchill government after 1945 would have governed along different lines from Labour. It is unlikely, for example, that local authorities would have obtained the sweeping powers of compulsory purchase they were granted by Lewis Silkin's Town and Country Planning Act. Nation-alization of industry would have been avoided, and attempts made to remove wartime controls over the economy as rapidly as possible. The Tory defeat of 1945 was therefore a major reverse from a party point of view. But was it inevitable that the Con-servatives would lose? And how far was Churchill himself respon-sible?

Given that Churchill was leader of the party from 1940 onwards, it is remarkable how far he managed to escape the blame for defeat. In part he was protected by a heroic status which made it very difficult for any substantial criticism of him to be aired in public. Many of his colleagues were privately critical of his conduct of the election campaign, but only revealed this in their memoirs many years later. Conservative propagandists also provided Churchill with a powerful if deceptive alibi of which he was later to make full use in his war memoirs. They argued that, acting from patriotic motives, the Conservatives had abandoned party politics in wartime. MPs and party officials had gone off to join the armed forces or devoted themselves to war work. Hence the machinery of the party had run down, leaving the party at an organizational disadvantage to Labour. Labour activists, mean-while, had never ceased to propagate party doctrines, while the party's organization in the constituencies was sustained and developed by trade unionists in reserved occupations.

There is just sufficient truth in this account to distract attention from the extent to which Churchill was personally responsible for the wartime decline of the party. The Conservatives faced a very strong challenge from the left, the nature of which can be quickly described. As has often been pointed out, the Labour Party benefited from the dual role it played as both government and opposition during the period of coalition politics from 1940 to 1945. On the one hand the official Labour Party was now a party of government with its leaders in the War Cabinet and other prominent positions. The leaders of the party could no longer be depicted, as they had been in the Tory press between the wars, as dangerous cranks and pacifists. Whatever private reservations Tories still felt, they had to be accepted as respectable and patriotic figures whose participation in the war effort was essential to its successful outcome.

The Labour leaders were also able to exercise much leverage within the coalition. Recognizing from the start that Labour's participation in government was an opportunity to influence the making of post-war domestic policy, they began to stake out positions on such questions as social security and full employment. While Churchill's thoughts were elsewhere, they were busy changing the agenda.

Attlee urged his followers to accept loyally the policies of the coalition. But the left wing of the party took very little notice of this. They provided, in fact, the core of the wartime opposition to the coalition. They included such prominent Labour MPs as Bevan and Shinwell. More broadly, the phrase 'Labour left' embraces the radical intelligentsia of academics, journalists and politicians who campaigned from 1940 onwards for a 'people's war': a war for the advancement of collectivist ideas and working-class welfare. Much of their criticism was directed at the Labour leaders in the coalition, whom they charged with 'selling out' to the Conservatives. But their primary aim was to undermine both the Conservative Party and conservative attitudes. Their main platform was the press, especially *Picture Post* and the *Daily Mirror*, but to some extent also they got their message across through official sources – broadcasting, lectures to the armed forces, the documentary films of the Ministry of Information.

The radical intelligentsia were brilliant myth-makers, telling partisan fables which they no doubt believed to be true in all the essentials. It was they who created the myth of the 'guilty men': the men of Munich whom they blamed for the many defeats which Britain suffered between 1940 and 1942; they, too, who impressed on a generation an image of the 1930s as an era in which the great mass of the population had endured poverty, mass unemployment and slum conditions. Finally it was they who invented the myth of the 'people's war': a war of social transformation in which class divisions and 'vested interests' were destined to give way to a sense of community.

So persuasive was the radical propaganda of the war years that it lived on for many years after the war, and entered into the work of academic historians. Even today our perception of the 1930s is haunted by images of the derelict shipyards of Jarrow, or the lawns of Cliveden, the great Victorian house by the Thames where supposedly the appeasers gathered to plot the latest shameful surrender to Hitler. But the left-wing imagery of the 1930s so widely disseminated during the war years was partial and distorted. As historians now recognize, for example, the 1930s were a period of economic recovery in which unemployment fell from a peak of three million to just over one million. Even the most blighted areas of industrial decline were recovering by the end of the 1930s, while the Midlands and the South of England were booming. In housing, education and social insurance, the policies of the national government were moderately progressive and far from the caricature of a regime committed to harsh economies at the expense of the poor. The foreign and defence policies of the national government remain controversial, but the Battle of Britain could never have been won without the preparations made in the 1930s, and if the appeasers had made mistakes, so too had the Labour and Liberal parties.

Here, then, was the challenge faced by the Conservative Party. As we can see, with the benefit of hindsight, it was a challenge that defeated them. To the challenge from the left there was very little co-ordinated or effective response. At some point between the phoney war, when the opinion polls showed a large Tory lead, and the summer of 1943, when the next round of opinion polls showed a large Labour lead, there was a dramatic swing against them. It is possible of course to write off the Conservative defeat as the inevitable consequence of the 'spirit of the age'. But the 'spirit of the age' owed much to the sudden passivity and impotence of a party which had dominated Britain for almost the whole of the period between the two world wars. How is this to be explained?

It would be quite wrong to suppose that the Conservatives in wartime were either absent on active service, or oblivious of partisan concerns. Though the party's ranks were depleted at all levels, there was always on the home front a Tory nation alive and alert, and full of the most robust opinions. It was a nation deeply alarmed by the advance of the left. Backbench Tory MPs, for example, saw how Labour ministers were seizing the initiative in domestic policy. From time to time they rebelled against the trend, as in the spring of 1942 when they succeeded in killing off Dalton's plans for the introduction of coal rationing. They were especially disturbed by the rise and rise of Ernest Bevin. In February 1943, no fewer than 116 Tory MPs voted against his Catering and Wages Bill, which laid down minimum wages and conditions in the catering trades.

What the Tory nation lacked was a leader. There were, of course, occasions on which Churchill himself exploded angrily against some real or imagined left-wing manoeuvre. He tried to suppress the *Daily Mirror*. He tried, also in vain, to forbid the making of the film *The Life and Death of Colonel Blimp*. He attempted more than once to put an end to the Army discussion classes organized by ABCA, the Army Bureau of Current Affairs. On all three occasions his interventions were ineffective. But he did succeed in marking out a line of resistance beyond which Conservative ministers in the coalition were unprepared to make concessions to Labour. He ruled out the nationalization of coal in 1943. He was also remarkably firm in resisting the demands of Bevin and the TUC for the revision of the Trade Disputes Act of 1927.

In all this, however, Churchill and the Conservatives were on the defensive, reacting to Labour and the left as and when issues arose. At no point during the war did the Conservatives succeed in organizing a counterattack: by the time of the general election campaign it was too late. After the election defeat, Conservatives complained that for five years they had been under attack from left-wing propaganda while the Conservatives themselves had abstained from attacks on their opponents. To a very great extent this was true: and the primary explanation lay in the fact that Churchill consistently neglected the interests of the party of which he was nominally the leader.

Why was this? As had already been remarked, Churchill was a profoundly egocentric statesman for whom parties were vehicles of ambition rather than causes to be served. When in 1940 he took over the leadership of the Conservative Party he did so solely for the purpose of ensuring that his authority as a war leader was buttressed by control over the majority party in the House. His closest political friends were maverick Conservatives like Bracken and Beaverbrook who, like him, were distrusted by orthodox Tories. He seldom got on well with such leading party officials as the Chief Whip, the Chairman of the 1922 Committee or the Chairman of the party organization.

It is not surprising therefore that Churchill seldom had the long-term interests of the Conservatives at heart. In the past he had frequently favoured coalition governments. When, during the war, he did occasionally peer ahead to the future, he was inclined to believe that the problems of the peace would best be handled by a continuation of the wartime coalition. From the Conservative Party's point of view it was also a problem that Churchill, unlike Neville Chamberlain, took little or no interest in social, industrial and economic affairs. He had lost the zeal for social reform that he had long ago displayed as an Edwardian Liberal. By the 1930s he was convinced that social and economic conditions had improved so much that little more needed to be done.

Such was Churchill's outlook that he repeatedly missed the opportunity to frame a Conservative strategy in the field of social and economic policy. The first opportunity occurred during the summer and autumn of 1940 when his old friend Duff Cooper, a true-blue Tory who was Minister of Information, proposed a declaration of British war aims including proposals to deal with unemployment, equal educational opportunities for all and greater social equality. Churchill's private secretary, John Colville, recorded in his diary: 'It is noteworthy that this paper has been written by a Conservative ... as in Disraeli's time perhaps the Tory party may prove to be the initiators of social revolution.'[9] Churchill, however, forbade any British declaration of war aims on the grounds that it would be premature and liable to stir up divisions at home.

The second opportunity occurred in July 1941 when the Conservative Party appointed R. A. Butler, the President of the Board of Education, to chair a committee to present Churchill with the party's views on post-war problems. Here again was a chance to develop a distinctively Conservative approach to domestic policy. The Committee did subsequently produce numerous reports but they never became Conservative policy for the simple reason that they were never endorsed by Churchill. In all probability he never read them.[10] Butler did of course go on to achieve one great triumph to the credit of the Conservative Party, the Education Act of 1944. But he did so by acting in defiance of Churchill, who had forbidden him to introduce legislation.

Churchill's leadership created a vacuum in the realm of post-war policy. The Conservative Party was unable to seize the initiative. It was seized instead by William Beveridge in his famous report, which appeared as a White Paper under the dry title of *Social Insurance and Allied Services*. Churchill has often been criticized for mishandling the report, but for once the criticism is exaggerated. This was one of the few occasions during the war when he gave some consideration to social policy. Like the majority of Conservatives he had serious reservations about the report; at the same time he had to ensure that the Labour Party remained within the coalition. He therefore hammered out a compromise which enabled preparations for post-war legislation to begin, while ruling out legislation in wartime. He also went on the radio to announce that the government was preparing a 'Four-Year Plan' of social reform for presentation to the electorate at the first post-war general election.

Though Churchill addressed the problem, he did so wearing his Prime Ministerial hat, rather than the hat of a Conservative Party Leader. He missed the opportunity of appropriating Beveridge for the Conservatives, though it would only have taken half a dozen speeches to tame party gatherings to achieve this. Churchill had little time for party gatherings and none for party policy. Henceforth official Conservative policy was virtually indistinguishable from the policies of the coalition government, outlined in a series of White Papers between 1943 and 1945. The Labour Party, meanwhile, continued to influence the making of post-war plans within the coalition, but took care to maintain within the party machine its own independent policymaking process.

It is clear in retrospect that, as the end of the war approached, the majority of electors were primarily concerned about the issues of housing and unemployment. More broadly, it was the agenda of the future welfare state which interested them. As it happened, Churchill at this time was the head of a government that was making extensive preparations for the extension of social welfare.

In a Prime Ministerial minute of October 1944, he himself defined the immediate post-war priorities as 'food, home and work'. It is fairly certain also that, had the Conservatives won the general election of 1945, a Churchill government would have established some form of welfare state. This is clear from the manifesto, *Mr Churchill's Declaration of Policy to the Electors*, which he and other party officials composed. Another indication of the shape of things to come was a Cabinet memo of 3 July to his colleagues in the 'Caretaker government', the brief interlude of Conservative rule between the end of the coalition and the announcement of the general election result. Churchill fore-shadowed an intensive housing drive in the style of a military operation, and the introduction of the National Insurance and National Health Service Bills.[11]

In spite of this, Churchill singularly failed between 1943 and 1945 to convey to the electorate any message at all about domestic policy. None of his wartime broadcasts after March 1943 gave pride of place to questions of social policy and few even mentioned them. Nor did Churchill make more than the occasional token effort to counterattack the radical myth-makers and their propaganda. In one respect, indeed, he was an accomplice in the attack on pre-war Conservatism: he made no bones about his condemnation of the appeasers and the Munich agreement. In the Edwardian period Churchill had argued that the best insurance against socialism was social reform. But this was a maxim he seemed now to have for-gotten. During the election campaign of 1945 he brushed aside advice that he should emphasize social reform and adopted a nega-tive, scaremongering approach, including the notorious claim that a Labour government would introduce some form of Gestapo, 'no doubt humanely administered in the first instance'.

How far was Churchill personally responsible for the Con-servative defeat of 1945? As we have seen, Churchill actively prevented the party from developing a strategy for dealing with the challenges from the left. A number of leading Tories – notably Anthony Eden, R. A. Butler and the Tory Reform Group –

wanted to see the party adopt a progressive strategy at home, based on the expansion of the social services and a measure of agreement with the Labour ministers in the coalition. On the assumption that the primary aspiration of the electorate in 1945 was a welfare state rather than a socialist state, such a strategy might have stood some chance of success. In view of the fact that Churchill was in fact preparing to deliver his own version of Beveridge in 1945 it would have been appropriate and indeed honest. Others would have liked the Conservatives to have fought a more partisan war, defending their record, attacking their opponents, and framing a programme in harmony with the social and economic policies for which Baldwin and Chamberlain had stood. Whether this more combative and ideological approach would have attracted popular support is more doubtful. But it might have succeeded under a leader who recognized, from 1941–2 onwards, that the domestic future was at stake. Such a paragon would have ensured that the Conservatives, like the Labour Party, continued to hold their annual party conference during the war years. (Conservative conferences occurred in May 1943 and March 1945 only). The Research Department would have been revived, ministers enlisted into a Shadow Cabinet for post-war policy, Conservatives' publicists mobilized and prepared for the fray. Chamberlain, had he lived, might have pursued such a course: it was inconceivable that Churchill would do so.

When he did address the strategic problems his party faced, Churchill wavered between the alternatives. At one point during the 1945 election campaign he gave Attlee a lift in his car. Speaking of his electoral tactics Churchill confessed: 'I've tried them with pep and I've tried them with pap, and I still don't know what they want.' Even allowing for the fact that Churchill was so exhausted at the time, with his thoughts dwelling on international affairs, this lack of feel for what was happening inside his own country remains something of a puzzle. Yet the consequences are clear. The Labour and Conservative parties both contributed greatly to the war effort and to ultimate victory. But the Labour Party knew where it was going after the war, while the Conservatives in 1945 were divided and uncertain of themselves.

Was this the price the Conservatives paid for Churchill? Only up to a point: the deeper cause was the war itself. Indeed the debate between the revisionists and the defenders of Churchill is actually a debate about the impact and significance of the Second World War, displaced into the realm of biography. The revisionists claim that Churchill must bear a large share of the responsibility for the decline of Britain. But as used in this context the 'decline of Britain' is not a historical fact but a highly partisan interpretation in which the loss of social and imperial ascendancies is equated with the decline of Britain both at home and abroad.

There is no need to accept this wholly negative audit of the impact of war. Let us itemize in parallel columns the 'cost of victory' as defined by the revisionists, and an alternative list of the 'benefits of victory'. (The table is intended only as an exercise to illustrate the possibilities, not as a final accounting of the audit of war.) Some of the consequences of the war which revisionists place in the debit column may, on alternative assumptions, be turned into credits. In other cases debits are balanced by credit items which the revisionists omit.

the costs of victory	*the benefits of victory*
dependence on the United States	independence of Nazi Germany
Eastern Europe under Soviet rule	restoration of independent and democratic Western Europe
decline of the British Empire	liberation of Britain from excessive overseas commitment
long-term damage inflicted by the war on the British economy	full employment and the 'long boom' of 1945–73
Labour victory of 1945: post-war social and industrial malaise	the welfare state and greater social equality

To sum up, the aim of the revisionists is to make Churchill into a scapegoat for national decline. On closer inspection, the 'national decline' of which they speak proves to be almost indistinguishable from the misfortunes of the Conservative Party in general, and the diehard right in particular, during the Second World War. Churchill did indeed bear a large measure of personal responsibility for the electoral – and ideological – defeat of the Conservatives in the general election of 1945. A sublime egotist, he was far too deeply immersed in the conduct of the war to pay much attention to the interests of a political party. But it was these very attributes that made Churchill unique and indispensable as a national leader at the head of a coalition government. As the giant who transcended party, he could be trusted to devote all his driving force to the one great objective on which all were agreed.

It is arguable that Churchill made mistakes, as a result of which the British paid a higher price for victory than they need have done. But it is hard to see who else could possibly have supplied the drive, the inspiration and the authority to keep the show on the road. But for Churchill, the British war effort might have petered out in faction, intrigue and defeatism in the summer of 1940. If so, Churchill was truly the saviour of his country.

CHAPTER IV

RECONSTRUCTING BRITAIN: LABOUR IN POWER 1945–1951

JIM TOMLINSON

The Attlee government, elected in the last weeks of the Second World War, was one of the most important administrations of the twentieth century. This was the first Labour government to have had a large majority and run its full term of office. The legacy of six years of total war provided an opportunity to reshape Britain, and in several major respects this is precisely what was achieved. The radical reform programme of the government left a lasting legacy, though whether this was mainly for good or mainly for ill is a highly controversial question. Ever since 1951 some commentators have characterized the policies pursued under Attlee as major causes of Britain's post-war 'decline'. Against this view, defenders of the government see it as having created the full employment and more equal welfare state of the 1950 and 1960s which greatly benefited the mass of the population.

Labour's programme in 1945 committed the party to extensive nationalization of basic industries, a significant expansion of social welfare, full employment and thoroughgoing planning of the economy. This programme, driven by the experience of mass unemployment in the 1930s, reflected the belief that only a much more state-owned and state-regulated economy could deliver economic stability, high employment and social security. Labour also recognized that better conditions for the majority required a modernization of the economy, because inter-war British capitalism had been both unjust and inefficient. All these elements of Labour's programme were connected. Full employment would be secured by economic planning and nationalization. Public ownership would bring government control over what were believed to be the 'commanding heights' of the economy, while making possible greater popular involvement in production. Planning and public ownership would also be the basis for modernizing the economy, and together these two policies should secure greater industrial competitiveness, underpin full employment and provide the resources for the expansion of welfare.

When Labour came to power in July 1945 many things were in the new government's favour. It had a huge parliamentary majority of 183 seats over all other parties (with 48 per cent of the vote), and for a while their unexpected defeat left the Conservatives in disarray. The new Labour government was able to tap into a popular desire for social improvement generated in the war years, though in the heady days of victory many Labour politicians and their supporters probably exaggerated the nation's desire for 'socialism'. Most people who voted for Attlee in 1945 were voting against the Tory record of unemployment and social insecurity of the 1930s, rather than in favour of a wholesale transition to a new social order. People wanted jobs, housing, social security and generally a better life for themselves and their families. They believed that Labour was much more likely to deliver these than the Conservatives, and this provided Labour initially with a great deal of popular goodwill. But the nature of this support meant that if these aims were not achieved the goodwill would diminish. In trying to deliver its programme Labour was helped by the wartime legacy of disciplined co-operation in many spheres of national life, underpinned by extensive state regulation. People had become used to the state controlling many aspects of their lives in pursuit of what, in wartime, was generally accepted as the greater good. Although this mood of acceptance continued into the early period of post-war reconstruction, it increasingly conflicted with a wish for a more relaxed, less regulated lifestyle – a yearning for a return to a full peace, rather than an indefinite continuation of wartime conditions.

While the political circumstances helped to create a honeymoon period for the new government, the economic conditions it inherited were much less favourable. The war left a legacy of rundown or destroyed capital equipment, massive damage to the housing stock, an exhausted labour force, and above all immense balance of payments problems. During the war Britain had sacrificed long-term economic advantages in order to win the war; once peace came there was no alternative but to rebuild the economy and to recapture export markets. In the short-term there was an inescapable need to borrow from the United States to help with the payments problem. Britain could not feed its population or provide raw materials for its industries without imports, and once the Americans stopped Lend–Lease at the end of the war with Japan (August 1945), and so ended Britain's ability to obtain its imports without paying for them, only the US could bridge the gap. Even during the war it had been recognized that to restore balance, exports would have to rise to 75 per cent above their 1939 level, but, whatever the policies pursued, such an increase could not happen overnight. Negotiations for the American loan had begun before the end of the war, under the wartime coalition, but the Attlee government finally accepted a deal of $3.75 billion at low interest rates and to be paid back over 50 years. The terms of the loan were quite generous by normal commercial standards, and came with few strings attached, but its acceptance by the new government emphasized both Britain's current economic weakness and the dominance of the USA in the post-war world.

Raising the level of exports to pay for much-needed imports and to escape reliance on loans from other countries became the first priority of the government. But this in turn required new investment in Britain's rundown capital equipment. In other words, as Labour well understood, economic survival demanded

79

a dramatic effort at industrial modernization – in the transport network, in the fuel industries and in manufacturing equipment. Exports and investment battled to be first in the queue for available resources, a battle usually won by exports because nothing was more urgent than feeding the population and supplying inputs to industry. Right at the back of the queue was consumption. This had already been squeezed heavily in the war, and Labour's policies continued the process.

Labour enjoyed an initial period of about eighteen months of government during which, despite great international tensions, above all with the start of the Cold War, the domestic programme of reform seemed to be running fairly smoothly. With vigour and enthusiasm Labour launched its programme of nationalization, the most important early examples being the Bank of England and the coal industry. The first of these, nationalizing the Bank, probably made rather little operational difference to policy, but it symbolized Labour's commitment to controlling the economy and not to allow private interests to stand in the way. Nationalization of coal was also hugely symbolic of Labour's intentions. In the inter-war years the condition of the coal industry had epitomized the failings of private enterprise, with its inefficiency, high unemployment and terrible industrial relations. Nationalizing coal was designed to end all that, and to allow the creation of a modernized industry, with real improvements in the wages, conditions and overall treatment of the miners. Coal was also seen as one of the key 'commanding heights' of the economy, a vital industry the demand for whose output was enormous and growing, in an economy still heavily dependent on coal for both fuel and raw materials. The photographs of miners marching to work under union banners on the first day of the new National Coal Board provide one of the most potent symbols of the world of the 1940s, not least in their expression of hope for a new beginning. It is extraordinary how quickly this industry, with over 900 separate mines and over 700,000 workers, was brought into public ownership, all the more so given that detailed planning for the execution of this long-advocated policy was very limited. This speed reflected not only the political importance of miners within the labour movement, but also the strength of the belief that only public ownership could put this ailing but crucial industry to rights.

Enacted in parallel with these early nationalizations were the key measures to reform and expand the welfare state. The most important of these was the creation by statute in 1946 of the National Health Service. This established the principle of comprehensive provision of medical services to everyone, without payment at the time of use. The finance for that service was to come overwhelmingly from general taxation. The setting up of the NHS was in many respects another instance of nationalization, as hospitals previously owned by local authorities were taken over by central government, along with voluntary and private establishments. There was debate in the Cabinet about maintaining local authorities as key bodies in the new system, but in the end the dominant view was that only a nationalized system could aspire to create equal standards of provision across the country, in place of the patchwork of services under the existing system.

Aneurin Bevan, the Minister of Health in charge of the creation of the NHS, became locked in a gigantic struggle with the doctors, both GPs and consultants, as he fought to establish the new service. He made substantial concessions on such issues as allowing private practice to continue and permitting GPs to be self-employed contractors to the NHS rather than state employees, but none of these agreements threatened the basic principle of a service free to all at the point of delivery. The new NHS seems to have been immensely popular from its inception, and the government's decisiveness in driving its creation through Parliament quickly is the best indication of the new government's determination and ability to deliver on its promises.

The National Insurance Act was also passed in 1946, creating a comprehensive system of social insurance, providing benefits during ill health, unemployment and retirement, as well as maternity and death benefits. As with the NHS, the new system replaced a patchwork of provision which had left many people, especially those not in full-time work, without coverage for some or all of these contingencies. The scheme was substantially based on the principles set out in the highly popular Beveridge Report of 1942, though Labour had been developing plans along similar lines for several years before that. Unlike the funding of the health service, access to the provision of resources from the social insurance system was tied to an individual's contribution record, rather than simply open to all citizens. But the aim was to incorporate everyone in the new system, and eventually to make other kinds of income maintenance redundant. The National Assistance Act of 1948 intended to provide for the shrinking number of those who fell through the national insurance net. Unfortunately, the nature of national insurance as established in 1946 prevented this shrinking from happening, because the benefit levels agreed in that year were too low to provide an adequate subsistence for the poor, especially poor pensioners. This was an unavoidable consequence of the flat-rate contributory system, because it meant that contributions had to be geared to what could be afforded by the lowest paid, which ensured in turn that benefit levels were kept low. But these problems were not immediately apparent in 1946, and the new system did offer security of income for many people in Britain.

In sum, after little more than a year in office, Labour delivered a major extension of public ownership and the key legislation for a new welfare state. These were significant achievements, and their enactment created a strong impression of a government delivering quickly on its manifesto promises. This positive perspective dominates the events of 1946, though even at this stage there were signs of emerging problems in one other key area where Labour had made big promises in 1945. This was housing.

Responding to the national desire to rebuild the blitzed cities and end slum-housing, Labour had promised to give high priority to housing, and to build a million new houses over a five-year period. Legislation to this end was quickly passed. Many new houses were started, but difficulties quickly arose. One complication was that house-building is very labour-intensive, yet in 1946 the government was desperate to get more workers into vital industries such as coal or into export sectors such as textiles. House-building also used lots of timber, almost all of which Britain had to import, and at a time of serious trade imbalances such imports were unwelcome. Perhaps the most worrying aspect of the situation for the new government was how unresponsive the building industry was to attempts to plan its activities. Labour wanted to give priority to local authority house-building, but many housing starts were left uncompleted as small, often one-person, building companies responded to more profitable demands from existing house-owners for repair work and improvements. Before the end of 1946 it was evident that the scale of house-building had to reined back, with inevitable disappointment for the millions living in sub-standard accommodation. But, although discouraging, the emerging difficulties over housing were the only serious blemish on what was otherwise a very successful initial period of reforming legislation.

Real problems for the government only began in the winter months at the beginning of 1947. A shortage of coal from the newly nationalized pits coincided with the worst weather since 1880. The government ordered extensive industrial shutdowns because the electricity-generating stations could not be supplied with enough coal, with serious consequences for both production and morale in industry. There was little the government could do about the coincidence of these two events, but the fact that the coal industry was now nationalized emphasized that changes in ownership were no panacea for economic problems. Moreover, the Minister of Fuel and Power, Emanuel Shinwell, showed little sign of the skills needed either to deal with the crisis or to stop it turning into a public-relations disaster for the government. For the first time, the government's ability to run the economy came seriously into question.

Eventually, the arrival of better weather in the spring of 1947 'solved' the problem, at least for the immediate future, but other serious difficulties soon followed. As a condition of the American loan, Britain had agreed to free the pound from controls and make it convertible into other currencies one year after the deal was ratified by the American Senate. When this date was reached in the summer of 1947, this commitment was honoured, and straightaway the international value of the currency plummeted, as holders of sterling fled into dollars because of the obvious weaknesses of the British economy compared with the buoyancy of the USA. After six weeks this outflow of foreign exchange forced a reversal of policy and the reimposition of controls. This crisis brought home to the government the continuing threat of the weak balance of payments, and the need to look again at economic policy. Total claims on Britain's economic resources were far outrunning available supplies, and this was having its most serious impact on the balance of payments, given that demand for imports was strong and that there was also pressure to divert goods needed for exports in to the home market. With full employment, consumers had the money to spend to try to make up for wartime deprivations, and companies too wanted to rebuild their stocks.

In the face of this second big crisis of 1947, the government tried to improve the mechanisms for planning the allocation of these scarce supplies by creating a new Ministry of Economic Affairs, headed by Sir Stafford Cripps, and at the same time established new planning bodies within central government. Many on the Labour side saw more effective planning and controls as the way to deal with the continuing weaknesses. In the same year, recognizing that these excessive demands on the economy were creating all sorts of distortions, ranging from the balance of payments deficit, to inflation, through to tightened rationing, the government started to use the national budget much more stringently to reduce overall demand in the economy. After the emergency budget of November 1947, especially, the government was taking far more out of the economy in the form of taxation than it was putting in from public expenditure. So from late 1947 Labour was adopting a two-pronged strategy: making a more intensified use of state control over resources by means of a 'Keynesian' approach (which puts the emphasis on government control of the overall size of total consumption and investment) but at the same time allowing more scope for market forces in the allocation of resources. After 1947 the second of these methods slowly came to predominate, and faith in planning to decline, though it should be emphasized that state control of the economy remained far-reaching right down to 1951 and beyond.

From 1947 the priorities already implicit in previous economic policy became very clear. Exports had to have the lion's share of any increase in resources, followed by industrial investment. The feeling of crisis evident in 1947 is shown by government's widespread use of the slogan 'Export or Die'. A massive campaign of exhortation was launched to convince the public of the vital need to increase exports. Workers in the Lancashire cotton industry were told that 'Britain's bread hangs by Lancashire's thread', and individual workers who had increased their output of cotton goods featured in leaflets distributed by the Central Office of Information. The government also supported the setting up of the Anglo-American Council on Productivity to encourage the adoption of American methods deemed superior in producing greater output from a restricted supply of labour. Such government-sponsored action was not wholly without effect, but equally it antagonized many who wanted to escape at last from selfless devotion to the national effort and turn their attention to more private concerns. Workers in Lancashire, for example, were not easily tempted back into a cotton industry with its long history of inadequate competitiveness, and which even in its current boom state often seemed far less attractive than better-paid jobs in engineering or, as far as many women were concerned, child care and domestic responsibilities.

The justification for this government emphasis on the improvement of the balance of payments was spelt out in the *Economic Survey for 1947*, which proclaimed that 'Failure to build up our export trade in the next two or three years so that we can afford to buy enough imports would mean continued food rationing, much less smoking and private motoring, widespread unemployment for lack of raw materials and inability to equip industry with the most modern machinery.'[1] This stark presentation of the policy dilemmas facing the government was accurate as far as it went, but it was incomplete. The balance of payments problems faced by Britain in the 1940s, which came to a head in 1947, were not just about paying for imports of industrial and consumer necessities. Deficits also resulted from two other features of the period – the massive outflows of funds to pay for Britain's overseas political and military ambitions, and the movement of capital from London to countries such as Australia and South Africa. The first of these led to Britain spending large sums of money everywhere from Europe to the Far East. The export of capital was largely a consequence of the Sterling Area, the arrangement by which countries, mainly in the Empire, held their foreign exchange reserves in sterling, and in return expected free access to the London capital market for their investment needs. The Attlee government was strongly committed to maintaining Britain's world role, and both the general overseas expenditure commitments and the continuation of the Sterling Area followed from these ambitions.

The balance of payments was therefore, in part, a political problem, an issue about how far Britain could continue its pre-war policy of remaining a great power. This policy had a significant economic cost, and these economic weaknesses in turn threatened to undermine the government's global political pretensions. Particularly galling was the subordination to the USA brought about by the need to obtain dollars. As Foreign Secretary Ernest Bevin said in 1947, 'we must free ourselves from financial dependence on the US as soon as possible. We shall never be able to pull our weight in foreign affairs until we do.'[2]

As already noted, the political and economic imperatives of improving the balance of payments, plus the determination to raise investment, meant that consumption came last in the claims on resources. To hold down consumption, wartime austerity had to be continued, and in many ways became the dominant feature of the domestic economy for the rest of the Attlee period. Austerity was evident in both collective (welfare provision) and personal consumption.

Austerity ensured, as we have seen, that benefits under the new insurance system were set at a low level. But there was no immediate political fall-out from this, above all because full employment enormously reduced the numbers dependent on benefit compared with the pre-war period. Elsewhere in the welfare state, austerity meant that improvements in housing, education and health care were less than had been hoped for in 1945, especially where there was a need for resources that would have to be imported or that could otherwise go into exports or investment. House-building was limited by the desire to save timber and to build up manpower in other sectors. School- and hospital-building was constrained by the need to economise on iron and steel, the key input in short supply in this period, and desperately needed for both exports and home investment. As a result, school-building was almost entirely limited to providing space for the rising number of pupils, with very little improvement attained in the low physical standards of the system. In health, the control over new building was even more stringent, with, strikingly, no new hospitals at all being started under the Labour government, although the 1946 Act had envisaged a nationwide system of district general hospitals to replace the hotchpotch of existing provision. In addition, very few of the local health centres, which had also been seen as a pivotal part of the new system as sketched in the legislation, came to be built, though the scale of resources involved in these was very small.

Austerity for consumers was also very severe. While the total output of the British economy rose by about 30 per cent under the Attlee government, personal consumption rose at only about a third as fast. This diversion of resources away from the consumer was only achieved by extensive rationing, at times going beyond even what had been imposed during the war. Rationing was unpopular partly for the obvious reason that it prevented most people from buying the goods they would have liked. One not wholly trivial example is pottery: all coloured and patterned wares were reserved for export, and only plain white china was allowed to be sold at home. This kind of policy provoked resentment, and could lead to law-breaking. Petrol is another conspicuous case: the ration for the ordinary consumer was reduced to nothing during the crisis of August 1947. In early 1948 two men stole a large number of bottles of whisky, not in order to drink or sell them, but to try and barter them for petrol. When chased, they threw more than two dozen bottles at the pursuing police.[3] Such incidents were not common, and although black markets in rationed goods existed during this period, their extent is often exaggerated. But it seems clear that black markets were widely tolerated even by those who did not participate in them, with the result that the legitimacy of evading government controls was perhaps increasingly accepted.

More serious for the government than illegal reactions to rationing were the political responses. One very important hostile response came from women's groups. Not only did women suffer from the shortage of goods which afflicted everyone, but in addition they were usually responsible for obtaining what goods were available, and this often meant queuing for hours. Long periods of queuing often ended in disappointment, though the pleasure obtained from being able to buy such 'exotic' goods as bananas was immense. Other features of austerity hit women particularly hard. For example, the desire to save on cloth led to appeals by the government for women to stick to short skirts and not to adopt the style of the 'New Look', which first appeared in 1947, with its long skirts and 'extravagant' use of material.[4]

The best known of the organizations stimulated by this anti-austerity feeling was the British Housewives League. This seems to have originated as a non-political body, largely concerned to protest at the behaviour of overbearing shopkeepers, which quickly obtained wide-ranging support, and was then taken up by the Conservative Party as a vehicle for its own anti-austerity and anti-government line. The League held marches and rallies which attracted a great deal of attention, and the government was forced on to the defensive, not only about the existence of such shortages of goods, but also about the allegedly bureaucratic way the problem was being dealt with. Labour, it was said, liked controls for their own sake. One sign that such pressures were having some effect came in 1948, when the President of the Board of Trade, Harold Wilson, announced a 'bonfire of controls'. The substance of this bonfire was very limited, much of it relating to paperwork required to produce vacuum flasks, but the very fact of its highly public announcement reflected the political difficulty the government was having in continuing with the wartime pattern of centralized controls over consumer goods in peacetime. Companies, too, were complaining about irksome controls over supplies of raw materials, imported goods and investment equipment. The comprehensiveness of these controls is brought out by the detail that permission had to be given to produce even a minor article like a cricket ball. Here, also, the government ceded ground, reducing controls progressively as soon as it deemed the economic consequences of relaxation at all acceptable.

After 1947 the government never regained the confidence and verve it had shown in the early months of power. The external economic crisis of 1947 was not repeated in 1948, thanks in part to the inflow of Marshall Aid from the US, which eased the balance of payments problem where it was at its most severe, in relation to the supply of dollars. The programme of domestic reform continued, with the nationalizations of gas and electricity, and the passing of the National Assistance Act. But Marshall Aid, though helpful, was not sufficient to prevent the return of problems on the dollar front, and these balance of payments pressures created a new, and again serious, external economic crisis in 1949. By that year, the very sharp rise in the level of exports, as well as controls on imports, meant that the overall balance of payments position had radically improved since 1945, but the dollar position was still precarious. When renewed downward pressure was exerted on the international value of the pound in 1949, the government was eventually forced to devalue the currency from $4.03 to $2.80 in September of that year. This decision can be defended as perfectly rational in economic terms. The competitive power of the American economy had improved enormously since the value of the pound against the dollar had been fixed at the beginning of the war, and economically it made sense to accept the implications of that change, and try to restore Britain's ability to compete in dollar markets by devaluation of the currency, thereby reducing the price of exports. But the affair was mishandled, and the decision taken only after a long period of resistance and argument within the government, which meant that, in the end, the devaluation was larger than might have been the case if the decision had been made at an earlier stage. Devaluation did eventually succeed in improving Britain's export position in North America and other dollar markets, but this required cuts in government spending to provide more productive capacity, and this process of public spending reductions was accompanied by another crisis in 1949. By the end of that year, the reputation of the government for competence in economic affairs was badly dented.

By the time of the 1950 general election most of the promises of Labour's 1945 manifesto had been fulfilled. With the most contentious nationalization measure, covering the iron and steel industry, on its way to completion, about 20 per cent of the economy was now under public ownership. A comprehensive, if not generous, welfare state had been established. The balance of payments was at last looking healthy, thanks to rigorous control of non-essential imports, devaluation against the dollar and a very successful export drive. Industrial investment had risen sharply, though from very low levels at the end of the war, and this was part of a policy of industrial modernization which had been enthusiastically pursued. As in wartime, austerity coupled to rationing had secured a much more egalitarian pattern of consumption than had ever existed before the war. This was reflected in health standards, which continued to show a closing of the gap in the conditions of different social classes, a trend begun during the war. But austerity had become increasingly unpopular, especially as the Conservatives had some success in portraying it as a consequence of 'socialist mismanagement'. Many senior Labour ministers were exhausted and/or ill by 1950, some having held onerous government jobs continuously since the formation of the coalition in 1940. The reforming drive so apparent in 1945 had greatly diminished, partly because so many of the intended legislative changes had been achieved.

Labour's manifesto for the 1950 general election had a 'steady as she goes' flavour, with no major new plans in domestic policy, and talk of further nationalization only in the relatively minor cases of cement, industrial insurance and sugar. While the last of these proposals stimulated the famous 'Mr Cube' anti-public ownership campaign by the Tate and Lyle company, the political storm caused was hardly a reflection of the importance of the industry. Whatever the merits of the nationalization case, sugar was hardly a 'commanding height'. On the other side, the Conservatives concentrated on the idea of 'setting the people free'. The 1950 election saw no big change in Labour's share of the vote since 1945, but in numbers of parliamentary seats the Liberals lost ground, mainly to the advantage of the Conservatives. While Labour seems to have held on to most of its working-class vote, and piled up huge majorities in its industrial and urban heartlands, it suffered losses in marginal seats, especially in suburban areas in the south of the country, where in 1945 it had made some of its mostly startling gains.

The last year of the Labour government, with its majority reduced to only five seats, was overshadowed by the outbreak of the Korean War, with Britain enthusiastically backing the US call for military resistance to the attack on the South, and by internal squabbling about the future direction of the party. The Korean War led to a reversal of the policy of spending less on armaments which had been steadily followed through the late 1940s – though even in 1950 Britain had a much larger military spending and manpower commitment to the services than ever before in peacetime. The majority of the Cabinet decided to respond to the war by a massive remobilization of resources behind the military effort. A large part of the reason was to impress the United States with Britain's capacity to play a world role, and therefore the country's right to be treated as an equal by America. Pursuit of these military ambitions required a tight rein on public expenditure growth, as well as a shift of resources out of civilian production into armaments.

The debate over the public expenditure implications of rearmament focused attention on the financial costs of the NHS, which had grown rapidly since the service began, and well beyond official expectations. Gaitskell, the Chancellor of the Exchequer, was determined to make a political point about the need to limit this expenditure, especially in the light of the Korean crisis. His opponent was Bevan, who by this time had emerged as the leading figure on the left of the party, and who argued not only that the money spent on health was necessary and appropriate, but also that Gaitskell's rearmament proposals were impossible to achieve because they would entail colossal diversion of resources from other sectors of the economy. Bevan lost the argument in the Cabinet, after widely publicized rows, and resigned, though his predictions about the unsustainable character of the proposed rearmament drive were later vindicated by the cuts in the programme brought in by the Conservative when they returned to power.

The resignation of Bevan and two other more junior ministers symbolized both the emerging divisions in the Labour party and its loss of clear direction. The majority of the leadership looked towards a policy of 'consolidation', with little more significant reform to be proposed. The left looked to further extensions of public ownership as the means of continuing to move towards a socialist society. By 1951 most of the Cabinet seem to have lost the will to go on and, rather than struggling with a small majority, decided to call another election. Labour actually increased its share of the vote in the general election of that year, though the continued collapse of Liberal support, which largely benefited the Conservatives, meant a comfortable Conservative majority of seventeen seats.

The reforms of the Attlee government were broad in scope, and their effects wide-ranging. One area of considerable advance was undoubtedly the welfare state, especially the NHS. Before the war access to health care for most working-class people was obtained through insurance cover. Many were excluded, especially married women, and the coverage for those included was patchy and incomplete. For example, even those entitled to spectacles had to pay almost half the cost. The costs of health care in inter-war Britain led to the exclusion of much of the population from some or all of its benefits. This was spectacularly illustrated by the explosion in demand, especially for dentistry and spectacles, when the NHS was established. In the case of dentistry, before 1939 many working-class people had simply let their teeth decay until the pain became unacceptable, and then had the tooth extracted, often by do-it-yourself measures which became a source of substantial folklore. The end was reached when the final teeth were extracted and dentures required, often second-hand and therefore ill-fitting and uncomfortable. Filling (or 'stopping', as it was then called) was expensive and relatively uncommon. With spectacles, it was common to use a ready-made pair from

Woolworths or a second-hand pair, and though these might improve sight to some extent, it was unlikely that the best available help would be obtained.

Given this history, it is not surprising that the early years of the NHS saw a dramatic surge in demand as people acquired dentures that fitted and spectacles suited to their needs. Even wigs could be obtained if deemed medically justified, though new 'silver curls for granny' were more talked about than seen. However, Utopia was not attained. The scale of reform was bound to lead to difficulties. In a laudable attempt to encourage filling rather than extraction of teeth, for example, the scales of payment to dentists under the new NHS were biased against extraction. However, this meant that the rewards to a dentist insisting on private extractions were particularly large, and there continued to be heartrending tales, such as that of the boy who had to wait in pain for five weeks before a dentist would extract a tooth for an NHS payment.[5] But the access of millions of the population to health care they had previously been excluded from was a major achievement of the Attlee government. Many members of the middle classes also gained substantially from the NHS, by obtaining a high standard of care without the need for the direct payment required before the war. But in many ways such an argument about who gained from the NHS misses the point. The primary aim of the NHS was to make available minimum standards of care to all, regardless of income, and that aim was largely achieved.

The welfare state of the 1940s, built in a period of austerity, was itself austere. As we have noted, in the rival claims for physical resources health and education were low on the priority list. Nevertheless, free secondary education, access to free health care and an adequate national minimum income (even if only through National Assistance) were promises fulfilled in ways almost unimaginable in the 1930s. The improvements in housing did not realize all the ambitions of 1945. But over a million houses were eventually built, making available what were usually high-quality houses at low rents to many more people on low incomes than all the house-building of the inter-war years put together. The beginning of many 'new town' schemes was also a major and successful initiative of this period.

The welfare state provision of the 1940s had a variety of effects on the distribution of income between different groups in British society. Middle-class consumers of health and education services did well if they substituted public for private provision, and therefore no longer had to pay grammar school and doctors' fees. The greatly increased numbers of professionals employed in the new services often did well, though the Renfrewshire dentist said to be earning a net income of £600–700 per month in 1948 (when a respectable working-class income was around £5 per week) was certainly an exceptional beneficiary of a piece-rate system in a time of unprecedented demand. The consequences of the welfare state were by no means straightforward, but overall it undoubtedly redistributed income from the rich to the poor. Although most of the money for national insurance came from flat-rate, and therefore regressive, employee contributions, most of the rest of welfare was for paid out of general tax revenues, which in aggregate were quite redistributive. Although income tax was increasingly paid by the better-off sections of the working class, the Attlee government focused its tax-cutting activities on raising the threshold at which income tax became payable, so for most working-class people the bulk of the tax they paid was through buying alcohol and tobacco.

Taking into account both expenditure patterns in the new welfare state and the tax system of the late 1940s, calculations suggest that anyone on below-average income gained a significant improvement in their living standards from the measures of the Attlee government. Labour ministers in the late 1940s sometimes went so far as to suggest that the limits of redistribution had been reached. This may have been exaggerated, but it reflected the growing political discontent of the middle classes, some of whom rightly saw that their privileges were being eroded.

Women were also major gainers from the new welfare provisions. They had commonly been excluded from the occupationally based insurance schemes of the inter-war years, but were now included in the comprehensive schemes of the 1940s. (Married women were allowed to opt out of the new national insurance scheme, but this did not affect their entitlement to health care.) Family allowances, legislated for by the coalition government, but first paid under Labour, helped to correct the gender imbalance in incomes. The welfare state provided for a big increase in women's employment, as many of the new jobs in health and education went to them.

The Attlee government's policies were not much influenced by the idea that women should as a matter of principle be encouraged to participate in the workforce. It *did* encourage women to work, but this was for pragmatic reasons concerning the shortage of labour, not because ministers believed such participation would liberate women. Despite the problems of child care for working mothers, nurseries were closed down because they were a highly expensive way of providing such care. Equal pay was supported in principle, but nothing was done to implement it because of fears about its inflationary effects and impact on the public sector pay bill. This is a fair summary of the approach of the Attlee government, but its attitudes did not fly in the face of contemporary feminism. Feminism was quite weak in 1940s Britain, but, insofar as it existed, its priorities were to improve the lot of women not as workers, but as housewives and mothers. Better maternity care and health provision, and domestic concerns such as shopping facilities, were the dominant feminist issues of the period, at a time when many women were anxious to escape the 'double burden' of paid work and domestic drudgery by giving up at least full-time work while trying to ease the pains of housework and looking after children.

For men probably the greatest gain in welfare in this period came from full employment. In 1945 the Labour Party had put the continuation of wartime full employment at the centre of its manifesto, and while the economic circumstances made securing this goal easy, its achievement is central to life in post-war Britain. The mass unemployment of the inter-war years had not only condemned many to idleness and poverty, but also immensely strengthened the bargaining power of employers in the workplace and society generally. The 1940s saw a substantial redressing of that balance. One of the great clichés of this era was that under full employment workers could no longer be treated as 'hands', hired and fired at whim. Many employers continued to hanker after a return of the slack labour market in which they called the tune, but there was widespread recognition that the agenda had shifted, and that everyone had to come to terms with the new strength of labour.

Full employment and redistribution through the welfare state went a long way towards eliminating poverty. In 1936 Seebohm Rowntree had estimated, in a social survey of York, that 31.1 per cent of the working-class population of that city lived in poverty. Repeating the survey in 1950, he put the figure at 2.8 per cent. While Rowntree's exact calculations may be disputed, and pockets of poverty remained, especially among the elderly, it is indisputable that conditions of life for those on low incomes had improved greatly since before the war. Many more people could now afford leisure activities, and the late 1940s saw all-time high levels of attendance at the cinema, professional football and first-class cricket. These 'goods' were not rationed, and they provided an avenue for getting away from the often bleak aspects of austerity living. Similarly, Butlin's holiday camps were immensely popular in these years, and the idea of a summer holiday at one of the traditional British seaside resorts became an established part of many people's lives.

Labour had always understood that raising popular living standards required improvements to Britain's economy. This 'modernization' objective was part of the reason for nationalization, but the government had also to try to improve the performance of the private sector, which even after the completion of Labour's nationalizations made up 80 per cent of the economy. Labour tried to persuade private employers of the need to change their ways, to invest in new methods and adapt to changing markets. They also argued that treating workers better would yield dividends in the form of higher productivity. Success in this area of altering the behaviour of private companies was only partial. Labour set up all kinds of consultative bodies to cajole employers, but many of them resisted what they regarded as illegitimate interference in company affairs. The government was reluctant to compel companies to change what they did, though in a few cases they used the rationing of supplies to, for example, force firms to export more. The government found that the worldwide 'seller's market' of the early post-war years, although helpful in the drive to expand exports, also meant easy profits, and so removed the incentive for companies to heed government exhortations.

The government's relations with the trade unions were much more positive, and as a result a successful incomes policy was pursued between 1948 and 1950. Labour sought to persuade trade unionists that they could get what they wanted in the way of better wages and welfare only from an efficient economy. Some success was achieved, though the enthusiastic support of union leaders for measures to raise productivity was not always matched on the shopfloor. Labour believed that the way to encourage efficient working practices was to involve workers in decisions at company level, and serious attempts were made to achieve this, for example by creating joint committees in pits and factories. Again, this project was not wholly unsuccessful, but many workers undoubtedly wanted to focus their attention on family and leisure activities, rather than on production issues.

Labour's attempts to modernize the British economy meant diverting resources into investment, but the materials such as iron and steel required for this purpose were also desperately needed as inputs to make exports. Short-term and long-term needs occasionally collided. 'Patch and mend' sometimes had to be the policy, even where more radical reconstruction would have been preferred. But the productivity performance of the economy did improve, total production grew, and much of this output was diverted into exports. Though distorted by the Korean War rearmament effort, the economy inherited by the Conservatives in 1951 was in a fundamentally healthy state, even if there were many areas where Labour's modernizing intent had not fully succeeded.

The Labour government's record has been criticized by both the left and the right. From the left critics tend to argue that Labour did not go far enough on the road to creating a socialist Britain.[6] The process of large-scale nationalization laid down in 1945 was achieved by 1951, and by 1951 few among the leadership of the party saw it as a policy which should be pursued indefinitely into more and more of the private sector. The reasons were not just their lack of commitment to 'socialism', but a recognition that popular support for such an extension was lacking. It was not only the Tories who criticized the existing publicly owned companies. Many trade unionists and workers, while recognizing the benefits in terms of wages and working conditions of taking industries like coal into state ownership, also saw the problems which the national control of such huge and complex industries posed. The call for 'consolidation' in the existing nationalized industries before much more extension of the process took place was based on a realistic assessment of the scale of the task already involved in making these industries function effectively. There was no great popular clamour to do anything else.

Claims from the left that the Attlee government became a 'puppet' of the United States in these years are also common. Clearly Britain was dependent on American economic help, without which austerity would have been far worse, and would probably have led to intolerable political strains on the government. Yet in return for its economic help the US got little from Britain. Conditions attached to the loan, such as that Britain should move towards a liberalization of the economy, were evident in the 1947 fiasco over the convertibility of sterling, but thereafter the Americans accepted that Britain would determine its own pace in opening up the economy to the outside world. Similarly, the promises given at the time of Marshall Aid, such as to pursue a balanced budget and keep inflation down, were aims that the British government fully accepted independently of any American wishes. Britain's anti-Soviet stance in the Cold War as it unfolded in the late 1940s was equally 'home grown', rather than primarily a response to American pressure. More plausible are criticisms which allege that Britain at this time was spending too many of its scarce resources on trying to remain a world power. Despite the granting of independence to India in 1947, there is no doubt the government saw the war as having reinforced rather than diminished Britain's imperial role. Alongside this was the perceived 'special relationship' with the USA, and the claim to be the dominant power in Western Europe. But the assumption that global status was Britain's proper role was almost universal at this time, including among people on the left.

From the right much criticism has focused on the government's commitment to radical improvement of the welfare state, allegedly at the expense of improving the industrial base of the country.[7] Such arguments carry little conviction. The Labour government's welfare commitments were clearly tempered by the recognition that scarce resources must be directed into exports and investment. As noted above, hospital- and school-construction and, to a lesser extent, house-building were all curtailed to save materials in short supply. At the same time Labour's concern to modernize and improve the economy is shown not only by the many statements of government ministers on this topic, but, more tellingly, by the pattern of resource use which demonstrates how exports and investment were given the highest priorities. Even the argument about the Attlee government's lack of attention to improving the skills of the British population, though not without some force, is exaggerated by people like Correlli Barnett. The number of undergraduate engineers and scientists rose sharply in the late 1940s; lower-level technical education, such as through evening classes, also grew. It is undoubtedly the case that the provisions of the 1944 Education Act for technical high schools came to little, either in the 1940s or later. But the assumption of central government was that the new secondary modern schools would train the skilled manual workers and technicians of the future, rather than providing a watered-down version of the grammar-school curriculum. The Attlee government was far from ignorant about the need to raise skill levels in the British economy, though it was arguably too optimistic about the ease with which obstacles to such an improvement could be overcome.

Overall, the Attlee government, while not achieving a social revolution (which few desired), did establish a society with much less poverty, and a much greater degree of equality, than had previously existed in Britain, without sacrificing the paramount need to restore the economy. It established the basis for the highly successful decades of the 1950s and 1960s, with their low unemployment, limited poverty and generally respectable economic performance.

CHAPTER V

'NEVER–NEVER LAND': BRITAIN UNDER THE CONSERVATIVES 1951–1964

DILWYN PORTER

'What went wrong?' The work of historians and other commentators who have concerned themselves with Britain in the second half of the twentieth century has been heavily influenced by the search for an answer to this apparently simple question. Its enduring appeal is partly explained by the idea that the question may be asked in a number of different ways according to political preference. Those who have approached it from the right have been largely preoccupied with Britain's retreat from Empire and great-power status. For the left it has often been about the failure to establish a social democratic New Jerusalem in 'England's green and pleasant land'. At times the question has been almost exclusively concerned with the apparent under-performance of Britain's economy and, in particular, the relative decline of the world's first industrial nation. Here, though right and left may have agreed about the question, there has been little sign of convergence about the answer. 'What went wrong with the British economy' is a mystery which, for a long time, has been at the very heart of political debate, lending focus and urgency to the conflicting policy prescriptions of right, left and centre.

Being miserable, by and large, has kept British historians in business, not to mention a legion of political, economic and social commentators. Those who have stood Canute-like against this tide of pessimism have often seemed a little eccentric. Who else on the left but Tony Benn could have attached the label 'years of hope' to the decade or so after 1949? But the optimists do have a point. There were some things in post-war Britain that manifestly 'went right' even for the Labour Party in the 1950s. In general the second half of the twentieth century has been characterized by social peace and by a prevailing affluence which, though not universally enjoyed, would have left earlier generations awestruck. This has led to an anomaly which historians are only just coming to recognize. Britain's fall from its previous status as a world power of the first order has coincided with a period when British people, with some exceptions, have accumulated many reasons to be cheerful about themselves. Perceptions of Britain in decline have coexisted with perceptions of personal well-being. This important feature of twentieth-century British history first became strikingly apparent in the 1950s and early 1960s, the era of the 'great leap forward' into affluence.

At the general election of October 1951 the business of government passed from Labour into Conservative hands. What was most noticeable, once the electoral froth had subsided, was how little had actually changed. Attlee's patriotic socialists gave way to Churchill's social patriots, but there was to be no attempt, beyond the denationalization of the steel and road-haulage industries in 1953, to redefine the relationship between government and people which had been established by Labour in the immediate post-war years. The incoming administration, with an overall majority of fifteen, inherited a welfare state underpinned by a mixed economy along with a continuing commitment to full employment as an objective of government policy. In line with Conservative manifesto commitments, rationing and other restrictions redolent of 1940s austerity were eventually abandoned but, even here, Churchill's government was simply following the precedent established by Harold Wilson's famous 'bonfire of controls' at the Board of Trade in November 1948. The new order, such as it was, was ushered in prudently with an eye on Britain's balance of payments, sufficiently precarious in the winter of 1951–2 to discourage any inclination to let consumption rip. 'Rab' Butler, Churchill's Chancellor of the Exchequer, found himself restricting credit in January 1952 and imposing import controls on carpets, clothing, shoes and toys. It was to be some time, in fact July 1954, before all food rationing came to an end.

The tentative approach adopted by Churchill's government after 1951 owed much to the circumstances in which it had been elected. Labour, despite antipathy between the left wing and the party leadership, remained a potent electoral force, having achieved, at 48.8 per cent, a slightly higher share of the popular vote than the Conservatives. Moreover, with trade union membership standing at over 9.53 million, organized labour remained a force to be reckoned with, especially in the full-employment conditions then prevailing. This was a fact of political life which Churchill readily acknowledged by assigning Walter Monckton to the Ministry of Labour. 'So conciliatory was Monckton', a recent historian of the Conservative Party has observed, 'that there were those who wondered if he was the Minister *for* Labour.'' What lay behind this was a recognition that Conservative politics were constrained to operate within the framework of Labour's post-war settlement, which had brought significant benefits to Britain's working-class voters, not least of which was freedom from the pressing fear of unemployment. Similar considerations prompted the government to resist the Treasury-inspired 'Robot' scheme for floating the pound in 1952. Butler, still reeling from the balance of payments crisis which had greeted him on taking office, was inclined to listen to those who urged him to 'let the exchange rate take the strain', but it soon became clear that the attendant prospect of rising prices and higher levels of unemployment represented a political albatross which an overwhelming majority of his colleagues, Churchill included, were unwilling to take on board.

Selwyn Lloyd, somewhat perplexed by Churchill's decision to send him to the Foreign Office as Minister of State, had protested an ignorance of foreign languages, a dislike of foreigners and a disinclination to travel abroad in peacetime. In short, as Churchill had perceived, Lloyd was perfectly qualified to represent the British people overseas. As with the management of the economy there was a strong element of continuity in Britain's external relations where the principal objective remained, as Ernest Bevin had once put it, to see that Britain did not get 'barged about'. If this meant shouting loudly at foreigners in English, so be it. Given the rationale that was to underpin foreign and colonial policy for much of the second half of the twentieth century a robust defensive stance seemed appropriate. Churchill, who articulated this rationale clearly, saw Britain standing at the intersection of three overlapping spheres of influence – the Atlantic, the Commonwealth and Empire, and (Western) Europe. It was a sophisticated concept and one which helped to sustain the illusion of world-power status for a number of years, though Britain's title to the pivotal location assigned to it by Churchill was rather more precarious than he was inclined to let on. Making sure that Britain did not get barged about was a question of keeping options open as long as possible, thus postponing the evil day when it would be necessary to commit Britain to one or other of the spheres of influence in which it maintained a stake.

It was largely a matter of keeping up appearances. In this sense Britain's first atomic bomb, exploded in October 1952, had a symbolic value, signalling, it seemed, a grim determination to match the emerging superpowers. But, as Anthony Eden, Foreign Secretary and Prime Minister-in-waiting, had acknowledged privately some months earlier, the everyday realities of diplomacy were less heroic and more in keeping with the reduced circumstances in which Britain now found itself. Referring to the co-operative security arrangements which he was anxious to establish in the Middle East and South-East Asia, Eden explained in a Cabinet memorandum that his underlying purpose was 'to persuade the United States to assume the real burdens in each organisation while retaining for ourselves as much political control – and hence prestige and world influence – as we can'.[2]

Churchill was similarly inclined to find cost-effective ways of maintaining a significant British profile at relatively low cost. Projected 'summit meetings', at which he could renew his wartime acquaintance with Eisenhower and Stalin, were a recurring theme, offering an anxious electorate the reassuring message that British influence might still count for something in an increasingly dangerous world.

The extent to which the details and nuances of policymaking at this elevated level were matters of everyday concern to the people of Britain remains an open question. Though the turnout at general elections (82.5 per cent in 1951, 76.7 in 1955 and 77.1 in 1959) suggested that most adults were generally aware of what was expected of them in a parliamentary democracy, relatively few took a more active interest. A survey of political activity in Derby, conducted in the spring of 1953, confirmed this impression. About 90 per cent of those interviewed claimed to have voted at the general election but only 11 per cent were members of a political party and of these around two-thirds rarely or never attending political meetings. The young (and it is worth remembering that the franchise was not extended to eighteen-year-olds until 1969) could appear somewhat indifferent. When Anthony Wedgwood Benn, as he then was, made contact with the 'younger generation' for the purposes of a radio broadcast in October 1954 he discovered high levels of ignorance and cynicism and a 'great gap between politicians and young people'. It was, as he noted in his diary, 'very revealing and disquieting'.

General impressions, as one contemporary analyst of electoral behaviour observed, were more important than knowledge of policy detail when people decided how to use their votes. These were formed, he suggested, mainly from the news as relayed by the press and radio 'and to some extent (and often most unfairly), through personal experiences – a change in the price of tea, or in the size of a wage packet'. 'Arguments in the pub and in the workshop' also contributed to 'a not too unfair picture ... of the character and competence of the rival teams'.[3] If, as has often been argued, the 1950s represented the high point of post-war consensus politics, there was little else to suggest that the voter could have exercised a real choice. 'Butskellism', an idea invented by *The Economist* in February 1954 and taken up more generally to suggest an absence of daylight between Conservative government and Labour opposition in the area of economic policy, is important here, not least because it implied that there was nothing to choose between the Chancellor of the Exchequer (Butler) and his 'shadow' (Gaitskell) when it came to the price of tea and the contents of a wage packet. The incentive to vote appears to have diminished between October 1951 and May 1955 – by about 5.8 per cent as measured by the fall in turnout. Why bother to vote at all if the general impression was that it was likely to make no difference?

It has been suggested that British politics in the twentieth century has been predominantly concerned with the unending struggle to balance the twin priorities of welfare and greatness. There was some evidence by 1953 to suggest that this was being achieved insofar as the new realities of a world dominated by the two Cold War superpowers permitted. The government's commitment to the welfare state was signalled by an increase in the total of public sector expenditure on health, social services and housing from £1,963 million in 1950–1, Labour's last full year, to £2,416 million in 1952–3. The achievements of Conservative housing policy, under the direction of Harold Macmillan, pointed in the same direction as the magic figure of 300,000 new houses completed, a manifesto commitment in 1951, was surpassed for the first time in 1953.

The great majority of completions in the early 1950s were new council houses and flats. Though Macmillan was criticized for diverting resources from other public sector projects, such as schools, in order to reach his target, those who lived on the new estates were better housed than those who remained in that proportion of the housing stock designated 'unfit', an estimated 847,000 dwellings in 1954. It is perhaps worth reflecting on what

Macmillan's housing policy tells us about the politics of consensus for, though there was no disagreement between the major parties regarding the need for more houses, Conservative policy placed a greater emphasis on the private sector. Whereas completions of new houses by private builders were running at around 12 per cent of the total in 1951, this proportion had increased to almost 20 per cent by 1953, establishing a trend that was to see the number of private sector completions exceed those for local authorities for the first time in 1959. Local authorities, once the subsidies for 'general needs' housing had been reduced in 1954, were expected to focus their efforts almost exclusively on meeting the needs of those displaced by slum-clearance. What became evident in the development of housing policy in the 1950s was a Conservative preference for private consumption over public investment. The differences between the two major parties were further accentuated after 1957 when the Conservative's Rent Act sought to liberate private landlords from the inconvenience of controlled rents. 'Butskellism' notwithstanding, there were limits to the bipartisan consensus.

Steadily increasing expenditure on education, housing and the National Health Service was providing, by 1953, solid evidence of the government's commitment to welfare. At the same time the Coronation of Elizabeth II, in June of that year, supplied a grand public spectacle which was a source of comfort to those seeking reassurance about Britain's important place in the world. The British Commonwealth and Empire was given powerful symbolic representation as its leaders, some of them demo-cratically elected, gathered to pay homage to their new con-stitutional sovereign. 'Soldiers of the Queen', drawn from every continent, were paraded in their thousands. For a day, at least, the eyes of the world, not to mention its newsreel and television cameras, turned towards London. Black-and-white images of red-white-and-blue flickered in homes up and down the country. It was the first great state occasion to be televised; an estimated audience of twenty-seven million watched for at least half a day.

And it was the best excuse for a 'knees-up' since VE Day.

'The use of a Queen, in a dignified capacity, is incalculable.' So Walter Bagehot had observed in his classic account of *The English Constitution*, first published in 1867. Elizabeth's Coronation and the juggernaut of sentiment, patriotic rather than nationalist, which it released seem to indicate that he had a point. For Bagehot the principal advantage of the monarchy, the 'dignified' part of the constitution, was that it reconciled British subjects, through personal attachment to their sovereign, to the necessary rule of government, creating 'a feeling of moral obligation to obey it'.[4] In this sense the Coronation might be regarded as an event of great political significance, essentially conservative in its ramifications, but simultaneously underpinning the social peace that generally prevailed in Britain at around the mid-point of the twentieth century. There were, of course, some places where the regal *hocus pocus* failed to work its magic. In Northern Ireland the minority community resolutely refused to join the party; Nationalist MPs issued a proclamation repudiating British sovereignty in Ireland. Street decorations, thoughtfully supplied by a Unionist-controlled local authority in Cookstown, were removed by people who found them offensive. The Royal Ulster Constabulary mounted guard until the great day was over to ensure that the hastily erected replacements stayed in place.

Closer to the old heart of empire, a few voices on the left were raised in protest. The *New Statesman* on 30 May, two days before the Coronation, protested that 'our society is floating in a tide of unreason'. Such views, it must be said, were deeply unfashionable; they were swept aside in the media by the rhetoric of a 'New Elizabethan Age'. Violet Markham, writer and broadcaster, who spoke on this subject to BBC Home Service listeners a few days before the event, helped to set the tone. Her talk, published by the *Listener* on 28 May, invoked the spirit of a new era 'as great as any that went before'. She urged:

Let us have done with unworthy murmurs that we, with our great past and great traditions, are now a second-class power because we have fewer ships and soldiers than our neighbours to east and west. A nation that had the enterprise during the last war to carry through a fantastic scheme like 'Mulberry' ... such a nation has reserve powers of will and imagination as great as any shown in the sixteenth century.

When, on Coronation Day itself, news arrived that John Hunt's expedition had conquered Everest, the 'New Elizabethan' fantasy was given further reinforcement. The nationalities of the two climbers who had reached the summit, Tenzing Norgay from Nepal and Edmund Hillary from New Zealand, seemed but a minor complication as newspapers fell over each other to tell their readers that Britain was back 'on top of the world'.

We should not assume, of course, that people necessarily believed what they read in the papers, but an agenda was set. The idea that it might be necessary to wake up one day to a more sober reality was not popular. Low's cartoon in the *Manchester Guardian*, captioned 'The Morning After', which made this point, provoked a hostile reaction, sufficient to prompt an editorial apology for any offence caused to 'Disgusted' of Cheadle. The effect lasted for some months, at least until the end of the summer, which, for many, was crowned in August at the Oval when England's cricketers reclaimed the Ashes from Australia after a gap of nineteen years. Slowly, a more complicated picture began to emerge. In faraway Kathmandu Tenzing's role in the Everest expedition had been appropriated by local politicians intent, according to reports reaching the Foreign Office, on discrediting a triumph which the British had claimed for themselves and stirring up ill-feeling among the natives. This necessitated careful modulation of media images when Tenzing arrived in London; a patronizing view predominated of an Asian innocent, second cousin to Gunga-Din, which subtly undermined his achievement. The arrival of winter brought a less complicated message for those inclined to measure a nation's prestige in terms of sporting prowess. Hungary's six goals (6–3) against England at Wembley in November shattered insular illusions of innate superiority over the 'continentals'. A further seven (7–1) in Budapest the following May rubbed in the idea that when it came to the 'people's game', other people now played it better.

The Coronation of Elizabeth II breathed new life into an ancient institution. It was now time to breathe new life into the Conservative government, but Churchill, who had suffered a stroke in June 1953, was in no hurry to retire. Though the long-awaited summit conference with the leaders of the United States and the Soviet Union remained out of reach, he had recovered sufficiently by December to meet the American President in Bermuda. It was made clear at an early stage that the so-called special relationship did not extend to the sharing of America's atomic secrets with its wartime ally, but Churchill and Eden, with French support, were able to achieve a modest success in persuading Eisenhower to withhold his threat to use the bomb in Korea, arguing that such a move would be widely regarded as 'morally repellent'. The lion, perhaps, had lost its roar but it could still whisper to some effect, as Eden's role in the Geneva conference which negotiated a settlement after the war in Indo-China seemed to suggest. He emerged from these high-profile occasions with his reputation for statesmanship enhanced and he remained ahead of the field when Churchill resigned the premiership in April 1955. A month later Eden led the Conservatives to a general election victory, increasing their overall majority to a more comfortable fifty-four seats.

Eden's party achieved a 49.7 per cent share of all votes cast in 1955. This remains a post-war record. In part this may be attributed to Labour's seriously damaged credibility. A left-wing revolt, smouldering menacingly since 1951, had exploded inconveniently for Attlee in March 1955, less than two months before the poll, when sixty-one Bevanites defied the party whip and abstained in a Commons vote on the key question of nuclear weapons. What has come to be known as the 'feelgood factor' also contributed. The international terms of trade had turned in

Britain's favour; its imports were relatively cheap and its exports relatively dear. Unemployment stood at 1 per cent, removing the dole queue to the realms of folk memory. Average weekly earnings were rising at a faster rate than retail prices thus ensuring, for most households, a useful increase in available disposable income. The British people, with some exceptions, were better housed and better fed than they had been four years previously. All this, and the idea that Britain still counted for something in the world, tended to work in the Conservatives' favour.

The relaxation of hire-purchase restrictions in August 1954 had encouraged an expansion of consumer expenditure, which rose by about 8 per cent between 1954 and 1955. Spending on durables such as cars, refrigerators, washing machines and television sets rose by about 10 per cent; new private car registrations exceeded half a million for the first time in 1955. It seems likely that the more democratic distribution of goods once deemed luxuries began to exert an upward pressure on Britain's relatively rigid social system. It started to creak in the mid- to late 1950s, though it did not give way. One indication of the pressure to which it was subjected was the enthusiasm with which Britain's upper classes took to the study of linguistics. Alan Ross, the academic who first compared 'U' (upper class) with 'non-U' habits of speech, introduced his work with the observation that members of the upper class were no longer 'necessarily better educated, cleaner, or richer than someone not of that class'. A few distinctive upper-class characteristics survived – 'an aversion to high tea, having one's cards engraved (not printed), not playing tennis in braces' – but, generally, speech was the most reliable indicator. 'Non-U *serviette*/U *table-napkin*' was, he suggested, 'perhaps the best-known of all the linguistic class indicators of English'. Of the use of the word *civil* it was noted that it 'is used by U-speakers to approve the behaviour of a non-U person in that the latter has appreciated the difference between U and non-U, e.g. *The guard was very civil*'.[5]

Nancy Mitford, writing in the monthly *Encounter* in September

1955, gave wider circulation to Ross's thesis. Life, it seems, could be very trying for those with impeccable U credentials: 'Silence is the only possible U-response to many embarrassing modern situations: the ejaculation of "cheers" before drinking, for example, or "it was so nice seeing you", after saying goodbye.' It was enough to drive one *mad* (U)/*mental* (non-U). Media interest lasted long enough to remind non-Us of their place; and to remind those experiencing for the first time a modest affluence of their obligation to be 'civil'. Deference was a precondition of the social peace, not least because, as Mitford observed, U-speakers supplied 'the sensible men of ample means who generally seem to rule our land'. These social stereotypes were powerfully enforced by contemporary British film-makers. Stock working-class characters, as Lindsay Anderson observed a few years later, made 'first-class soldiers'.

> On the march, in slit trenches, below decks, they crack their funny Cockney jokes or think about the mountains of Wales. They die well, often with a last mumbled message on their lips to the girl they left behind them in the Old Kent Road; but it is up there on the Bridge that the game is really played, as the officers raise binoculars repeatedly to their eyes, converse in clipped monosyllables ... and win the battles.[6]

There was no work, as yet, for working-class heroes.

Eden, with his faded matinée-idol good looks, would not have seemed out of place on the bridge. It became evident, however, in the course of the international crisis initiated by Nasser's nationalization of the Suez Canal in July 1956, that his judgement was suspect. Within six months Eden had resigned, his health ruined and his foreign policy in shreds. He had conducted himself, in Malcolm Muggeridge's phrase, like a 'benzadrine [*sic*] Napoleon', choosing a course of action which led to military fiasco and exposed the pretence of Britain's strength overseas. British troops had been progressively withdrawn from the Canal Zone under the terms of the 1954 Anglo-Egyptian Agreement as the process of cutting overseas defence commitments got underway. This made it difficult to bring direct pressure to bear on Nasser, seen by Eden as a 'Moslem Mussolini' whom it would be dangerous to appease. In these circumstances British foreign policy was forced into less orthodox channels in pursuit of what had become its immediate objective – the removal of Nasser.

During October 1956, while the polite rituals of international diplomacy were apparently being observed, Eden and Selwyn Lloyd, his Foreign Secretary, began secret negotiations with their French counterparts with a view to securing a suitable pretext for military intervention. This was to be achieved with the assistance of Israel, the third party to this covert scheme. An Israeli attack on Egypt was to be followed by an Anglo-French ultimatum calling for a ceasefire and the withdrawal of all troops from the Canal Zone. Egypt's inevitable failure to comply with these terms would then open the way for an Anglo-French occupation in the interests of 'peace' and international freedom of the seas. It was, perhaps, just preferable, but only just, to the assassination of Nasser through the use of nerve gas, an option apparently under consideration at MI6.

After Israel, as secretly agreed, attacked Egypt on 30 October, the British armed forces mobilized for the occupation of the Canal Zone. When this got underway, a week later, Eden's government was virtually isolated in the court of world opinion and the Anglo-American special relationship had been all too plainly jeopardized. The advantages of the moral high ground, occupied briefly by the capitalist West after the Soviet Union's invasion of Hungary in late October, had been seriously compromised. A humiliating retreat began under intense diplomatic pressure from the United States and the threat of a catastrophic run on the pound as Britain's dollar reserves evaporated. It was difficult to argue that anything useful had been achieved by Eden's elaborate exercise in gunboat diplomacy. Nasser was still in place, his reputation in the Arab world considerably enhanced now that he had successfully seen off the dinosaurs of the old imperialism.

As for the Canal itself, which had been open to international traffic before the Anglo–French intervention, it was now closed, the Egyptians having sunk block-ships as part of their defensive response.

For the British government the outcome of the Suez crisis was a painful lesson in the realities of the new world order. For some British people it was a traumatic experience, mercifully short-lived, which challenged widely held assumptions about the nation to which they belonged. Public opinion, though confused, had rallied to Eden at the height of the crisis, responding not just to headlines of the 'EDEN GETS TOUGH' and 'ITS *GREAT* BRITAIN AGAIN!' variety, but to deeply rooted patriotic instincts and a sense of Britain's rightful place in the world. 'Let the Russians just start something, that's all,' said one of the playwright Dennis Potter's older relatives in the Forest of Dean, 'and then they'll have *us* to face. Like Hitler did – oy, and the bloody kaiser. And there yunt an army in the world as ool touch the British army, you mark my words.' But this confidence had been seriously undermined. 'We should have gone right on in there,' said a young miner about Suez, 'but this country is not capable of it any more. Not even against the bloody wogs.'[7]

The first requirement after Suez was to change the captain on the bridge. This was smoothly accomplished in January 1957 with due attention to the constitutional proprieties. Cabinet ministers and senior figures in the Conservative Party were consulted. Having considered the question put to them by Lord Salisbury – 'Is it Wab, or Hawold?' – most of them plumped for 'Hawold', for Macmillan rather than Butler. This outcome was conveyed, as she had requested, to the Queen, who then exercised the royal prerogative in favour of Macmillan. Only then was he accepted by the Conservative Party as its leader. This convoluted process, a little confusing for those who believed that they lived in a parliamentary democracy, prompted Labour to declare that, if similar circumstances arose while they were in office, a vote of the Parliamentary party would be required to ratify the sovereign's choice of Prime Minister.

It was a small but important gesture and an indication that the adulation which the monarchy had enjoyed since the Coronation had faded a little. But, as both Lord Altrincham (John Grigg) and Malcolm Muggeridge discovered, those who approached the sacred institution with even a modest degree of scepticism tended to activate an especially raw, defensive reflex. Altrincham, writing for the *English and National Review* in August 1957, had perfectly respectable motives. He sought to modernize the monarchy rather than bury it, to rescue the Queen from 'tweedy' influences prevailing at court which, he believed, discouraged her from assuming the mantle of a modern constitutional sovereign. Some criticisms, especially of the Queen's style of public speaking, which he found 'a pain in the neck', were more personal, earning him a well-publicized slap in the face from an irate Empire Loyalist. Muggeridge, in a two-year-old article recycled in the New York *Saturday Evening Post* during the Queen's autumn 1957 American tour, challenged the institution more directly as the source of snobbery and outmoded social convention, implying that it exercised a real constraint on Britain's capacity to adapt and modernize. The venom of the response, prompted by what Muggeridge had supposed were 'sensible and amiable observations', caught him a little off-balance, not least on account of the hate-mail which rejoiced at the recent death of his son. Although about a third of the letters received by the two miscreants were supportive, the thought that they should suffer some dire fate, preferably on the wrong end of a horsewhip, was more typical. 'They say you are a known homosexual; we believe it . . .' was another common refrain.[8]

Altrincham and Muggeridge, it could be argued, had been sacrificed on the altar of middle-class post-Suez *angst*. The note-paper favoured by their accusers indicated bourgeois origins. Its most obvious proletarian manifestation came a little later, at the end of the summer of 1958, when Afro-Caribbeans and Africans in Nottingham and in Notting Hill, West London, were subjected to violent attacks from native English youths. Much of the trouble in Notting Hill, it was noted in *The Times* on 3 September, was caused by 'gangs of youths, many of them from the Elephant and Castle and other tough districts', but local feeling against the immigrant population also ran high. Older men in pubs spoke of their determination to 'Keep Britain White' and 'made all sorts of wild charges against their coloured neighbours'. It could not have been easy in these circumstances for local people to make a stand against what *The Times* called the 'Storm Troop mentality', so the courage of a greengrocer's wife who gave shelter to a terrified African student, barring her door against the pursuing mob, should be acknowledged. A *Times* leading article attributed the violence to 'a tiny submerged hooligan element' which the 'civilized majority' would hold in contempt. This offered a degree of comfort but bypassed the less obvious, everyday manifestations of race discrimination which sprang from deep roots embedded in the culture of an imperial working class.

Dan Jacobson, a South African novelist who published an account of the trial of some of the Notting Hill 'nigger-hunters' in the December 1958 edition of *Encounter*, was struck by the ordinariness of the young men in the dock; 'they weren't sunken nobodies; they were rather jaunty anybodies'. They were trapped, he argued perceptively, in 'a complex of attitudes and beliefs which seem to be in the very bone and marrow of what we call "our civilisation"'. This did not augur well for the estimated 180,000 people of African, West Indian, Indian and Pakistani origin who were living in Britain by 1958 or for those that were to follow them.

Though violence of the kind witnessed at Notting Hill was exceptional it seems clear that dark-skinned immigrants triggered a variety of unfriendly responses ranging from cold indifference to outright hostility. Folk myths, which often contradicted each other, abounded, testifying to an uneasy relationship between host community and newcomers. *They* took our jobs but *they* were also on national assistance. *They* were lazy but *they* also worked too hard. *They* were after our women but *they* did not mix. A local shopkeeper, identified by the *Birmingham Mail* in a feature on 28 November 1961 as one of 'the bitter five per cent', indicated that the adjustment of attitudes required if he was to live happily with his new neighbours was almost too painful to contemplate:

> We were very kind to them when they first came, but now I just get in my car at the weekends and drive to where I cannot see a black face. Some of them are very decent folk, but others have this inferiority complex and they try to make up for it. They are rude and cheeky.

Perhaps such feelings were linked, if only unconsciously, to perceptions of British decline after Suez and to nostalgia for Empire and some of the less attractive values on which it had been built. The persistence of this undercurrent of opinion was recognized by Macmillan's government, which legislated in 1962 to place restrictions on entry from black and Asian Commonwealth countries.

It was arguably surprising that the Conservatives did not pay a higher price for Eden's Suez policy or for the disillusionment which its failure generated. Eden's successor, it must be said, made light of his own part, often characterized as 'first in, first out', in the débâcle. Persistent Labour leads in the opinion polls throughout 1957 and the first half of 1958 were eventually reversed and the Conservatives were well placed by October 1959 to win a third successive general election victory, retaining the share of the vote which they had achieved in 1955 and increasing their majority to 100. Explaining this outcome requires balancing what went wrong for Britain in the 1950s, a story in which Suez looms large, against what went right. Whatever the discomfiting news from abroad, relayed into people's homes by the BBC and by ITN, there were material compensations to be derived from higher levels of personal consumption. 'Most of our people', as Macmillan was able to point out in a well-publicized speech at

Bedford in July 1957, 'have never had it so good.' There was some substance to this claim, which was reinforced by a further relaxation of credit in October 1958 and by Heathcoat-Amory's pre-election budget in April 1959, which fed the consumer boom with tax cuts of around £350 million.

Consumer expenditure had grown steadily throughout the 1950s. What was especially evident after 1957 was an enormous surge in spending on durable goods. This was running in 1957 at around £1,004 million per annum (at 1958 prices) but had increased to £1,465 million by 1960, up by about 45 per cent. Significant thresholds in terms of the ownership of various durables were passed between 1958 and 1959 as consumers responded to the government's efforts to stimulate a pre-election boom. In the period from September 1957 to November 1959, according to a survey published in the *Financial Times* on 9 December 1959, the number of households owning a car increased by 25 per cent, while the figures for televisions, washing machines and refrigerators were 32, 54 and 58 per cent respectively. Though household availability of these goods remained some way off the near-saturation levels reached by the 1990s they were beginning to be perceived as necessities rather than luxuries.

Much of this increased spending, especially among working-class consumers, was financed by hire-purchase and other credit arrangements. The 1950s had seen an enormous expansion in mail-order retailing with the charge-free credit offered by the major catalogue companies proving especially attractive to upwardly mobile working-class customers who had turned their backs on the 'tallyman' but had yet to gain access to the banking and credit facilities available to the middle class. As reported in the *Economist* on 27 February 1960, mail-order sales had expanded by about 15 per cent per annum since 1950, twice as fast as sales from conventional retail outlets. This paved the way for John Bloom's Rolls Razor, Colston, Duomatic and other direct-sales operations of the early 1960s which offered washing machines and refrigerators at competitive prices with credit facilities if required. Hire-purchase arrangements, the infamous 'never-never', were especially important for the sale of cars, motorcycles, furniture and carpets. There was no shortage of jeremiahs to warn that it would all end in tears. 'The present scramble in hire-purchase finance ...', ran a letter to *The Times* on 1 September 1958, 'seems designed to entice more and more excursionists into the alluring but unhealthy Never-Never Land.' Law courts, the writer believed, were kept in business by those 'who are persuaded by persons whom they do not know to enter into contracts that they do not understand to purchase goods they do not want with money they do not have'.

The consumer prosperity of the late 1950s and early 1960s was, in reality, more securely based than such criticism implied. Though most indicators do suggest that a major watershed in consumption was crossed at some point between 1958 and 1960, this happened at the end of a decade characterized by full employment and a relatively low rate of inflation. More people than ever before were sufficiently confident about their personal finances and future prospects to take on the responsibility of a mortgage. Building societies alone provided a record 326,125 new mortgages in 1960, advancing over £544 million. With owner occupation of the housing stock at 42.3 per cent in 1961 and rising, the 'property-owning democracy' advocated by middle-of-the-road Conservatives since the mid-1940s seemed a realistic project. Moreover, though life was far from comfortable for those on low incomes, the welfare reforms of the 1940s, effectively consolidated by Conservative governments after 1951, had, as even critics recognized, raised national minimum standards of subsistence above pre-war levels.

At the start of the decade, in the last month of the Attlee government, opinion-poll evidence had indicated that the 31 per cent of those interviewed who believed their standard of living was improving were in a minority, outnumbered almost two to one by the 57 per cent who took the opposite view. Though the gap tended to narrow during the 1950s it was some time before this state of opinion was decisively reversed. As late as March 1958 Gallup reported a small majority of pessimists over optimists, but at some point during the following fifteen months the mood changed. By June 1960 the 34 per cent who believed that their standard of living was going up clearly outnumbered the 13 per cent who thought things were getting worse, a trend that was enhanced in the course of the following eighteen months. There seems little doubt that this optimistic tendency worked in the Conservative government's favour in October 1959 and for some time afterwards as the Labour Party struggled to come to terms with working-class affluence. Labour's share of the vote was still respectable at 43.8 per cent, though this represented a 5 per cent drop from the peak achieved nine years earlier. A post-election survey conducted by Mark Abrams for *Socialist Commentary* revealed that 40 per cent of manual workers now considered themselves to be 'middle class', thus eroding the relationship between class and voting behaviour on which the Labour Party had come to rely. There was a sense in which socialist high-mindedness sat uneasily alongside the material aspirations of the people whom Labour claimed to represent. It was all very well to denounce the government for promoting a 'live now, pay later' mentality at the expense of investment in British industry, but this cut little ice on the doorstep. Cowards may have flinched and traitors sneered but there was an evident determination, even among those manual workers who remained loyal to Labour, to keep the twin-tub turning in an ever-increasing number of working-class homes.

Having reached this peak of mid-twentieth-century affluence, it is as well to break from the onwards and upwards trajectory of this narrative to consider those who, for one reason or another, were excluded from its benign dispensation. Though ownership of key consumer durables was widening, it was by no means universal. Low incomes were an important factor here. The *Financial Times* survey of December 1959 cited earlier revealed that ownership levels among manual workers tailed off sharply where the annual income of the head of household was under £350. Among this group ownership of a car (1 per cent), a refrigerator (2 per cent) or a washing machine (11 per cent) was rare; only 34 per cent of such households owned a television set, though this did not preclude rental. Those who were at a disadvantage in the labour market for other reasons, principally race or gender, were more likely to find themselves in such low-income households. Even when it came to the purchase of goods and services, some people found themselves in an unfavourable position. When Mrs Delsie Ankle, a Handsworth shopkeeper, applied to the Scottish Insurance Corporation for fire cover, she was at first accepted but then turned down. The company explained, according to a *Times* report on 18 July 1963, that its 'detailed survey of the premises' had revealed 'that the insured is a West Indian and unfortunately we do not underwrite fire insurance in these cases'. When Mrs Ankle, 'a cheerful Jamaican', contacted her MP, the company denied that it operated a 'colour bar' and insisted that the application had been turned down on other grounds, blaming the unfortunate misunderstanding on 'a clerkess' at its Birmingham branch.

The ramifications of structural disadvantage were, perhaps, most evident in Northern Ireland – though few British politicians at the time cared to look. Having established the principle of parity with the rest of the United Kingdom in respect of its social services in the late 1940s the Unionist government in Belfast had presided over a marked improvement in terms of education, health and welfare. It would, however, be difficult to argue that the benefits of this improvement were enjoyed equally by both the Catholic Nationalist minority community and the Protestant Unionist majority. As F. S. L. Lyons, the eminent Irish historian, noted, very few Catholics achieved relatively well-paid employment:

> There is a vicious circle here. They have not been able to aspire
> because so many are in poorer-paid occupations. Because they are in

> the poorer-paid occupations [their children] have to leave school as
> early as possible. Because they leave school as early as possible they
> cannot aspire to the quality of education which would admit them to
> the more prestigious jobs.[9]

Thus, by the early 1960s, though Catholic children had benefited from the general improvement in education, they remained at a disadvantage when they entered a labour market where discrimination in favour of the Protestant Unionist community was often blatant.

For a while Macmillan's government, having secured re-election in 1959, basked in the sunshine of public esteem, apparently unworried by these ominous shadows. The Prime Minister worked hard on his image, cultivating a personal style which some described as 'Edwardian', reaching back to a period before the great divide of 1914—18 when one could be sure that Britain, and its traditional ruling order, still counted. Macmillan was himself supremely conscious of the limits of British power and of the need to redefine its international role. The trick was to accomplish this without undermining political stability at home in a way that would endanger the Conservative Party and those institutions and interests which it existed to preserve. Retaining the confidence of the electorate while this readjustment was achieved required a leader with the skills of an illusionist or, as some have suggested, an 'actor–manager'. These were much in evidence after 1959 as Macmillan flew from one capital to another in his role as the 'honest broker' of international relations. His performance at the United Nations in September 1960, when Khrushchev interrupted his speech by banging a shoe on the desk, was out of the top drawer, the English patrician establishing an apparently effortless superiority over the Russian peasant.

The outline of this strategy had been evident even before 1959. In April 1957, only a few months after the withdrawal from Suez, Macmillan's government had undertaken a comprehensive review of Britain's defence policy. The intention was to roll up the map;

the expensive deployment of troops east of Suez was to be reduced and compulsory national service abandoned. At the same time the government committed itself to the maintenance and development of an independent nuclear deterrent which, it was widely believed, would ensure a continued presence at the top table while containing defence expenditure within a self-imposed limit of 7 per cent of GNP. The rationale which underpinned this strategy was widely accepted at the time even within the Labour Party. When Hugh Gaitskell, who had succeeded Attlee at the end of 1955, came under pressure to adopt a unilateralist stance it was 'Nye' Bevan, the darling of the Labour left, who came to his assistance. He was not prepared, he informed the party conference at Brighton in October 1957, to send the next Foreign Secretary 'naked into the conference chamber'. Thereafter, those who believed that Britain should take the moral lead and abandon weapons of mass destruction were sidelined into pressure-group politics under the banner of the Campaign for Nuclear Disarmament, founded in February 1958.

Britain's independent nuclear deterrent was important for Conservatives to the right of Macmillan, a weighty body of opinion both at Westminster and in the country. After the humiliation of Suez there was some comfort, apparently, to be derived from the idea that Britain had the capacity to inflict serious damage on the Soviet Union and its hapless citizens. This, it was argued, effectively deterred the Soviets from launching an attack and lent real weight to British diplomacy at or near the summit of world affairs. There were even those like Randolph Churchill, son of Winston, who claimed that Britain, at a stroke, had become once again a major power. It was especially important to sustain this body of opinion as the orderly retreat from Empire got underway. During the Macmillan years the Union Jack was lowered in Ghana and Malaya (1957), Cyprus and Nigeria (1960), Sierra Leone and the Cameroons (1961), Western Samoa and Uganda (1962), and Kenya and Zanzibar (1963). Britain, it was clear, had no intention of resisting what Macmillan called the 'wind of change'. In these circumstances its independent nuclear deterrent had more than military value. Britain may have lost an empire but it had gained a bomb.

It was unfortunate, therefore, that the credibility of Britain's nuclear threat came to depend so heavily on American technology. The 'special relationship' with the United States, by no means unproblematic after Suez, required careful attention if the necessary co-operation was to be secured. Macmillan, as he made clear in a Cabinet memorandum at the very end of 1960, was under no illusions about 'the uncertainty of American policies towards us – treated now as just another country, now as an ally in a special and unique category'.[10] It was to this source that his government had turned for help after abandoning its plans for a British surface-to-surface missile in February 1960. The American Skybolt system, famously described by Robert McNamara, Kennedy's Defense Secretary, as 'a pile of junk', temporarily filled what had become a gaping hole in Britain's defence policy. When, in November 1962, the United States consigned Skybolt to the scrapyard, the hole reappeared, much to the embarrassment of Macmillan's government, forced hastily to acquire a new American missile system, Polaris, for which the Royal Navy was not yet equipped. This sorry saga reflected badly on Macmillan, who had not been slow to intimate that the was a close friend of America's dynamic young President. It raised doubts about the 'independence' of the nuclear deterrent and reinforced the impression that Britain was being marginalized, as it had been during the Cuban missile crisis a few months earlier.

This was exactly the impression which Macmillan had wanted to avoid, not least because it raised awkward questions about competence. It came at a time when confidence in the government's management of the economy had already receded from the heady days of the consumer boom which had provided such a helpful context for the 1959 general election. It had become clear in the course of 1960 that Britain's balance of payments was deteriorating rapidly, a reflection of the high level of imports generated by increased consumer demand. Britain's deficit on visible trade (commodities and manufactures) rose from about £117 million in 1959 to £406 million in 1960. Thus the small improvement of £7 million in Britain's invisible trade (mainly financial services), which remained consistently in surplus throughout the period, was wiped out. With sterling under pressure on the foreign exchanges, Selwyn Lloyd, now Macmillan's Chancellor, was required to apply the brakes to expansion, incurring an unpopularity for which he eventually paid the penalty in July 1962, when he was sacked, along with six of his colleagues, by an ungrateful Prime Minister on the infamous 'night of the long knives'. Lloyd had introduced a number of emergency measures which sought to discourage demand and bring inflationary pressures under control. The most controversial of these, and the most damaging in electoral terms, was the public sector 'pay pause' introduced in July 1961 with a view to influencing settlements in the private sector.

Though it lasted only eight months, the embargo on public sector pay increases sowed the seed of disaffection among many of those who might normally have been expected to support the Conservatives. By the time it was replaced by the so-called 'guiding light', which set an indicative 2.5 per cent limit, the damage was done. Civil servants and local government officers, nurses, teachers and university lecturers – not to mention railwaymen, coalminers and other workers in nationalized industries – all felt the pinch. 'Orpington Man' cast a proxy vote of protest on their behalf in March 1962 when the Liberals won a famous by-election victory in leafy London suburbia, the Conservative share of the poll falling by 22 per cent from the 1959 figure. It could be argued that the pay pause and other policies designed to restrict demand had the desired effect in that the balance of payments account was back in surplus by 1962. A readjustment had been effected which did not appear to have impaired the general level of prosperity; spending on consumer durables, for example, having dipped from £1,465 million in 1960 to £1,403 million in 1961, resumed its upward surge, reaching a new peak, at £1,469 million, in the following year. It is clear, nevertheless, that some damage had been inflicted on the government's reputation. 'You've never had it so good!', the slogan which had won the 1959 election, now seemed a little shallow. Commentators began to draw attention to Britain's 'stop–go' economy.

This situation was compounded by the publicity given to its rather sluggish record of economic growth as Macmillan's government sought entry to the European Economic Community after July 1961. Inevitably, unfavourable comparisons were drawn with the EEC countries, especially West Germany, which was said to have experienced an 'economic miracle' in the post-war years while Britain had muddled along complacently, achieving annual growth rates of around 2 to 3 per cent of GDP. Germany had developed the capacity to double its industrial production every ten years; at growth rates then current it would take Britain at least three times as long. EEC membership appealed to economic modernizers, like Edward Heath, who hoped that greater exposure to competition from modern industrial states in an expanding European market would supply the stimulus required to make the British economy more efficient. In such quarters there was a feeling that Britain had 'missed the bus' at the time of the crucial Messina Conference in 1955, which had prepared the way for the Treaty of Rome two years later. Such criticism was not entirely fair in that the success which the EEC subsequently achieved was by no means assured at the start. By 1961, with the counter-attractions of Empire and the special relationship somewhat diminished, it was possible to contemplate an approach to the EEC.

It should be stressed that Macmillan did not anticipate that membership of the 'European Common Market' (as it was usually referred to in Britain at the time) would preclude a wider world role. There was nothing contrite or defeatist about Britain's bid, no sense that it was coming to terms with a future as a middle-ranking European power. In these circumstances the pain of exclusion was all the sharper when de Gaulle, after fourteen months of difficult negotiations, used the French veto to keep Britain out in January 1963. Coming only a month or so after the Skybolt muddle it provided ammunition for the growing stage army of satirists, like Peter Cook, whose stock-in-trade was a knowing impersonation of an ageing and increasingly ineffective Prime Minister.

As the illusions of British power faded one by one, the government became increasingly accident-prone. Within a few months of de Gaulle's snub, Macmillan had almost, but not quite, been 'driven out of office by two tarts', as Julian Critchley later put it. Critchley, then a young Tory MP, was referring to Christine Keeler and Mandy Rice-Davies, inhabitants of a somewhat seedy milieu to which John Profumo, the War Minister, sometimes retreated to escape the pressures of office. Rumours about Profumo's relationship with Keeler, who was simultaneously involved with Yevgeny Ivanov, Assistant Naval Attaché at the Soviet Embassy, had begun to circulate in July 1962. By the spring of 1963 they had become impossible to ignore, not least because Labour MPs, with George Wigg to the fore, scented blood. Profumo, a married man and, no doubt, somewhat embarrassed, made a personal statement in the Commons at the end of March denying any impropriety in his relationship with Keeler. But, by the beginning of June, it had become obvious that this had been less than frank. Macmillan, who confessed to an unworldly innocence in such matters, seemed out of date and out of touch. Lord Denning's inquiry, set up after Profumo's resignation to investigate the security aspects of the scandal, simply prolonged the government's ordeal by rumour.

For the Labour Party, twelve years in opposition, a glimpse of a Conservative minister with his trousers round his ankles was immensely heartening. Harold Wilson, elected to the leadership after the death of Gaitskell in January 1963, sought to capitalize on Tory misfortune though it seems unlikely that the trend of public opinion, running in Labour's direction since the introduction of the pay pause two years earlier, was much altered by these events. For many people the scandal was something to be enjoyed rather than politicized. Stories beginning 'Have you heard ...?' enlivened many evenings in saloon and public bar alike. The one about eight High Court judges at an orgy caused Macmillan particular distress. Though it was sex which made the affair so interesting, there is some evidence to suggest that the public were rather less shockable by the early 1960s than they once had been. The two million copies of *Lady Chatterley's Lover* sold in the year after the celebrated court case in July 1960 indicated a healthy curiosity at least. Research conducted among a sample group of middle-class, middle-income men in Cambridge and published by the *Sunday Times* 'Insight' team in their instant paperback *Scandal 63* suggested that 'it was clearly the most exotic elements that people were aware of'. Insofar as they were willing to place the affair in a political context, and they showed some reluctance to do so, it was apparent that Profumo's sexual behaviour caused them less concern than the idea that he had behaved dishonestly by lying to Parliament.

Though confidence in Macmillan and his government was shaken by the affair, its negative impact should not be exaggerated. A Gallup survey undertaken immediately after Profumo's resignation suggested a Labour lead of just over 20 per cent. This was impressive but represented only a small increase, around 1 or 2 per cent, on the substantial lead which had been established before news of the scandal broke. Macmillan's personal credibility suffered greater damage. For a time, in the summer of 1963, he was the least popular Prime Minister since Neville Chamberlain in 1940. But, by the autumn, a recovery was underway. Labour's lead had been cut to about 13 per cent and Macmillan's standing had been enhanced by his high-profile role in the negotiations which led to the tripartite Nuclear Test Ban Treaty signed in August. In the end it was not 'tarts' but the Prime Minister's prostate trouble which brought the Macmillan era to a close. 'La commedia è finita,' he told reporters after his resignation, a parting shot in the best traditions of the actor–manager. Roughly translated, the party was over or, perhaps, the game was up.

Britain's decline from world-power status in the second half of the twentieth century required careful management if the essential interests of its ruling order were to be protected. The retreat from Empire, it should be recalled, had disastrous consequences for the Fourth Republic in France. No one in the 1950s and early 1960s had more to gain from an era of domestic social peace than those who were attached to Britain's amorphous 'Establishment', U-speakers to the last man and woman. Eden's Suez policy, having engaged the patriotic sympathy of an imperial working class, had exposed the pretensions and, to some extent, the incompetence of its rulers. The principal achievement of the Macmillan govern-ment after 1957 was to defuse a potentially damaging reaction. While 'Supermac' remained centre-stage, juggling apparently successfully with the often conflicting requirements of welfare and greatness, Britain's 'Angry Young Men' were kept waiting in the wings, relatively isolated from mainstream public opinion. After 1960 it became progressively more difficult to sustain this performance and the critics of complacency had their day. Hugh Thomas, in his introduction to a collection of essays on *The Establishment*, first published in 1959, and in paperback a year later, had set the tone:

> To those who would desire to see the resources and talents of Britain fully developed and extended, there is no doubt that the fusty Establishment, with its Victorian views and standards of judgement, must be destroyed; the authors of the following essays make their own suggestions as to how (as well as why) this should be done…[11]

This theme was picked up and developed in different ways by Michael Shanks's *The Stagnant Society* and Anthony Sampson's *Anatomy of Britain*, both published in 1961, and by the Penguin 'What's Wrong?' series. Britain's ancient institutions, ten years earlier a cause for celebration, had become a cause for concern.

The body of opinion which this emerging literature of modernization helped to nourish was simultaneously democratic, meritocratic and technocratic. It was assiduously exploited by Wilson in the long campaign which preceded the general election of October 1964. Macmillan had been succeeded in October 1963 by his Foreign Secretary, the fourteenth Earl of Home, a tweedy and somewhat remote figure selected in a mysterious way by a clique of senior Conservatives among whom Old Etonians featured largely. This gave Labour the opportunity to intensify its attack on the Tories' 'thirteen wasted years', generally characterized as a period in which Britain's anachronistic class system had been shored up to the detriment of its stagnating economy. The Conservative Party of the 1960s, it seemed, could only walk backwards into the future. It was, however, far from finished. Sir Alec Douglas-Home, as he became when he renounced his peerage, was to run 'the fourteenth Mr Wilson', as he called him, very close at the general election, won by Labour with a majority of four. For much of the period after 1951 the Conservatives had succeeded in persuading the electorate that, on balance, more was 'going right' than was 'going wrong' and that the right people were in charge. In 1964 Labour, by the narrowest of margins (0.7 per cent of the popular vote), persuaded them to reverse this judgement. It was an historic victory, not least because it suggested a quickening impulse to modernization and a willingness to look forward rather than back.

CHAPTER VI

THE WILSON YEARS: 1964–1970

KENNETH O. MORGAN

The 1960s, like the 1930s, have a unique place in folk memory. They are popularly thought of in two ways – they were 'swinging' and they were socialist. They are seen as a precious era both for the experimental young and for the intellectual middle-aged, a time both of cultural and sexual liberation and of planned social engineering. But were the two by any chance related? Whether the ideals of emancipated youth were an intrinsic part of the Wilson governments of 1964–70 depends on where one looks for evidence. Those Cabinets included Roy Jenkins, whose liberal régime at the Home Office saw artistic censorship and legal repression put to flight, and Tony Crosland, whose *Future of Socialism* (1956) argued that socialism should be fun, an expression of 'grace and gaiety' instead of the drab austerity associated with the Webbs' Fabian tradition. But they also contained symbols of the nonconformist conscience, the teetotal Methodist George Thomas, the Calvinist Willie Ross (both former schoolmasters) and above all the old Portsmouth Baptist, James Callaghan, who declared in 1969, to Labour as well as Tory approval, that the tide of permissiveness had gone too far. In this as in much else, Harold Wilson was an enigma, although appearing with the Beatles when they each received an MBE was an attempt to make Labour the natural party of youth, linking the Liverpool of Wilson's Huyton constituency with that of the clubs of Penny Lane.

What is clearer is that these two abiding images of the 1960s, the personal liberalism and the public socialism, had very different effects. The new libertarianism was to transform British society – marriage, family, neighbourhood – for good or ill. It brought forward long-excluded social groups – blacks, Celts, the sexually unorthodox – on to centre-stage. From the 1960s onwards, the social world was turned upside down as never before. On the other hand, the Wilson governments, hailed as a second coming after the post-war triumph of 1945, left a tangle of half- or unfulfilled expectations. They created a political sea-change from which the British centre-left took thirty years to recover.

The 1960s took their style from Harold Wilson himself. He dominated the decade. He was elected Prime Minister in October 1964 with a majority of four, gained a large majority of almost 100 in March 1966, and remained in office until a quite unexpected defeat in the general election of June 1970. Although he was to return to office, again unexpectedly, in March 1974 and to remain premier for just over two more years, he was then far less vigorous. It was in his 1964–70 administrations that he was in the ascendant, and it is by these that he must be judged. The general election of 1964 had been in large measure a presidential-style contest in which Huddersfield Harold, a shrewd, folksy, modernizing populist, was ranged against the grouse-moor image of the Tories' aristocratic Prime Minister, Alec Douglas-Home, known in Labour rhetoric as 'the fourteenth Earl'. In fact, Wilson's victory, as noted, was a very close-run thing. When his new Foreign Secretary, Patrick Gordon Walker, was defeated in a by-election in Leyton in early 1965, the Labour majority almost disappeared. Wilson, however, continued to emphasize his personal leadership. He compared himself to a succession of American presidents – the 'hundred days' of Franklin D. Roosevelt in 1933, the New Frontier of John F. Kennedy (Rhodesia, Wilson once said, was 'my Cuba'), even to Lyndon B. Johnson, 'flying by the seat of his pants'. He adopted an accessible classless style, complete with Joe Kagan's Gannex raincoats, while his reflective pipe-smoking image and sharp wit made him a natural on television.

In fact, his political background was complex. He had gained a reputation as a left-winger when he resigned with Nye Bevan in protest against Gaitskell's budget of 1951 with its unsustainable rearmament programme and charges on the health service. When Wilson was elected party leader in February 1963, he took Crossman, Foot and Barbara Castle of the old Bevanite left over to a portrait of the dead Nye to drink a toast to him.[1] He was wont to see himself as a latterday Bolshevik in a Tsarist Cabinet. But in reality his politics were pragmatic, even right-wing. He emerged during the war as a Whitehall planner under Beveridge. As President of the Board of Trade under Attlee, he was best known for dismantling some of Labour's post-war controls. In the party turmoils of the 1950s, he steered a careful course. He was never really a Bevanite, and caused anguish on the left when he joined the shadow Cabinet in succession to Bevan in 1954. He voted for Gaitskell in the 1955 leadership contest and was rewarded with the shadow Chancellorship. He was elected leader in 1963 as the left's candidate over the right-wing George Brown and Jim Callaghan, and often uttered leftish noises on race relations, South Africa, Vietnam and nuclear weapons. But the keynote of his charismatic leadership of the opposition in 1963–4 was an attempt to bypass old and ideological divisions – what he called 'theology' – with a new apolitical appeal. Socialism, he declared, was about science. His remarkable speech at the Scarborough party conference in October 1963 linked socialism with technological advance, with automation and the computer, instead of the sterile world of class conflict and Clause Four. It epitomized his empirical, value-free style, and left his critics wrong-footed. In addition to a relative unconcern with policy, Wilson had shown a zeal for internal manoeuvring, with 'leaks' and 'moles' fed by close advisers such as Marcia Williams, and his political bloodhound, George Wigg. Even in October 1964 observers sensed that there might be troubles ahead for this unpredictable media-sensitive leader. When *Private Eye* dubbed him 'Wislon' it seemed to strike a natural chord.

His team in October 1964 was talented, but variegated. It included most of the elements that made up the Labour coalition in its golden age, from the Celtic neo-Marxism of Jennie Lee to the philanthropic Catholicism of Lord Longford. Wilson's two main ministers were George Brown and James Callaghan, both of broadly working-class origins, both of the party right, but rivals for the throne. In making Brown head of the Department of Economic Affairs and Callaghan Chancellor of the Exchequer, Wilson ensured that there would be a permanent state of jostling for position – what he called 'creative tension' – between them. They were an uneasy, if gifted, troika. The old Bevanite left found its main voices in Richard Crossman, a maverick intellectual and former Oxford don, variously Minister for Housing, Leader of the House, and Minister for Social Services, and Barbara Castle, who rose largely through sheer executive ability to become Secretary for Employment and Productivity in 1968. Wilson saw her as a custodian of the Bevanite conscience; the public speculated that she might become Britain's first woman prime minister.

These broadly leftist ministers were more than balanced by up-and-coming figures on the right. There was Tony Crosland, who became Secretary for Education and Science in 1965, the most powerful socialist intellectual of his time. There was Denis Healey, Minister of Defence, another intellectual, versed in the technicalities of weaponry and international security as no other ministers were. The most rapidly rising force was Roy Jenkins, regarded as something of a languid littérateur in the opposition years but whose rapid promotion to the Home Office in 1965 and then to the Treasury in succession to Callaghan in November 1967 established him as perhaps the Minister most likely to succeed if Wilson fell under the proverbial bus. 'Mind you,' Wilson told Callaghan in July 1967, 'I take care not to go near buses nowadays.'[2] It was a heady mix that would give the Prime Minister's aptitude for tactical manoeuvre, along with his paranoid fear of crown princes claiming the throne, the freest of reins.

The main issues of the Wilson years were those that concerned most post-war administrations: managing and modernizing the economy; redefining Britain's international role; and adapting to social, ethnic and generational change. It is on these essential priorities that this chapter will focus.

The economy preoccupied the Wilson government from its very first day in office, Saturday, 17 October. It was known that the outgoing Tory government, under its Chancellor Reginald Maudling, had left a huge balance of payments deficit of over £600 million as a result of its 'dash for growth'. In fact, Callaghan discovered in his first private talks with William Armstrong his private secretary that the real figure was closer to £800 million. From the first, therefore, Labour took office in 1964 as in 1945 amid an air of crisis. Many advisers, among them Nicky Kaldor and Donald McDougall, felt that Britain must devalue. Nevertheless, at a secret meeting on the morning of 17 October Wilson, Callaghan and Brown rapidly agreed that devaluation of the pound was unthinkable. It would make Britain's balance of payments worse; it would mean severe deflation for the workers; above all it would leave Labour with the political albatross of being the devaluation party, in 1964 as under Cripps in 1949. Callaghan also felt that Britain's pledges to Commonwealth holders of sterling and to the United States that the exchange value of sterling would be held were inescapable moral obligations. All the Treasury personnel, from William Armstrong and Alec Cairncross down, agreed with the decision not to devalue, as did important economics ministers like Douglas Jay and Anthony Crosland. But many economists were to feel that a decision to hold the pound at an unsustainable level and keep it as a reserve currency crippled the government's economy policy from the outset. At any rate, Wilson declared that devaluation henceforth would be the great unmentionable. No official papers would discuss it. As patriotic defenders of a $2.80 pound, a national virility symbol, Wilson's team would soldier on.

The outcome was a difficult first winter which saw the government in desperate straits to hold the economy together in the face of a manifest lack of overseas confidence. Its measures were liable to be painful for Britain and for others. There was uproar from Britain's European Free Trade Area partners when it was suddenly announced that Britain would be imposing a 15 per cent surcharge on all foreign imports. Callaghan's first budget on 11 November 1964 had the wrong effect. Although its impact was on balance mildly deflationary, the markets were more struck by the announcement of two forthcoming Capital Gains and Corporation Taxes, and by new social expenditure of £345 million on pensions and benefits. This did not seem to be the time for a Labour government to parade its social conscience to the world, after less than a month in office. Massive pressure on the reserves followed and there was a fall in the value of sterling. The raising of bank rate to 7 per cent did not check it. Finally on 25 November, a huge package of international aid was put together amounting to $3,000 million from the US Federal Reserve and European central banks. At last the pressure on the pound subsided and the Labour government had some breathing space. But it was a troubled start that set the tone for Wilson's administration – the finances under pressure, a massive international bailing-out operation, a sense that the economy was almost out of control and the government on the run.

The early months of 1965 were more tranquil. The pound strengthened and the markets recovered. Callaghan's second budget of April 1965 aroused some admiration for its innovative quality: its main features were the new 30 per cent Capital Gains and Corporation Taxes, previously announced, along with sharp increases in income and other taxes, but also cuts in the defence budget. But international confidence in Labour's management of the economy continued to be low. Callaghan and Wilson discovered this at first hand in Washington where they paid separate visits to President Johnson in June and December. The Americans left no doubt about their anxiety about the scale of Britain's indebtedness, and the need for economies at home, along with a wage-restraint policy. There were strong hints that continued American generosity might depend on Britain's maintaining a world role in its defence commitments in Asia, while some murmured about Britain showing its US allies quite how a good a friend it was by giving help in Vietnam.

Hopes for modernizing the British economy, including the promotion of science and technology, did not, however, rest with the traditional operations of the Treasury. Labour's claims to provide long-term economic planning, instead of Tory 'stop-go,' were vested above all in the newly created Department of Economic Affairs, run by the energetic but highly unpredictable George Brown. It got off to a bad start. The first three months in office down to mid-December were preoccupied with turf wars with the Treasury, heightened by the known political rivalry of Brown and Callaghan. The line between the two departments was in any case so vague that it would have caused trouble had Brown and Callaghan been two plaster saints. The remit that the DEA would handle the long term and the Treasury the short term would have been difficult in any circumstances. Eventually, in early December a so-called 'concordat' was worked out between the two departments, drafted by the Treasury official (Douglas's son and Callaghan's son-in-law, Peter Jay).[3] Since the Treasury would continue to handle such key areas as exchange-rate policy and taxation, the DEA's role was circumscribed from the start. Labour sought to break free from what was traditionally seen as the stifling control of a deflationary-minded Treasury and to promote stable expansion and growth. In practice, with powerful officials like William Armstrong orchestrating matters, the Treasury was the inevitable winner.

Even so, the DEA pressed on throughout 1965 with its proposals for a strategy of growth. George Brown used his powers of persuasion to get the CBI and the TUC to agree on a long-term programme. Central to it would be some kind of income restraint for wages and salaries, euphemistically termed 'a planned growth of wages'. In September 1965, Brown proclaimed his National Plan to the world. It would mean a 4 per cent annual growth rate, a 25 per cent increase in output between 1964 and 1970. But its effect was muted from the start. Indeed, the financial events since October 1964 had already made so dramatic an increase in economic growth inherently improbable. The Plan had no teeth, either to restrict incomes or to increase production or productivity. By the end of 1965 it lacked all credibility. Brown was to move from the DEA to the Foreign Office, a defeated man, in August 1966. The DEA under the successive direction of Michael Stewart, Wilson himself for a while and then Peter Shore, slowly faded out. No successor was proposed by the Blair government in May 1997. With the end of the Plan, Labour's pledges for economic planning withered away, as they had between 1947 and 1951. Much of its zeal for science and technology went with it. The new Ministry of Technology made limited headway under the trade unionist, Frank Cousins, though distinctly more under the youthful leadership of Tony Wedgwood Benn after 1966. On balance, Wilson's proclaimed 'white heat' of a new technological revolution remained tepid. Professor Blackett, its scientific mastermind, left the government in disillusion.

Labour's control of affairs appeared sufficiently secure for it to win the general election of 31 March 1966 with a much enlarged majority of ninety-eight. For the first time, Wilson felt himself truly in command, Labour the natural party of government. Callaghan's third budget that May confirmed his reputation as a tax reformer at least, though his main innovation, a Selective Employment Tax invented by Nicky Kaldor to boost employment in manufacturing, proved a temporary expedient. Then in July a huge crisis blew up, from which the government and Wilson's long-term reputation were never to recover. Stimulated by a lengthy seamen's strike, there was massive run on the reserves and the exchange rate of sterling. In June the monthly trade deficit doubled. Things went from bad to worse. Frank Cousins resigned from the government in protest at its incomes policy. A by-election in Carmarthen saw a Welsh Nationalist defeat Labour. Wilson himself went off to Moscow on 16 July to discuss possible peace initiatives in Vietnam with the Russians; in the three days he was away all manner of rumours flourished. It was believed that some kind of coup against him was attempted in his absence, possibly at the home of Anne Fleming, which suggested echoes of James Bond. The dread word 'devaluation' now returned to the political vocabulary.

The crisis of July 1966 when the government, in Wilson's phrase, was 'blown off course', says much about the personality clashes and paranoid style that increasingly undermined the Labour government. When Wilson returned from Moscow, a series of rushed economy measures were announced. Instead of devaluation, there would be cuts of £500 million. The Economist, with some exaggeration, called it 'perhaps the biggest deflationary package that any advanced industrial nation has imposed on itself since Keynesian economics began'.[4] Eventually by August some stability returned to the markets, with massive American and some European help. Sterling, which had slumped, staggered up to $2.70 again. But a mood of crisis and intrigue hung over the government thereafter. Not merely 'blown off course', it appeared liable to sink without trace. The main casualties were Wilson, who seemed obsessed by short-term party considerations, and the erratic and alcoholic George Brown, whose move to the Foreign Office covered a loss of face. Callaghan came out of it rather better but with a reputation as the potential leader of anti-Wilson MPs, if neither the Brutus nor the envious Casca of journalistic legend. At a time when Britain seemed at its most 'swinging', joyously celebrating England's victory in the World Cup final at Wembley, its Labour government appeared beleaguered even with years in office still to run.

Devaluation of the pound hung over the administration thereafter. More and more key ministers supported it. They included George Brown, Roy Jenkins and everyone who favoured entry into the European Common Market. Most economists regarded it as inevitable. But the Treasury remained implacable, preferring international assistance to help Britain conquer its endemic problems with its own policy of growth. Harold Wilson still preferred to go to almost any lengths to avoid a political as well as economic defeat. Callaghan's spring budget in 1967 was prepared against the background that devaluation was still off the agenda. But this would not last long. In May he was told by a key adviser, Alec Cairncross, 'that's the last of the good news' and so it proved.[5] That summer saw a series of unrelated blows. President de Gaulle's veto of British entry into the EEC in May blocked one key avenue of escape. In June, the Six-Day War between Egypt and Israel, which resulted in a temporary oil embargo, shattered hopes of a balance of payments surplus in 1967. Then in September a series of unofficial strikes in the docks savagely afflicted exports at a critical time. The monthly trade deficit for October was £107 million, easily the worst on record.

On 2 November Cairncross was the first Treasury mandarin to yield to the inevitable. He told Callaghan that the game was up and devaluation inescapable. The resolution was a messy one. A casual question by Robert Sheldon about foreign loans in the Commons on 16 November cast the markets into turmoil and perhaps cost the nation £500 million. It was said to be the most expensive parliamentary question in history. Two days later the pound was devalued, from $2.80 to $2.40. It shook the world and caused temporary panic in Washington, which feared the dollar might be next in line. Callaghan announced a standby credit of $1,400 million with the International Monetary Fund (IMF) with severe terms attached, and then resigned on 30 November. He was in deep depression, regarding devaluation as a tremendous national and personal defeat. But the real casualty, perhaps, was Harold Wilson. His television broadcast at the time of devaluation, blithely telling the viewers that 'the pound in your pocket has not been devalued', appeared merely irresponsible. His credibility largely evaporated at that precise moment.

Callaghan's successor at the Treasury, Roy Jenkins, was a literate economist and a lucid communicator. His budget of March 1968 warned of 'two years of hard slog'. In all, £923 million would be taken out of the economy, a massive deflationary package which rained blows down on consumer and industry alike. In fact, the balance of payments continued to be depressed for the rest of the year. Edmund Dell was later to criticise Jenkins for delay in bringing in his economy measures and for failing to be rigorous on inflation.[6] There was talk of a further possible devaluation. But in 1969 the tide began to turn. Helped by the benefit to exports from Callaghan's devaluation of the pound, Jenkins launched a further attack on domestic demand and added £340 million to taxation in his 1969 budget. Through this severe medicine, the balance of payments improved dramatically. In 1969, there was a surplus for the first time in the decade, amounting to around £400 million. It appeared that Labour under Jenkins had indeed turned the economy around. But this had been achieved via a traditionally deflationary Treasury rather than through the up-beat expansion of the DEA, when George Brown had once cheerfully announced 'Brothers, we're on our way.' Brown was now no longer even a minister, having resigned needlessly the previous year. His cherished DEA had disappeared with scarcely a whimper. The annual growth rate, planned for 4 per cent, was only a little over 2 per cent. Nor were foreign creditors reassured. The pound still looked overvalued to many objective observers. The underlying problems of the economy, including over-full employment, especially in the public sector, and rising inflation from wage settlements of 12 per cent in the winter of 1969–70 were still there. For ordinary citizens the years 1964–70 were not at all a bad time, with apparently continuing affluence. But its handling of the economy and its failure to modernize its structure were the roots of Labour's long-term weakness.

The second task for the government was a reassessment of Britain's international role and responsibilities. Chief among its priorities was the alliance with the United States. For all the old anti-Americanism of socialists like Nye Bevan, Labour had established itself as the Atlanticist party. It had set up Marshall Aid and created NATO in the Ernest Bevin era. Labour politicians felt close to the American Democrats, while John Kenneth Galbraith had become a guru for British left-wing critics of the inequalities of the 'affluent society'. Wilson, Brown, Callaghan, Healey and other ministers were well known in Washington, and took the supposed special relationship as the pivot of their policy.

That relationship, however, was most one-sided. The client role of Britain since the humiliation of Suez was evident enough. Wilson entered Downing Street with vague promises to do away with the British nuclear deterrent, but these were promptly jettisoned as a policy of weakness. As has been seen, much of his first three years in office were spent in trying to persuade the Johnson administration to prop up the ailing British economy. Until the summer of 1967 it seemed to work. Wilson was received in the White House by the President with fulsome references to Shakespeare, Milton and (inevitably) Winston Churchill. But he was coming as a debtor and a suppliant. American aid was directly linked to domestic economic policy (it was US insistence which led to the Prices and Incomes Bill to curb wage demands in 1966) and to defence arrangements. McNamara, the US Secretary for Defense, insisted that the conditions of US aid would be Britain's keeping its troops on the Rhine and, even more, retaining all its highly expensive defence establishments east of Suez, from the Persian Gulf to the great naval base at Singapore. This line eventually could not be held. When Wilson was musically entertained at the White House in 1968, the New York Met. baritone, Robert Merrill, had to omit from his repertoire 'I've Got Plenty of Nuthin'' and 'The Road to Mandalay'.[7] These were felt to be inappropriate for a prime minister who had devalued the pound and was withdrawing from east of Suez.

Other than financial aid, the other essential feature of the Anglo-American relationship was Vietnam. Despite accusations to the contrary, there is no decisive evidence that the support from Wilson, Michael Stewart and others for the American policy of protecting the corrupt régime in South Vietnam was ever directly linked to American aid. Britain studiously refrained from sending a military force into Vietnam, on the lines of British involvement in Korea or indeed Australian participation in Vietnam. The best Wilson could do was, while remaining a loyal ally, to try to use his talents as a peacemaker, using his long-established contacts with members of the Russian government. He tried to intervene directly to produce a ceasefire, using such improbable emissaries to Vietnam as the left-wing minister Harold Davies. Wilson was most actively engaged in those critical days of 16–19 July 1966 when his government was reeling from the attacks on the pound. It led nowhere. Many felt that it was a cosmetic attempt by Wilson to win favour with the Parliamentary party at a time when he was under pressure from the left. Walt Rostow, a White House adviser, observed in February 1967, when asked about possible British mediation in Vietnam, 'We don't give a goddam about Wilson.'[8]

After Johnson left office, Anglo-American relations became more distant. Richard Nixon's main priorities lay in Asia, in building up relations with the Chinese and somehow trying to extricate his country from Vietnam (and shortly Cambodia). It was clear that the reality of the supposed special relationship was of Britain as a client, no longer (as Oliver Franks had declared back in 1950) ahead of the 'queue' of European powers.[9] Even under Macmillan there were pretensions that Britain was one of the 'big three'. But, though still important through its Commonwealth connection and potential European status, it was no longer so in the Atlantic context.

More directly important, it seemed, were relations with the Commonwealth, still a major worldwide connection linking the developed and developing world, and a market for a quarter of British exports. Harold Wilson was a Commonwealth man by instinct. He cherished the Queen as its head; he took the meetings of heads of ministers seriously. But the Commonwealth was in manifest decline. Throughout the Conservative years, there had been a massive process of decolonization in Asia, in the Caribbean and above all in Africa. The relationship was a much more indirect one now. Dominions like Canada and Australia felt their ties with the mother country were more remote and sentimental, especially after post-war immigration. Race relations caused frequent difficulties, especially the immigration restrictions imposed on East African Asians and others (discussed below) and relations with South Africa. Commonwealth pressure helped Wilson keep arms and other exports to the Republic limited, although the continuing defence relationship continued to rumble. The views of black African and other nations in the Commonwealth were major factors in persuading the Wilson government to cut off sporting contracts with South Africa, especially the decision to bar the all-white South African cricket team from visiting England in 1970. An especially painful problem was the civil war in Nigeria in 1969–70. Savage fighting there after the breakaway of the Ibos of Biafra and the broad support of the British government for the central government in Lagos led to much bitterness. The unity of the Commonwealth otherwise was undermined by the unilateral decision to devalue the pound in November 1967 without apparent regard for Commonwealth holders of sterling. Meanwhile the threat that Britain would withdraw its forces from east of Suez seemed to underline the fragility of the Commonwealth as a cohesive force.

The major problem of Commonwealth policy, without doubt, was Rhodesia. The Conservatives had left southern Africa in a mess after the winding up of the Central African Federation. Trouble in the old Southern Rhodesia seemed inevitable. Harold Wilson faced the unilateral declaration of Rhodesian independence by the white minority government of Ian Smith in November 1965. It was a major challenge to British authority and claims of sovereignty. The fact, however, that he had long ruled out military intervention, to the fury of many African nationalist leaders, removed an important weapon from his armoury from the outset. The essential pressure now could only come from economic sanctions: Wilson declared that this would bring Ian Smith's illegal régime to its knees 'in weeks rather than months'. But the imposition of sanctions was less impressive than it seemed. South Africa kept up trading relations with Rhodesia, while there was evasion of sanctions through Mozambique and from European powers such as West Germany and Switzerland. Wilson was later to be severely criticized for the contravening of sanctions by British oil companies such as Shell and BP. The Rhodesian government thus kept going without much internal difficulty.

Wilson felt morally committed to a settlement in Rhodesia that would ensure a peaceful transition to majority black African rule. He had two efforts at face-to-face summit diplomacy with Ian Smith. They met first on HMS *Tiger* off Gibraltar in December 1966 when Wilson put pressure on Smith to concede the essential 'six points' to provide unimpeded progress to African rule. But as soon as Smith got home he disavowed any agreement and the impasse went on. Front-line African states such as Zambia and Tanzania complained that Britain was allowing another apartheid regime to emerge undisturbed. Wilson made a further attempt to persuade Ian Smith to retreat when they met again on another vessel, HMS *Fearless*, in August 1968. These talks proved less tetchy than before and went on for thirty hours. Wilson appeared to have gained key concessions, notably Smith's agreement to extend the African franchise, and to add to the number of Africans in the elected legislature. But again as soon as Smith got home he refused to budge. 'The fight goes on,' he told the white Rhodesians in Salisbury, many of whom had originally been right-wing émigrés after the war fleeing from the socialist terrors of Attlee's Labour government. With South African support, the illegal régime in Salisbury remained in power against a background of growing internal discontent and eventually violence. African critics like Kenneth Kaunda of Zambia were scathing about the failures of Britain's government. On the other hand, with the military option ruled out, it is difficult to see what more Wilson could have done in diplomatic terms, eventhough the monitoring of sanctions evasion was clearly inadequate. Rhodesia was in some ways a heroic failure on his part, but a failure it undeniably was.

The changing character of the Commonwealth was illustrated most powerfully by the announcement in January 1968, soon after the devaluation of the pound, that Britain would withdraw its forces from east of Suez. This was a clear acknowledgement that it could no longer play a worldwide role; with aircraft carriers being scrapped, Britannia no longer ruled the waves. It was a decision that had long been anticipated. Britain's economic problems made inevitable a massive cut in defence commitments, as even the reluctant Americans had come to recognize. The pattern of international defence needs, based on global nuclear retaliation rather than armed forces on the ground, made a string of defence establishments from Kuwait to Malaysia unnecessary. The most recent security problem had been a confrontation with Indonesia in Borneo which came to an end in 1966. Thus it was announced that, by the end of 1971, British troops would be withdrawn from the Persian Gulf, Malaysia and Singapore, whose naval establishment had been expensively refurbished since its capture by the Japanese during the war. There was some Commonwealth anger at so historical a shift in British priorities. Lee Kuan Yew, the Premier of Singapore, along with the government of Malaysia, protested vehemently, not least over the loss of employment in the Singapore naval base. This was of some significance since these two countries were major holders of sterling, important markets for exports, and centres of £7,000 million of British investment. In the end, however, only a modest concession was made in delaying the British departure. The Labour government was, indeed, recognizing the inevitable course of history, as decolonization proceeded apace. What was left of the old imperial heritage was marginal: Hong Kong, due to pass back into Chinese hands in 1997; the naval base of Gibraltar, the subject of a long-running dispute with Spain; Belize, claimed by Guatemala; and scattered outposts such as the Falklands to which hardly anyone paid attention. In a roundabout way, Labour's old anti-imperialist crusade had reached its fulfilment.

With the Anglo–American alliance of diminishing importance, and the Commonwealth fading away, the obvious area for British overseas involvement was Europe. But Labour, like the British public in general, was slow to take the point. Back in 1962 it had formally opposed Britain's application to enter the Common Market, and greeted de Gaulle's veto with relief. Gaitskell had spoken of 'a thousand years of history', and the historic ties with the Commonwealth, symbolized by the glories of battles in the First World War at Gallipoli and Vimy Ridge. But, especially with Britain's continuing economic difficulties, the need for creating a relationship with Europe became ever more pressing. No longer could it be argued that devaluation of the pound (an inevitable consequence of joining the financial arrangements of the EEC) was a barrier. Important ministers now favoured an application, including Roy Jenkins at the Treasury and George Brown, who spent much time at the Foreign Office in 1966–7 soliciting goodwill in European capitals. On 30 April 1967, by a majority of 13–8 (the majority included Tony Benn),[10] the government agreed formally to apply to join the EEC. Two weeks later, another veto from de Gaulle followed. He cited Britain's role in the sterling area and the presence of the pound as a reserve currency; underlying it was a fear that Britain in Europe would be America's Trojan horse. Many greeted his veto with relief, especially on the Labour left. The Common Market was, after all, a capitalist enterprise, while its agricultural subsidies to farmers would end a century of cheap food in Britain.

For all that, Labour, and indeed the country generally, henceforth had a potential European destiny. Opponents such as the passionately anti-European Douglas Jay were dismissed. Key figures like Wilson himself, Callaghan, Healey and Crosland were prepared at least to keep an open mind about European membership if the right terms could be negotiated. European socialist leaders like Brandt and Schmidt were much in favour of Britain's joining if only as a counter to de Gaulle. Business and the City, along with much of the press, were strongly pro-European. There was no change in the situation in June 1970 when Labour left office, even though de Gaulle had now left the scene. A major positive legacy of the Wilson era was a fundamental and lasting reassessment of Britain's European role.

The third aspect of the Wilson years was the one which mostly captured the headlines. This was an era of personal liberation, in the view of some critics one of moral anarchy. The popular consumer culture of the Beatles, Mary Quant and Carnaby Street was allied to the sexual freedom provided by the pill. The Wilson years were seen by the world as a time of 'permissiveness', no doubt with exaggeration (after all, only 9 per cent of single women took the pill in 1970). The children of the post-war baby-boomers trampled over the remnants of Victorian puritanism and inhibition. Working-class young people in full employment embraced the pop music and fashion of the new consumerism. The middle-class young went to university on full grants, often in a new mood of rebellious liberation. The anguished response of critics like Mrs Mary Whitehouse suggested that Britain faced a cultural crisis. In an age of relativism, its moral climate would never be the same.

The government did not create the mood of libertarianism. But it did try to respond to it as best it could, without losing touch with the respectable conservatism of the silent majority. The main legislative response came during, and in part from, Roy Jenkins's time at the Home Office between 1965 and 1967. During this period, the old censorship of the Lord Chamberlain and others over the arts, symbolized in the Crown's prosecution of the publishers of *Lady Chatterley's Lover* back in 1959, disappeared, with Roy Jenkins presiding over their eclipse like a liberal crusader. The Lord Chamberlain's last gasp came with his censoring of Edward Bond's play *Early Morning* in 1967 for depicting a lesbian Queen Victoria. Other kinds of freedom were also given tacit encouragement. Homosexuals, the victims of intolerance and persecution since the days of Oscar Wilde, won partial liberation in 1967. A private member's bill, moved by Leo Abse and supported by almost all Labour members, decriminalized homosexual relations in private by consenting adults. Another private member's bill by the Liberal David Steel to allow the abortion of unwanted pregnancies also went through. It was greeted with dismay by the Roman Catholic Church, for which it was clearly a severe defeat. In 1969 the government allowed amendment of the divorce laws, which many had long seen as intrusive and inhuman. It also supported penal reform in decisive fashion. Sydney Silverman's bill for the ending of capital punishment was passed in 1965; the change was made permanent under Callaghan in 1969. The Wilson years therefore saw the disappearance of the brutality of the rope from British history.

These were freedoms that ended persecution or repression. The government also tried to respond in more positive fashion. Its idealism needs to be remembered as a major feature of the Wilson years. The setting up of a Ministry of Arts, under the inspired choice of Jennie Lee, meant a huge public boost for culture, including for the funding of the Arts Council, and the British Film Institute. It was a distinguished period for British theatre, for example through the National Theatre Company. London boasted five major orchestras of world renown, while elsewhere orchestras in Manchester, Birmingham and Bournemouth, along with the vitality of opera companies such as the Welsh National Opera, testified to the international pre-eminence of classical British music-making. At the very least, the Wilson government provided the funding. So it did, emphatically so, for education. The expansionist creed of the 1963 Robbins Report to promote higher education was pursued. Six new universities were created in Warwick, Sussex and elsewhere. The Colleges of Advanced Technology were granted university status with the aim of encouraging science. Some criticized the élitist 'binary divide' that remained between the universities and the vocational polytechnics. Still, a much higher participation ratio in higher education resulted. More fundamental was Jennie Lee's creation of the Open University, a locally based institution for everyman (and woman) based on distance-learning techniques including television and credit-based modular courses. It was to prove a startlingly successful instrument of social mobility and cultural enlightenment for working men and (especially) home-based women, the envy of the educated world.

Labour also acted with vigour and commitment elsewhere. In the state secondary schools, the apostles of modernization had long championed the comprehensive ideal and the ending of the hated 'eleven plus' exam for schoolchildren. Anthony Crosland (Highgate School and Trinity, Oxford) made it his business as Education Secretary to promote comprehensivism across the land. He informed his wife, 'If it's the last thing I do, I'm going to abolish every fucking grammar school in England. And Wales. And Northern Ireland.'[11] This legacy of the socialist 1960s was much criticized in later years. It was said to level down, to downgrade quality and standards, to encourage teachers to adopt unduly experimental methods, and to weaken the state system at its base while, curiously, leaving the private schools (which flourished in this period) intact. On the other hand, calls to restore the divisive and unfair 'eleven plus' were always rejected, while the attempt by local authorities to make universal neighbourhood high schools on the American model attacked at its root perhaps the fundamental cause of social inequality.

These areas of cultural and educational life were in a sense traditional, emerging from the professional and other aspirations of the white, male middle class. Other pressures of the period were far more novel. These involved the hitherto unfamiliar themes of race, Celtic nationalism and Ireland.

Race emerged as a major political theme for the first time in the Wilson era. The build-up of Commonwealth immigration from the West Indies and the Indian subcontinent in particular in the 1950s had led to a rapid growth of the black and brown population. It rose from around 60,000 in 1951 to 336,000 a decade later, with evidence of black ghettos already emerging in cities from Bristol to Bradford. Racial tensions continued to fester: in the 1964 election there was racialist incitement in the Smethwick area of Birmingham with the slogan, 'If you want a nigger for your neighbour, vote Labour.' There was particular apprehension at the prospect of up to 300,000 Asian holders of British passports coming to Britain to settle, as was their legal right, after the granting of independence to Kenya and Uganda.

The government's response was a mixture of positive and negative thinking. It set up a strengthened Race Relations Board, followed by a Community Relations Commission under the direction of the former Minister of Technology, the Transport Workers' leader Frank Cousins. This was shrewd because some union branches were known to be particular centres of racism. However, the Commission proved to have inadequate powers, and Cousins left it two years later. The negative side of the government's policy caused far more of a stir. Callaghan, who had been badgered by Labour MPs for Midlands constituencies, rushed through a Commonwealth Immigrants Bill in February 1968. This meant that the entry of East African holders of British passports would be reduced under a voucher scheme to only 6,000 or 7,000 a year. This caused fury in many constituency Labour parties. Callaghan was denounced as a reactionary. It was assumed that had the Kenyan Asians been white, there would have been no problem. Callaghan was no racist himself and sat for the ethnically mixed constituency of Cardiff South-East, which included areas such as Tiger Bay. But this apparently morally neutral response to the immigration problem caused dismay. The government's bacon was saved by the gratuitous racial campaign launched by the maverick Tory Enoch Powell. He attacked black immigration in flamboyant language and spoke dramatically of the 'river Tiber foaming with much blood'. Powell's rhetoric was disowned sharply by his party leader, Ted Heath. In political terms, it enabled Labour to get off its self-created hook and try to reclaim the moral high ground by denouncing Powell's extremism. But the episode was an unhappy one. Race now entered British politics centre-stage. Ritual 'Paki-bashing' took place in towns like Bradford and Luton. Labour had left dangerously unfinished business here.

The same was true of a different kind of ethnic challenge. This was the emergence of significant movements of both Scottish and Welsh nationalism, for the first time in the twentieth century. Both the Scottish Nationalists and Plaid Cymru had performed poorly at general elections down to 1966. Now disillusion with the economic and social consequences of the dominant Labour Party caused a dramatic transformation. In Wales, it was reinforced by the growth of Cymdeithas yr Iaith Cymraeg (the Welsh Language Society), with a strong student following, in the early 1960s following an influential radio broadcast, *Tynged yr Iaith* (The Fate of the Language), by the veteran right-wing Nationalist leader, the poet Saunders Lewis. The Welsh-language movement saw direct physical action against government building, post offices and television masts in support of Welsh-language driving and television licences, tax forms and the like. English–only road signs were defaced or destroyed all over Wales, to the bafflement of visiting motorists.

In Wales, the Carmarthen by-election of July 1966 saw the election of Plaid Cymru's much-respected leader, the pacifist Gwynfor Evans. He was able to build on public disillusion with Labour economic policy and its newly created Welsh Office. In 1967–8, there were signs that Welsh nationalism was growing not just in Welsh-speaking rural areas but in Labour's industrial heartlands in the valleys. In Rhondda West in 1967 and Caerphilly in 1968, Plaid Cymru came very close to winning these traditionally rock-solid Labour seats. Official Labour seemed old and demoralized. In Scotland, the Nationalist challenge was more powerful still, since here political nationalism had a more rooted tradition. A Labour majority of 16,000 at Hamilton was overturned by Mrs Winifred Ewing of the SNP in November 1967, and sweeping Nationalist gains in local elections followed. Unlike Plaid Cymru, the SNP showed long-term strength not only in rural areas such as the Western Isles, but also in cities like Glasgow and Dundee, and the new towns of Cumbernauld and East Kilbride. Clearly Labour without its Welsh and Scottish bastions would face disaster. In response Wilson turned to the old remedy of a Royal Commission on the constitution, initially under Lord Crowther and then, after his death, under Lord Kilbrandon. This would consider the issue of Scottish and Welsh government, or self-government, in broad terms, but would take several years over it. There were more subtle strategies. One effective initiative in Wales was the work of George Thomas, the Welsh Secretary, who orchestrated the investiture of Princes Charles as Prince of Wales at Caernarfon Castle in July 1969, as a boost to unionist feeling. The Prince spent a term trying to learn Welsh at Aberystwyth university college. It was all very effective unionist propaganda. By 1970 Welsh and Scottish nationalism seemed to be on the wane. Nevertheless, a new genie had emerged from the bottle. Scottish and, to a lesser degree, Welsh government and national identity were on the agenda as they had not been since the early years of Lloyd George in the 1890s. The United Kingdom, torn by divisions of class and race, looked that much more disunited.

More serious than either Wales or Scotland was the eruption of troubles in Northern Ireland. Since the Free State Treaty in January 1922, Ulster had receded into the background of British politics. It remained dormant under one-party Protestant Unionist rule. Catholic complaints of discrimination in jobs and housing, of political gerrymandering by Unionist politicians and of a one-religion police force were ignored. Then in the summer of 1968, the long campaign of civil rights which had begun in 1967 in conscious emulation of the campaign of blacks under Martin Luther King in the United States exploded into violence in the Catholic areas of Londonderry's Bogside and the Falls Road in Belfast. There were violent clashes between local nationalists and the Royal Ulster Constabulary; ten people were killed, including a nine-year-old boy who was asleep at the time. Law and order, any kind of political consensus as known elsewhere in Britain, had broken down.

Callaghan as Home Secretary handled the crisis with great skill. There were no guidelines for him to follow. Northern Ireland had been left to the Unionist government in Stormont. In the Home Office files, it appeared only under 'general' along with the more troublesome Isle of Man and the Channel Islands. Callaghan visited Northern Ireland twice in rapid succession and virtually took control, creating an air of confident authority in contrast to the parish-pump Unionists in Belfast. The British troops were sent in, to take over from the Royal Ulster Constabulary. The hated B Specials, a Protestant paramilitary force loathed in Catholic areas, were abolished while the RUC was left unarmed on the lines of the traditional British bobby (whose Police Federation Callaghan had earlier represented in Parliament). At the same time, he turned vigorously to the socio-economic causes of discontent. A Downing Street Declaration led to a new non-party commission for housing, an attack on discrimination in jobs and political manipulation, and long-term economic initiatives to combat Ulster's heavy unemployment problem. Lord Scarman and Lord Hunt, two liberal-minded men, inquired into the troubles in Londonderry and the police force respectively. Calm returned, and the British army was hailed as protectors of their freedom by Catholic communities in the province. When Callaghan told the Protestant leader, the Rev. Ian Paisley, that they were all the children of God, Paisley rejoined angrily that they were all the children of Wrath. But Callaghan was a tough man and Paisley emerged from their meeting white and shaken.

In the early months of 1970, it seemed that peace had returned to Northern Ireland. Wilson hailed Callaghan as having given the government its first clear political success since the 1966 election. But far more was needed. The age-old political and constitutional impasse between Protestants who supported the Union with Britain and Catholics who wanted an end to partition and absorption into the Republic in the south still had to be tackled. Catholic enthusiasm for British troops stationed in their midst was now less than total. By the summer of 1970 there were alarming signs of activity from the left-wing and terrorist Provisional Sinn Fein, while Ulster loyalists were also believed to be arming. Northern Ireland was still the polarized, bitter province it had been for centuries. For all that, here was a sphere of policy where the government seemed both effective and enlightened. Perhaps for the first time in modern Irish history, it had left Ulster better governed than when it took office. Had Labour retained office in 1970, it is possible that the opportunity might have been seized for a long-term reconciliation. Instead, the advent of Tory rule, repression and internment culminating in 'Bloody Sunday' in Derry in 1972, plunged the unhappy people of Ulster back into the abyss.

One common feature seemed to link the troubles involving race and the various Celtic nations. This was the phenomenon of youth, especially middle-class youth. It was young people, often students, who were prominent in Scottish demonstrations against the Polaris submarines in Holy Loch, who climbed television masts on behalf of the Welsh language, and who joined civil rights marches in Ulster. Generational revolt had occurred before. But now it took political form. University campuses erupted in the summer of 1968, largely copying the much more violent student protests in the United States, Germany and France. International student leaders like 'Danny the Red' or Rudi Dutschke became celebrities. There were 'demos', 'sit-ins' and occasional riots even in Oxford and Cambridge. The main political target was the American war in Vietnam. A series of massive protests resulted in a huge march to the US Embassy in Grosvenor Square on 27 October 1968. In the event, the government, and Callaghan in particular, handled matters with much calmness. The march went ahead, but the police held firm, and the demonstration dissolved without violent disorder. From that time onwards, student protest seemed to pass its peak. Too often, young idealists had been joined by aggressive ideologues anxious for a punch-up with the police. Some middle-class citizens turned against publicly subsidized students causing mayhem on university campuses. Students, in Britain unlike South Africa, were not victims of institutional violence. The repressive powers of the university authorities consisted in Oxford, for example, of nothing more terrifying than the white-tied proctors and their few elderly bowler-hatted 'bulldogs'. There were some victories for politicized youth. The government responded to the Latey Commission's proposal for the voting age to be reduced to eighteen. Universities overhauled their disciplinary procedures for the better; student representation on university and college senates and committees became the norm. But, in the longer term, student indiscipline harmed the universities and weakened their standing as against central government.

Ministers responded humanely in key areas of sexual liberation. But over drug use and abuse 'permissiveness' seemed to be reaching its natural limits. When the Wootton Committee recommended the legalization of soft drugs like cannabis, Callaghan rebuffed it sharply, with his condemnation of 'permissiveness' referred to above.[12] Parents, middle class and working class, even the majority of younger people themselves, seemed by 1970 to be turning against unkempt and aggressive student demonstrators, and against cultural experiment in general. Overseas gurus such as Timothy Leary, the apostle of the drug culture of San Francisco, or the legendary Maoist rebel Che Guevara, had little relevance to the British scene. Even the Beatles began to lose their sheen when 'boy meets girl' ballads gave way to the psychedelic message of 'Lucy in the Sky with Diamonds' (LSD). By the 1970 election, youth seemed more orderly, and permissiveness under control, for good or ill. The government had come through the fires with a shrewd balance of tolerance and order.

By 1970, when thoughts were turning towards another general

election, it seemed that the government, for long deeply unpopular, was finally restoring its position. Callaghan had given it a major policy success with his handling of Northern Ireland. He added the bonus of refusing to redraw Parliamentary constituencies as he should have done, to help Labour's chances at the next election. More important still, Roy Jenkins had put the national finances back on course with a resounding balance of payments surplus after all the crises of the past. Harold Wilson, fearful of leaks to the media, neurotic about conspiracies and intrigues, still seemed the dominant politician of his day. Partly this was because the Conservatives had made only limited headway since the 1966 election. Their leader, Edward Heath, a bachelor of wooden personality, was not popular. Further, in approaching the next election, they had produced the Selsdon Park programme of anti-statism and cutbacks in public expenditure. This could mean mass unemployment and social unrest. Harold Wilson declared, as Oliver Cromwell had once done, that the Lord had delivered the enemy into his hands.

There had been one major crisis in the summer of 1969 which had somehow been negotiated. Barbara Castle, Secretary of State for Employment, was determined that the firm smack of socialist planning should be extended not only to business but to the increasingly militant trade unions as well. Their pressure for higher wages along with unofficial strikes in connection with demarcation disputes and other issues, was believed by many to be a major cause of economic weakness. Barbara Castle, an old Bevanite, had no especial reason to love the unions. The dominant role of powerful union leaders like Jack Jones of the Transport Workers and Hugh Scanlon of the Engineers, almost beyond the reach of government and the law as industrial potentates, alarmed her. She was furious when the Donovan Royal Commission on the unions ruled against penal sanctions to curb union power, and called for maintaining the voluntary system of collective bargaining, with the emphasis on the workplace and plant bargaining rather than national agreements. It seemed to her an opportunity missed.

She produced a White Paper, *In Place of Strife*, which led to an Industrial Relations Bill in the spring of 1969. Much of it was intended to strengthen the hand of the unions. But attention focused on three penal provisions: a twenty-eight-day conciliation pause, imposed settlements in inter-union disputes, and enforcement of strike ballots. There was much to be said in equity and logic for all these proposals. But they roused intense fury in union circles by introducing the force of law into a traditionally voluntary industrial relations system. Mrs Castle was strongly backed by Harold Wilson and (at first) by Roy Jenkins. A united Cabinet would surely get its way even over the industrial muscle of the unions. But the Cabinet was far from united. The first key dissentient was Callaghan, a former union official, who spoke out strongly at Labour's National Executive against the penal aspects of the Industrial Relations Bill. Wilson condemned him and removed him from the Inner Cabinet, but he was simply too powerful to sack. Callaghan was joined by his ally and old patron, Douglas Houghton, chairman of the Parliamentary Labour Party, and then by a series of Cabinet colleagues alarmed at breaking their historic relationship with the unions. The TUC voted it down by almost 8 million votes to only 846,000. The Parliamentary party was mostly hostile. In the Cabinet, Mrs Castle was left with Harold Wilson as a lone ally. Even Roy Jenkins 'elegantly sidled on to the fence'.[13] Exposed, almost alone, Harold Wilson had lost. The bill was humiliatingly withdrawn and a 'solemn and binding' agreement cobbled up with the TUC to provide a voluntary system monitored by them. Solomon Binding was obviously a man of straw. A rising tide of inflationary wage settlements followed over the winter. It was clear that Mrs Castle's bill, with unions, party and Cabinet against it, was simply a non-runner at that time. On the other hand, its opponents provided no valid alternative. As Prime Minister, Callaghan was to reap the whirlwind in the 'winter of discontent' ten years later.

Harold Wilson went to the country in June 1970, taking advantage of cheerful polls boosted by the improvement in the economy, and near-tropical weather. Memories of the union débâcle, it was hoped, were fading. The public was invited to return Labour again on the Stanley Baldwin-style basis of safety first. But the opinion polls, not for the last time, proved highly deceptive. Labour's campaign lacked the old passion. Wilson himself had lost the charisma of 1966. The young canvassers and local enthusiasts, disillusioned perhaps by Vietnam or immigration, were not there this time. The plodding campaign of Edward Heath made quiet headway during the campaign, especially when economic indicators seemed to show bad trade figures again. Even the football went wrong. England, victorious in 1966, went out of the World Cup in Mexico, at the hands of the Germans again as luck would have it. Although the Nationalist challenge in Scotland and Wales was comfortably rebuffed, Labour lost ground overall. Significantly, there was a 3.8 per cent drop in the voting, which reached only 72 per cent. Many Labour voters had simply stayed away, out of apathy or worse. In fact, Labour's poll had fallen by almost a million since 1964; it was nearly a million less than that of the Tories. The Conservatives under Heath won 330 seats to Labour's 288, a manageable enough majority. Wilson's hopes of a third victory, to confirm Labour as the natural party of government, had been deflated. A television programme was to turn the knife, condemning Wilson's team as 'yesterday's men'.

Harold Wilson's six years of government have had a bad press, both from the Thatcherites in the 1980s and from some advocates of 'New Labour' in the 1990s. In reality, the Wilson years were in many ways successful and creative. Important and correct decisions were taken in overseas policy, notably the withdrawal east of Suez and the first serious Labour commitment to joining Europe. At home, it was in many ways an era not of spiritual degeneration but of social and sexual freedom. As Paul Johnson wrote in the *New Statesman* after the election, 'We no longer terrorise homosexuals. We do not force mothers to bring forth unwanted children into the world ... We do not murder by the rope.'[14] It was a very good time for the arts and for many aspects of education, the Open University in particular. Socially, there was an advance towards a more mobile, less class-ridden world: Wilson's people believed there was indeed such a thing as society. In Northern Ireland, there was unexpected, if short-term, progress towards peace and reconciliation. Devolution for Scotland and Wales began to creep on to the public agenda. The first attempts were made to deal with the strains of a multi-ethnic society, although the restrictive policy on immigration was widely condemned. The economy was often not under control, and the failure to devalue long before November 1967 was regarded as a profound error. Nevertheless, enough remained of the affluence of the 1950s to make this seem a good enough time compared with the 'stagflation' of the next decade, and the mass unemployment and social exclusion of the Thatcher era. A conference held to celebrate Sir Alec Cairncross's eightieth birthday in 1991 was to see the 1960s, for all the shortcomings, as part of the economic 'golden age'.[15]

Yet there was always an insuperable problem. The government responded to change in most areas, and was successful in many of them. But the Labour Party itself was no longer as effective a vehicle for reform. Structural decline was underway. Membership continued to fall sharply, even taking the bogus figures provided by Transport House. Constituency parties in inner cities often reflected client groups such as council house tenants or members of public sector unions. The failure to reform the unions and the adversarial tone of industrial relations showed up starkly the immobilism of a movement trapped in the old time-warp of Keir Hardie's pre-1914 'labour alliance'. If the *élan* and the composition of the Labour Party were in decline, so too was its ethos. It had come to office to achieve sustained growth through planning, a fusion of thirties Keynesianism and forties socialism. Partly through external pressures in the global economy, it failed. This collapse of the panacea of planning left a hole at the heart of Labour's ideology.[16] It never regained the democratic socialist impulse of 1945. Men no longer sang 'England, arise'.

The ultimate casualty of the decade was Harold Wilson himself. He was a decent, kindly man of great ability. Unlike Mrs Thatcher, he identified with ordinary people and respected their civil liberties. His regime always retained a sense of humanity and a commitment to social justice. It looks almost noble when compared with the monetarism, privatization and dogma of inequality promoted by the Thatcherite zealots who were to follow later on. If Wilson's children were the young students of campus 'sit-ins', Thatcher's children were the hungry, homeless residents of cardboard boxes in the Strand. And yet distinguished biographies have not really restored Wilson's reputation. The supreme political tactician of his generation, he dominated these six years. He embodied its classless style, part nonconformist revivalist, part Max Miller, a latterday darling of the halls. But tactics and cosmetics, like patriotism, were not enough. For all the best and most idealistic endeavours of the planners of the 1960s, their revisionist New Jerusalem remained mostly unbuilt.

CHAPTER VII

'YOU'VE NEVER HAD IT SO BAD'?: BRITAIN IN THE 1970S

NICK TIRATSOO

Almost everyone who has reflected seriously about Britain in the 1970s agrees that the decade was little short of a disaster. The tone was set at the time when a variety of influential academics and journalists wrote as if the country was about to implode. They created a fashion for supposedly analytical books with lurid titles and pessimistic themes, such as *Britain Against Itself, The Future That Doesn't Work: Social Democracy's Failures in Britain* and *Is Britain Dying?*. Across the Atlantic, long-standing critics of Britain's welfare state and mixed economy joined the chorus of disapproval. The *Wall Street Journal* waved 'Goodbye Great Britain, it was nice knowing you'. Nowadays the decade is regularly referred to as the country's nadir. Conservative politicians, in particular, often refer to the failures of these years in the hope of dramatizing their alleged successes after 1979.

Looked at in detail, the conventional charge sheet against the 1970s is long and damning. Britain was beset by economic failure. The trade unions acted like robber barons, holding the rest of the country to ransom. Inflation stalked the land, destroying the social fabric. Ordinary people constantly found themselves bullied by powers outside their control. This was a period of strikes, power-cuts and discontent. What makes all this particularly reprehensible, in the critics' view, is their belief that it was entirely avoidable. Britain needed strong government in the 1970s, but its politicians dithered and trimmed, flunking difficult decisions and necessary confrontations. They were ultimately culpable. The experiences of the 1970s are, therefore, taken to illustrate one central lesson: that political leadership must always be absolutely resolute and uncompromising.

Many of these points are now almost accepted as common sense. Fairly typically, one middle-aged woman told the *Independent* in July 1996 that the events of the decade had permanently changed her political outlook. She explained: 'I can still remember those awful strikes. That was the only time I ever tried to dye anything. I got the machine out and the damn bedspread and we had a power-cut.' Nevertheless, this is a case which repays closer scrutiny. Nobody could sensibly claim that Britain was at its finest in the 1970s, but it is also clear that the country's problems have frequently been exaggerated and distorted. We have come to see the decade in a way which magnifies the bad and neglects the good. Moreover, key events are too often presented without any context. The following chapter aims to dispel some widely held myths about Britain during these years and thus achieve more balanced conclusions.

The 1970s began with something of an electoral surprise.[1] Harold Wilson's Labour Party, in power since 1964, had weathered a long series of financial crises, and now looked likely to benefit from a gradually improving economy. Wilson was a wily politician who remained very popular with grass-roots Labour supporters. However, when he finally chose to call an election in June 1970, it was the Tories who triumphed, winning 46 per cent of the vote and a thirty-seat Parliamentary majority.

The significance of this result was particularly pronounced because the Conservatives promised to make a clean break with the previous twenty years' style of government. During a policy review shortly before the election, the party had moved decisively to the right, away from old-style 'One-Nation Toryism' and towards a fixation with free markets. In a famous phrase, the Conservatives pledged to end support for 'lame ducks', whether these be inefficient manufacturers or work-shy welfare claimants.

The new Prime Minister seemed to personify the change: Edward Heath was no Tory grandee, in the style of Macmillan or Home, but the grammar-school-educated son of a lower-middle-class Kent tradesman.

Once in office, the Conservatives quickly showed that they were serious about their radical intentions. A dock strike broke out shortly after the election but the incoming Minister of Labour refused to intervene, thereby clearly distancing himself from Wilson's long-standing and almost automatic strategy of direct conciliation. Other significant measures quickly followed. The government abolished the Prices and Incomes Board – a pillar of their predecessors' anti-inflation strategy – and then introduced relatively severe public expenditure cuts, sweetening the pill with a reduction in standard-rate income tax. The message was clear: the nation must be persuaded to 'stand on its own two feet'.

These bold ideological moves were applauded by the party's hawks but soon generated practical problems. Some trade unions had been inclined to moderate their wage claims in Wilson's last year but, with no incomes policy to restrain them, began seeking to make up lost ground. As a consequence, inflation accelerated, increasing from 5 per cent in 1969 to double digits in mid-1971. Meanwhile, unemployment was also rising sharply as the government's neo-Darwinian approach to competition started to bite. It appeared likely that the total might well move beyond the politically sensitive one-million mark. Worse still was the fact that all this harsh medicine did not seem to be generating any great compensatory surge in entrepreneurial activity. Left to their own devices, Britain's employers were not rising to the task. Indeed, the country's growth rate was actually decelerating, from 2.5 per cent in 1969 to 2.0 per cent in 1970 and 1.7 per cent in 1971.

Given these circumstances, Heath decided that he had no option but to alter course or, in an expression that will be forever associated with him, execute a 'U-turn'. A government which had begun by boasting of its 'hands off' approach was suddenly transformed into one pursuing a fairly conventional degree of interventionism. The change involved several notable policy initiatives. The Chancellor, Anthony Barber, presented a budget which was highly reflationary, hoping that tax cuts for the better-off would provoke a boom. At the same time, the government indicated that it would now bale out private companies if the worst came to the worst, and there were much publicized state-led rescues of Rolls-Royce and Upper Clyde Shipbuilders. However, the most spectacular redefinition of policy occurred over the industrial relations issue.

Conservatives had never quite been able to make up their minds about trade unions. Most Tories shared a gut feeling that the unions were undemocratic and probably corrupt, potential bullies that clearly needed reform. On the other hand, it was understood that any move to draconian controls in this area might be politically inexpedient – after all, the Tories needed working-class votes to stay in power. Moreover, there was some lurking sympathy with the view that free collective bargaining had a perfectly legitimate place in a market-led system. Nevertheless, under Heath Mark Two, all these tensions were resolved at a stroke as the government lurched towards legislative solutions. A new Industrial Relations Act introduced unprecedented legal regulation. Unions were required to register themselves formally and then adhere to various rules about the conduct of industrial disputes. A National Industrial Relations Court was to oversee the scheme, imposing compulsory ballots of union members and American-style cooling-off periods as it saw fit. A long tradition of largely voluntary negotiations between unions and man-agements had been unilaterally ended almost overnight.

Heath's hope was obviously to tame the unions, but he soon found that government interference in collective bargaining brought its own problems. A minority of unions refused to register as instructed, thus placing themselves in a legal black hole. Some rank-and-file militants were jailed for contempt of the new act but then had to be released because of protests from sympathizers. Further embarrassment followed when the High Court reversed two Industrial Relations Court decisions. If this was not enough, Heath next found himself pitched into a damaging conflict with the miners.

Britain was still heavily dependent on coal in the early 1970s, yet those who worked in the pits were largely forgotten, underpaid in a dangerous occupation. Watching the general wage scramble in 1970–1, the miners' union decided that there was need for redress, but its resulting claim was turned down by the employers, the state-owned National Coal Board, under pressure from the government. Carefully staying within the recently introduced legislative framework, the union then decided to call an industry-wide strike, the first since 1926. Few predicted that their action would have much impact, but the miners improvised effective picketing and were soon able to restrict coal supplies to some power stations. Heath's response was to ration electricity, using power-cuts to domestic consumers and an enforced three-day week in industry. The dispute dragged over into 1972, but the government was unable to impose its will and in the end had to sanction a settlement worth between 17 and 24 per cent to the miners. The final consequence of this episode occurred some months later when Heath performed yet another volte-face and introduced a statutory incomes policy – the very measure Conservatives had been openly ridiculing when they took office.

The Prime Minister's fortunes did not improve during 1973. A passionate European, he proudly led Britain into the EEC at the beginning of the year. Nevertheless, there was little celebration: both parties remained divided over Europe, while the public was mainly distrustful. Meanwhile, there could be little doubt that Barber's 'dash for growth' was turning sour. Tax cuts had fuelled a property boom and overseas speculation rather than solid investment in British industry. Moreover, the Chancellor's strategy also seemed to be harming the balance of payments: the stoked-up economy was sucking in imports at the very time when commodity prices were, for entirely fortuitous reasons, moving against the developed world. Towards the end of the year, two further events added to the Prime Minister's woes.

In October 1973, the Yom Kippur War between Israel and Egypt led to a debilitating oil embargo and a four-fold increase in the price of oil, a huge inflationary shock. Shortly afterwards, the government found itself once again locked in conflict with the miners. This dispute, again over wages, developed on familiar lines. The miners' union enforced an overtime ban to pressure the Coal Board, while Heath implemented a three-day week to conserve stocks. In the new year, both sides raised the stakes. The miners' union decided on a complete stoppage, after a poll revealed that 80 per cent of its members supported such a move. Heath's reaction was to call an election for late February, specifically on the question 'Who governs Britain?'

At first, it was generally felt that the Prime Minister had acted astutely. The miners received some public support but they were also deeply loathed in many parts of the South. The widely publicized fact that their unions' executive included Communists appeared to play into Heath's hands. However, as the election campaign developed, several events decisively weakened the Conservatives' case. To start with, when the miners' strike actually began, it proved to be a low-key affair, with little that the press could pick on as unruly behaviour. Then Wilson underlined his claim to have a better relationship with the unions by intervening to prevent an entirely separate dispute on the railways. Finally, just before the election, a set of trade figures were released which showed that the economy was beginning to run out of control. The balance of payments deficit for 1973 was a record £1.5 billion, a figure made much more worrying because the full impact of the Middle East war had yet to be felt. In the end, therefore, the election proved to be a very close-run thing. Both the big parties lost support, with the Conservatives recording their lowest share of the poll since 1929. The Liberals attained an unprecedented 19 per cent of the votes cast and several other small parties also did well. Labour finished as the biggest party in Parliament, with 301 MPs to the Tories' 297, but this was well short of an overall majority. Intense negotiations saw Heath try and fail to form a coalition and Wilson finally accept the challenge of leading a minority government.

Labour had inherited a poisoned chalice – a lame economy and a divided nation – but within a few months appeared to be making some progress. The miners were offered a generous settlement and returned to work. More generally, Wilson began to shape a new and genuinely innovative strategy for coping with inflation. This revolved around a 'social contract' between government and unions, with the latter moderating their wage claims in exchange for legislation which would add to workers' social and legal rights. Encouraged by these successes, Labour decided to call another general election in October and this time was rewarded with a narrow parliamentary majority of three.

Wilson must have hoped that his newfound status would allow a period of calm and relatively stable government, but he was soon to be disappointed. As everyone recognized, Labour was hardly united. The European issue continued to prove troublesome. In addition, there was a yawning gap evident over the question of strategy. Wilson and most of his senior ministers – particularly Denis Healey at the Treasury and Jim Callaghan at the Foreign Office – were in favour of a cautious approach, believing that the electorate wanted bread-and-butter issues, like the cost of living, to be addressed as a matter of urgency. On the other hand, there was strong pressure for greater radicalism. The party as a whole had moved to the left in the early 1970s and thrown up the charismatic Tony Benn, Minister for Industry in the new Cabinet, as the rank and file's champion. What the left wing wanted above all was much greater government control of the economy, including selective nationalization and the immediate redistribution of wealth in favour of the working class.

This was a potent cocktail, but Wilson had much experience of handling difficult colleagues, and proved adept at keeping the Cabinet functioning. Benn was allowed to busy himself with various interventionist schemes – for example, the creation of cooperatives at Norton Villiers Triumph and the *Scottish Daily News* – while his colleagues concentrated on the wage–price spiral. Various solutions to the latter were debated, but in the end it was agreed that the first step must be to take the sting out of the situation by a dose of deflation. Healey therefore introduced one of the most stringent budgets on record, raising taxes by £1.25 billion and pruning a roughly equivalent amount off public expenditure. Of course, the cuts ran counter to Labour's traditional proclivities, but the Chancellor and his colleagues argued that they were simply unavoidable given the state of the economy. One encouraging fact was that the trade unions appeared to be broadly supportive. At its September 1975 conference, the TUC backed a policy of voluntary wage restraint, limiting increases to a flat-rate £6 per week for all categories of workers. Labour began 1976, therefore, in a mood of quiet confidence.

However, the sense of foreboding soon returned. In April, Wilson suddenly decided to retire. This was a grievous blow, not least because it reignited tensions in the party as left and right jockeyed for power. In fact, the subsequent leadership election only underlined the scale of the divisions: Jim Callaghan beat the left's Michael Foot in a ballot of Labour MPs, but only by 176 votes to 133. A few months later the new Prime Minister found himself facing a further round of economic difficulties. A flare-up of industrial relations trouble, including a seamen's strike, precipitated a loss of confidence in sterling, with the pound falling to an all-time low of $1.70. In this situation, the government had little option but to placate the markets, and interest rates were raised to 15 per cent. The problem, of course, was that this also hit domestic consumers and so threatened Labour's electoral support. The trend in public opinion was dramatically illustrated at a by-election in Walsall, which saw a record 27.3 per cent swing against the party.

At this point, the government decided that its only way forward would be to buy time, using a loan from the International Monetary Fund (IMF) to create a breathing space secure from outside pressure. Early negotiations with the IMF indicated that it would be willing to help, but only at a price. The highly orthodox Fund officials were not sympathetic to left-leaning governments and believed that welfare provision could easily hinder growth. They talked, therefore, of Britain needing to deflate by a further £2–3 billion. After long negotiation, Healey was able to moderate these demands but not by very much. The final package granted $3.9 billion of credit in exchange for a £2.5 billion cut in government expenditure.

This decisive initiative stifled the markets and laid a potentially sound basis for subsequent economic improvement. On the other hand, it did little to improve relations in Labour's own ranks. The left was furious, arguing that the Cabinet had betrayed socialist principles and allowed itself to be ordered around by foreign bankers. Healey was intermittently heckled when he appeared at that year's party conference. Moreover, the crisis had certainly dented Britain's reputation in the rest of the world. Some foreign observers believed that Britain's problems were essentially temporary, but others loudly proclaimed that the government was leading the country to economic bankruptcy.

However, the more sensational predictions were quickly shown to be ill-judged. In fact, the following two years were ones of modest progress. Several factors were responsible for this welcome change in fortunes. Firstly, Callaghan proved to be an unexpectedly steady Prime Minister, a leader with roots in the labour movement who had a significant degree of cross-class appeal. The fact that he had once been Parliamentary adviser to the Police Federation said a good deal. Secondly, the government's wider stability was greatly helped by the 'Lib–Lab' pact of early 1977, an agreement with the Liberal Party which gave Labour a few extra Commons' votes in exchange for some relatively minor concessions over policymaking. Finally, and perhaps most significantly, the economic outlook benefited from the fact that Britain now began enjoying the benefits of North Sea oil. The first field had opened in 1975 and nine were in full production three years later, with the country rapidly moving to a position where it would be on par with countries like Iraq and Kuwait as a major world oil power. What all of this meant in hard financial terms was there for all to see. The balance of payments and the inflation position both improved, while the pound rose to nearly $2. Given such relative success, Chancellor Healey was able to pay back the first $2 billion of the IMF loan with some ease.

The linchpin holding this recovery together was the pay policy agreed between the government and the TUC in 1976. This voluntary code, revolving first around flat-rate increases and then a virtual pay freeze, held firm for far longer than expected but was beginning to come under strain by late 1977. Trade union leaders like Jack Jones of the transport workers fought hard to protect what had been achieved, but he was not able to stem the pressure from some well-organized and militant groups dissatisfied with their low settlements. The task of the trade union leadership was made all the more difficult when Callaghan announced bluntly, in July 1978, that pay increases would be limited to just 5 per cent over the next twelve months. Anger on the union side was fuelled not just by the small size of this figure but also by the fact that it seemed to have been plucked out of the air and imposed without negotiation or consultation.

In fact, Callaghan's behaviour appeared to be more than a little ill-judged. He was clearly looking to the next election – the Liberals had withdrawn from the pact – and perhaps saw the 5 per cent figure as a vote-winner. However, he then dithered and announced that Labour would continue with its tiny majority until some time in 1979. The Prime Minister had lost the chance of calling an election when the economy was unarguably in recovery and also irritated a union leadership that already felt ill-rewarded for its efforts on the government's behalf.

What followed has been etched in public memory as the 'winter of discontent'. The 5 per cent figure was rejected by the Labour Party conference and then opposed by various key groups – firemen, lorry drivers and Ford workers – who obtained settlements well into double figures. Public sector workers, always at the bottom of the pay league, tried to follow suit, and in the early weeks of 1979 there was a rash of local selective strikes by health service staff, dustmen and even the gravediggers of Liverpool. Schools were closed and rubbish mounted in the streets. Finally, the government gave in and granted a 9 per cent rise, thus fatally compromising its own pay policy.

Correctly or not, many saw this chain of events as a great Labour failure. The government had been unable to act in the face of selfish industrial militancy. The whole episode boosted the Conservatives and, in a vote of confidence in the House of Commons on 28 March, Labour finally fell, defeated by one vote, and the first administration to leave office because of a Commons division since 1924. In the election that followed, the party was duly punished. Labour polled just 36.9 per cent of the vote, its worst post-war performance. This allowed the Conservatives, with 43.9 per cent of the vote and 339 seats in Parliament, to form a government with an overall majority of forty-four.

What should we make of this hectic succession of events? The conventional view is that the 1970s were years of crisis, a period when, in the words of the Oxford historian Norman Stone, 'all kinds of things just fell apart'. In detail, this assessment depends upon a number of interlinked propositions. The failings of these years were failings of government. Both Conservative and Labour administrations had no real compass and so spent much of their time muddling through. All ended up with lamentable records. What makes this particularly galling, the critics add, is the fact that most sensible people knew perfectly well what needed to be done. The trade unions were the central problem in British society, and so governments should have acted resolutely to curtail their powers. Had Mrs Thatcher taken office earlier, it is usually concluded, then the whole story would have been very different. But was any of this actually the case?

Before examining how governments acquitted themselves in the 1970s, some context is necessary. Britain has long been part of the world economy and this has generally set the limits on what administrations at Westminster can or cannot achieve. Broadly speaking, the world economy grew relatively smoothly from 1945 to about 1973, and as a result most countries (including Britain) benefited enormously. However, for the rest of the 1970s, the situation was very different. Buffeted by the impact of oil-price rises, the world economy became unusually turbulent, generating much more problematic conditions for individual nations. Japan's growth rate fell from an annual 10.6 per cent in the 1960s to 4.7 per cent in the 1970s. Unemployment in the United States rose from 4.6 per cent in the 1960s to 6.6 per cent between 1974 and 1979. What such figures tell us is that some of Britain's difficulties in the 1970s were beyond anyone's control. The country could not buck world trends. Nevertheless, this does not let the different governments of the time off the hook completely. Administrations had *some* room for manoeuvre even in the most difficult years of this troubled decade. Are the critics right in their assertion that opportunities were invariably squandered?

Certainly, the Heath government of 1970–4 can only be judged an abject failure. As we have seen, Heath was over-ideological at first and then hypnotized by the miners. The trade union reforms of these years caused more problems than they cured. Moreover, the 'Barber boom' left a troublesome legacy which took years to overcome. About the only good thing that can be said for Heath is that he showed a degree of sensitivity when it came to unemployment. Unlike some Conservative Prime Ministers of other years, Heath was not prepared to use the dole as a means of achieving selective economic gains.

The Labour administrations that followed, by contrast, must be rated much more favourably. Both Callaghan and Wilson made mistakes, but their achievements outweighed their lapses. Labour's prime aim was to moderate inflation without jeopardizing employment. Much emphasis was placed on the social contract as a means of controlling pay claims, but the government was also steadfast in pruning its own budgets. Public expenditure as a proportion of the country's gross domestic product actually fell fairly fast during this period, from 44.9 per cent in 1974 to 42.8 per cent in 1979 (about the level it remained in the late 1990s). Of course, such deflation might easily have led to large-scale job cuts, but the government went out of its way to soften the blow wherever possible, for example supporting ailing companies and maintaining an active regional policy. The results were quite impressive. Inflation was running at 24 per cent in 1975 but just 8 per cent three years later. Meanwhile, unemployment had grown, though not by disastrous proportions. The annual average figure for 1974–9 was 4.5 per cent, high against the 1960s, but low when compared to what many other countries were experiencing in the same period.

On top of this, Labour was also achieving gains in other areas. For example, some significant social legislation was passed during these years on issues ranging from racial equality to redundancy. Probably the most important developments here related to women's rights. Labour had passed the Equal Pay Act in 1970 and five years later strengthened this legislation with a Sex Discrimination Act. Largely as a result of these new laws, women's earnings as a proportion of men's grew from 63.1 per cent in 1970 to 73.5 per cent in 1980. Other, more detailed measures had an equally dramatic impact. A Labour MP, Jo Richardson, piloted through the Domestic Violence and Matrimonial Proceedings Act in 1976, which made it much easier for women to get legal protection from violent husbands. About 300 had applied for injunctions against such men in 1972, but this number jumped to 3,000 in the first year of the new legislation's operation. In retrospect, Richardson's act was clearly a very significant milestone in dealing with a long-hidden problem that had secretly blighted many lives.

One final point requires emphasis. In the conventional view, it is usually asserted that the pre-Thatcher governments had 'lost the confidence of the British people'. Looking at the situation in detail reveals that this is far from true. The Conservative Party retained a clear lead in the opinion polls during 1976 and 1977, and recorded some spectacular by-election victories. In 1978, on the other hand, as the government's approach was seen to succeed, the position changed. Now Labour looked to have the support necessary for an election victory. In an editorial at the beginning of August, the current affairs weekly *New Society* noted that the government had 'a sporting chance of being re-elected', and then went on to explain the underlying trends. Callaghan, the magazine noted, was a popular leader, but Labour's real advantage lay in its handling of the economy:

> According to the polls, inflation and jobs vie with each other as the top issue in voter's minds. Gallup's latest findings are that on both issues Labour is seen as having the best policies. On inflation, Labour's lead is substantial, although on jobs the Conservatives have been catching up. To underline Labour's strengths, a detailed breakdown of similar polls this year ... shows, perhaps surprisingly, that Labour does better among those voters who regard inflation and jobs as important issues, than among those voters who don't.[2]

Of course, some of this goodwill disappeared in the months that followed. All the same, it remains unarguable that, up to January 1979, many were convinced that Labour was more than competent to run the country.

The assertion that the 1970s was a period of wholly bad government is, therefore, simply inaccurate. Politicians made mistakes during the decade, but this was hardly anything new. The important fact remains that, after 1974, Labour had a coherent strategy which it implemented in difficult conditions with some success. Both Wilson and Callaghan showed that a consensual style of leadership, predicated upon the idea of a social contract, could achieve real results. Is the conventional view any more believable on the subject of trade unions?

Critics of the trade unions in the 1970s make several different observations. It is often suggested, firstly, that unions tended to act irresponsibly over wage bargaining. Grass-roots pressure for pay increases was inevitable at this time because of inflation. The unions could have helped the nation by encouraging discipline and restraint. However, most were simply interested in the selfish pursuit of their members' interests. The result was an endless cycle of 'devil take the hindmost' bargaining which undermined stability. A second line of argument focuses on the everyday impact of unionism at company level. The allegation here is that unions were deeply implicated in a number of practices which eroded economic health. They wanted to achieve more and more control at the workplace and were prepared to use strike action at the drop of a hat in pursuit of their aims. Are either of these contentions actually true?

The unions' role in relation to pay bargaining during the 1970s is certainly not beyond criticism. Some unions *were* only interested in narrow ends and disregarded the consequences of their actions. Sectional behaviour became particularly pronounced in 1978–9. However, it is important to remember that these years also saw long periods of almost universal restraint. As has been shown, the TUC's endorsement of Labour's pay guidelines was a crucial element in the recovery of 1976–8. More fundamentally, we need to ask whether the unions really had the capabilities to deliver on pay in the way that the critics now maintain. There is an assumption that those occupying leadership positions in union headquarters could easily influence the rank and file, but this was, in fact, by no means always the case. The reality of the situation was that the unions were both weaker and more fragmented than is usually recognized.

Most unions had been created in the early years of the century and continued to run on highly traditional lines. Each collected small amounts of money from their individual members and then used the sum of these contributions to provide a modest range of benefits (payments for sickness, accidents and so on). Little was left over for things like office equipment or house journals. The movement as a whole only employed about 3,000 full-time officials to service twelve million members. Inevitably, much of the day-to-day business was carried out by volunteers, principally about 300,000 shop stewards. These people were often highly dedicated, but they normally had to work in a near vacuum, bereft of any back-up or support services. A survey of shop stewards in a prominent public sector union during 1974 found that one-third had no noticeboard, half had no access to a phone, and two-thirds lacked a room for meeting in. Given these circumstances, it is easy to see why transmitting an instruction from the top of a union organization to the bottom was often fraught with difficulties.

Having said that, it is apparent that many ordinary members were not in any case particularly inclined to listen to their leaders. Some joined unions because of the movement's historic ideals, but the majority saw their involvement simply as a means of obtaining benefits. Robert Taylor, a labour correspondent with the *Observer*, summed up the prevailing point of view when he wrote that the union card was 'a kind of commodity' which members paid for 'in order to gain tangible rewards'. In these circumstances, few had much sympathy for the idea of restraint: the whole point of unions was to gain maximum returns. Of course, several leaders tried to overcome this situation by appealing to their memberships on the basis of politics – they should support 'their' Labour government's battle for socialism – but this approach, too, had its pitfalls. Many ordinary unionists were apolitical or even in sympathy with the Conservatives. Indeed, only 48 per cent voted Labour at the February 1974 election. More generally, few in the rank and file had much sympathy with the idea that they were somehow engaged in a struggle with capitalism as a system. The leadership's talk of building a better society generally fell on deaf ears. In a 1976 poll of manual workers belonging to trade unions, 82 per cent agreed that profit was not a dirty word; 86 per cent accepted that it was important to live in a free-enterprise society; and 89 per cent concurred that it was fair to pay dividends to shareholders. This was not a membership which would necessarily take much notice when exhorted to make sacrifices in the name of the general good.

We may conclude, therefore, that the case against the unions in relation to pay bargaining is far from clear-cut. Indeed, there are good reasons to argue that it should be stood on its head. The problem was that the unions had too *little* power, not too much, and so were unsuited to enforcing government policy. From this perspective, the degree of restraint, particularly in the later years of the decade, is remarkable, and testament to the movement's general sense of social responsibility.

The charge that unions damaged economic health at company level revolves around two issues. Much debate from the mid-1970s onwards centred on the alleged iniquities of forced union membership – the closed shop. The controversy began when, as part of the social contract, Labour passed legislation making closed-shop agreements legal. The unions were pleased with the development and moved to capitalize on it. By contrast, press comment was almost wholly negative. Closed shops would strangle entrepreneurship, it was asserted, and undermine managerial authority. Moreover, the new legislation was clearly authoritarian: the right *not* to join a union remained fundamental in a democracy. As the columnist Paul Johnson thundered: 'The compulsory enforcement of the closed shop by parliamentary statute is the greatest disaster which has befallen liberty in my lifetime.' Such points are still repeated today.

Once again, however, we are dealing with hyperbole. The growth of closed-shop agreements in the second half of the 1970s was pronounced but by no means pervasive. At the end of the decade, about three-quarters of all workers were *not* so covered. Secondly, the idea that closed shops were invariably imposed on managements is largely fanciful. Research by academics at Warwick University showed conclusively that executives often actually preferred a closed shop. This was because dealing with workers through their unions in a standardized way did much to ensure stability and discipline. It is noticeable that employers were far less worried about closed shops than some excitable and partisan figures in the media.

This brings us, inevitably, to strikes. Many have alleged that the unions were continually provoking disputes at this time, and indeed popular memories of the 1970s frequently harp upon industrial strife. Quite obviously, there is something in this: no other decade has seen two long miners' strikes, for example. Nevertheless, the evidence is nowhere near as damning of the unions as might be imagined. This is a case where fiction needs to be very firmly disentangled from fact. The first essential step is to measure the actual extent of the problem. It is certainly true that the average number of disputes per year in the 1970s was higher than in the 1960s. On the other hand, we cannot infer from this that Britons in general were becoming more strike prone. Most conflict was concentrated in relatively few plants and sectors. Indeed, a Department of Employment study showed that, between 1971 and 1973, as many as 98 per cent of manufacturing establishments were without any disputes at all. Britain, it seems, had several troubled industries – coal, the docks and cars – rather than an all-embracing industrial relations pathology.

Another way of approaching this question is to focus on strikes themselves, in order to get some idea of their impact. Big disputes were no doubt damaging but luckily they were statistically rather unusual. We tend to think of strikes in terms of the great setpiece confrontations – typically, the miners' disputes – yet this misleads. The majority of conflicts during these years lasted less than three days. Moreover, it is well worth emphasizing that strikes were, anyway, responsible for only a small proportion of the total days lost at work. In a fairly typical year during the 1970s, accidents and certified illness accounted for about 320 million days, thirty times more than industrial disputes.

Thirdly, we can ask how Britain's experiences with strikes rated in international terms. The popular image is that the country was particularly afflicted, but this is not borne out by the evidence.

In an international league table of days lost through strikes between 1970 and 1979, Britain occupies a middling position, above Australia, Canada, Italy and the United States, though below Germany, France and Japan. The British cannot then be called exceptionally strike prone in comparative terms.

Finally, there is an important point to be made about causation. It is generally assumed that most strikes were provoked by the unions. A union official, so the story goes, would spot a minute failing, say a stale roll on sale in the canteen, and tell the membership to stop work. However, the reality of the situation was very different. Many unions went out of their way to keep the peace. Local officials and shop stewards spent much of their time trying to nip trouble in the bud. They were, in the words of two independent academic industrial relations experts, 'more of a lubricant than an irritant'. Moreover, union executives were by no means always ready to support the aggrieved: only a small proportion of disputes, perhaps 5 per cent, received official backing. Trouble, therefore, often occurred *in spite* of union efforts rather than because of them.

In fact, if we are to attribute blame for Britain's industrial relations problems during these years, there is a good case for seeing employers and managers as far more culpable than the unions. Only a few British executives held any form of academic or professional qualification, and most operated by 'rule of thumb' methods which could often seem arbitrary and inconsistent. The general lack of finesse was nowhere more apparent than in dealings with the shopfloor. Many managers believed that they had only two options over labour relations: to be a 'bastard' or a 'hard bastard'. There was much talk in management circles of 'sorting out the peasants'. American visitors to British factories were often appalled by the way the employees were treated. Hugh Parker, a former managing director of McKinsey's consultancy operation in the UK, was quoted as saying: 'Too many managers don't identify themselves with the interests of the managed. They stay aloof – at arm's length from the workers.' At the very least, it can be concluded, management attitudes were hardly conducive to harmonious industrial relations.

What all of this suggests is that criticism of the unions in the 1970s has frequently been overdrawn. Much comment on the subject clearly needs to be taken with a pinch of salt, because of bias and distortion. The scale of myth-making can be illustrated by one episode during the 'winter of discontent'. When some lorry drivers went on strike in early January 1979, a whole number of different experts predicted doom. A month later, *The Economist* looked back on these forecasts and compared them with what had actually transpired. The results were hardly flattering to the parties involved:

> -On January 10th the CBI [Confederation of British Industry] predicted that 1 m workers would be laid off 'by the end of next week'. Lay-offs were still only 200,000 four weeks later.
> -Sir John Methven, the CBI's director-general, was in even more apocalyptic mood at the start of the strike: he talked of it bringing Britain to a halt within 10 days.
> -ICI, also on January 10th, threatened to shut up shop within 10 days. It didn't.
> -On January 16th Mr Derrick Hornby, president of the Food Manufacturers Association, warned that food was being run down fast and predicted '600,000 lay-offs will be a reality in a comparatively short time – and I'm talking of days'. But the supermarket shelves stayed well stocked (except for a few items) and Mr Hornby's lay-offs turned out to be illusory as the CBI's.[3]

The final strand in the conventional view of the 1970s concerns Thatcherism. The argument here is really about lost opportunities. The critics contend that once Mrs Thatcher took over the Conservative Party leadership in 1975, there was a better way. Thatcher, it is said, broke the mould of politics, offering fresh and innovative solutions to Britain's problems. The tragedy, in this view, is that everyone had to wait another four years before these could be put into practice. However, a careful look at the historical record reveals that this, too, is largely based on fallacies.

Thatcher's elevation to the Tory leadership certainly excited many on the right of her party. Here was a leader, it was felt, who would be sympathetic to free-market radicalism. Nevertheless, it soon became clear that Thatcher was rather less ideologically driven than some had imagined. What she ostensibly championed was a partial reassertion of traditional right-wing views, tempered by a heavy dose of expediency. Thus the important outline strategy of 1978, *The Right Approach to the Economy*, contained little that was in any way new. Typically, the section on nationalization was short and vague, mentioning but hardly elaborating on privatization. Twenty-three lines on how the nationalized sector could be improved ended with the following rather muted observation: 'the long-term aim must be to reduce the preponderance of State ownership and to widen the base of ownership in our community. Ownership by the State is not the same as ownership by the people.'

The essence of the chosen approach was particularly evident over the issue of the trade unions. There is no doubt that Thatcher and many of her colleagues loathed trade unions. On the other hand, they were well aware of the need for working-class votes. Accordingly, tough policy prescriptions were almost entirely avoided. The Conservatives, it was stressed, favoured reforming industrial relations *in general*. However, they wanted to proceed by consensus and consultation. Barney Hayhoe, Conservative spokesman on employment during the 'winter of discontent', explained that the party was united on the need for moderation:

Conservatives have repeatedly emphasised that we do not plan to launch yet another wholesale legislative upheaval on returning to office. Back in February 1976 Mrs Thatcher stated ... that we do not intend to introduce any major legislation – there would be 'no new Industrial Relations Act'. Again, she re-affirmed this point at Paddington, when she stated that 'Society is not changed by laws alone; far too many have recently been enacted'. We shall review the recent legislation on industrial relations in the light of experience and see what amendments are needed. Any amendments will only be introduced after consulting all the parties involved. In the nature of things, further changes will probably become necessary in time, but again it would be folly to proceed without the fullest consultation. As Mrs Thatcher has noted, 'many trade union leaders are conducting negotiations every day in this country with a complete sense of responsibility'.[4]

Given such timidity, there were those who began to wonder whether Thatcher was actually capable of beating Labour. The Monday Club, on the extreme right of the Tory Party, declared its loyalty. The Club had been critical of Conservative leaders in the past, but this time it would be different: 'Not only do we whole-heartedly support the leader as an individual, but her policies are identical to those which we have advocated for so long, sometimes in the face of stern criticism from other sections of the Party.' However, others voiced doubts. Many ordinary voters, it was said, were unsure about where the Conservatives stood. Moreover, the leader herself seemed to be at fault. According to the distinguished political commentator Ronald Butt, Thatcher had the unfortunate and confusing habit of 'giving forthright answers to straight questions . . . and then, having stuck her neck out, withdrawing it somewhat precipitately in order not to upset established opinion'.

In the end, of course, Thatcher did go on to win the 1979 contest, but this was hardly the sweeping victory for a dynamic, new political force that some now claim. The Conservative manifesto was a cautious affair which gave few hostages to fortune and, according to one party insider, gave priority to 'the felicitous phrase' at the expense of 'ideological hammer blows'. The leader herself reiterated long-standing right-wing prescriptions and played on some of the public's growing irritation with the unions. There was virtually no mention of any fresh policy departure. Significantly, the most radical member of Thatcher's circle, Keith Joseph, was kept well hidden throughout. Enough of the electorate were persuaded by the Tory promises, but, as we have seen, even this was no foregone conclusion. As is often the case with elections, the eventual result probably turned more on the losers' failings than the victors' strengths.

What all of this shows is that the dimensions of the 'Thatcher revolution' in the late 1970s were fairly modest. The Thatcherites were not offering innovative solutions, merely repackaging the policies of their predecessors. Thatcherism, whatever happened afterwards, remained at this stage more a matter of expediency and reflex than ideology. The Conservative Party under its new leader did have objectives that were different from those of Labour, but the gulf between the two was not nearly so wide as some now pretend. The idea that there was an obvious better way for Britain after 1975 needs much qualification.

The preceding pages have concentrated on the conventional view of the 1970s and demonstrated that it is inaccurate on many counts. How is it that the story has come to be told in this particular way? What accounts for the elaboration of so many myths? The group which has probably done more than any other to shape popular perceptions of the 1970s is the Tory right.

The Conservative Party was reasonably united in the early 1970s but all this changed with Heath's twin defeats of 1974. The Tories were shattered by these failures and quickly launched an inquest on what had gone wrong. Debate polarized opinions. Some believed that Heath had been defeated by circumstances; there was no need, therefore, to tamper with the party's approach. Others, by contrast, took a more critical line. The most prominent voices here belonged to a faction of right-wingers who argued for a fundamental change of direction.

The right-wing analysis began from the perception that Britain was in a total mess. Socialism had gained a substantial foothold and now threatened all forms of free expression. As the influential political philosopher Shirley Robin Letwin explained in the *Spectator*, the next stop was dictatorship: if left unchecked, socialists would take over all businesses and 'drown democracy in a flood of legislation, regulation by fiat and ad hoc administrative decisions'. In these circumstances, the right-wingers believed, the imperative was to go on the offensive. Since the war, too many compromises had been made. Heath, Macmillan and even Churchill were culpable, in that none had done enough to overturn Labour gains. A future Conservative government must stop trying to placate the enemy and instead vanquish it.

After Mrs Thatcher's election victory in 1979, the right wing was able to gain an almost complete ascendancy. The new leader was no instinctive innovator, as has been noted, but nor was she soft on socialism. Right-wingers found that they could influence her and simultaneously strengthen their hold on the levers of power. In this way, Conservatism gradually metamorphosised into Thatcherism, a strident variant. For the purposes of the present enquiry, the most significant aspect of this change was that it legitimized and institutionalized a particular version of the recent past. The stories that right-wingers had told each other about the 1970s were now trumpeted by Conservatives at every level of the party. The Prime Minister herself provided a typically trenchant exposition at the 1985 Blackpool conference. She asked:

> Do you remember the Labour Britain of 1979? It was a Britain in which union leaders held their members and our country to ransom; a Britain that still went to international conferences but was no longer taken seriously; a Britain that was known as the sick man of Europe and which spoke the language of compassion but which suffered the winter of discontent. Governments had failed to tackle the real problems. They dogged difficult problems rather than face up to them. The question they asked was not 'will the medicine work?' but 'will it taste all right?'[5]

In the space of only a few years, history had been comprehensively rewritten. The 1970s were painted in hues of blackest black, with Labour depicted as the evil ogre and Heath simply airbrushed out of the picture.

This tells us something about where the conventional view of the 1970s came from, but why did this interpretation become so popular? Who responded positively to the Tory vision? For an answer, we need look no further than the British middle class.

For most of the post-war period, the middle class had hardly been visible as a coherent social interest group. Middle-class people shared certain aspirations – to better themselves, to give their children a 'good education' and so on – and generally felt that these were comfortably attainable. In the 1970s, the mood began to change. The middle class increasingly felt under threat and many argued that it needed to reassert itself. The *Sunday Telegraph* journalist Patrick Hutber published a book in 1976 with a title that exactly captured the predominant feelings of anxiety and aggression – *The Decline and Fall of the Middle Class and How It Can Fight Back*.

One precipitating factor behind this new militancy was inflation. Professionals and the self-employed were rarely members of trade unions and thus saw their incomes diminishing in real terms, especially at the beginning of the decade. Nevertheless, it is clear that such economic hardships were hardly overwhelming. Both home ownership and patronage of public schools increased to 1980. In fact, what middle-class people tended to feel most concerned about was the perception that they were losing control. Society, it seemed, no longer had much time for the middle-class virtues. Better elocution and education were not, as once, guarantees of lifelong success. Much of the blame for this trend rested with Labour. The party had built comprehensive schools and polytechnics; raised higher tax levels; and, most inexcusably, engaged in a serious dialogue with the trade unions. It had allowed too many of the 'wrong kind of people' into positions of authority. To make matters worse, there were good reasons for believing that Labour was becoming the 'natural' party of government, the most likely winner of future elections. The terrible prospect, therefore, was for more of the same, and the eventual threat of total liquidation.

The sense of fear was observable almost across the board. Peter

Yorke made his name during these years with an acutely observed book on the 'Sloane Rangers' – the young and affluent of West London. According to Yorke, the Sloanes were generally a happy breed, who preferred to party in the Fulham Road. Yet, as he reported, even Sloane life was not without its darker side. A gaggle of subversives waited to pounce:

> Intellectuals and politicians, trade unionists, the new kind of academic with facial hair; these people are all 'chippy', 'bolshie' or 'stroppy'. It reflects, no doubt, personal misfortune — over-education or a poor deal physically – that has turned the balance of the mind; but none-theless, the enemy need watching. Rangers do not like Tony Benn (a class traitor Ranger), Arthur Scargill or anyone who's a thinker not a doer.[6]

In practical terms, the way the middle class reacted to this situation varied. Many simply kept their heads below the parapet and hoped it would go away. There was a pronounced vogue for the eighteenth century in all things cultural, a yearning for a time before industry, cities and the workers, together with a fashion for criticisms or satires of the modern. Married Sloanes' lavatories, according to Yorke, invariably contained Osbert Lancaster's *From Pillar to Post* and P. G. Wodehouse's *Carry on Jeeves*, two witty celebrations of aristocratic eccentricities, alongside the obligatory old *Punches* and *Private Eyes*. A less pleasant trend was a growing fascination with retribution. A correspondent to Hutber described his fantasy: 'In evil moments one is tempted by the image of a society where militancy on the labour front is countered by the edict "Work or Starve", where individual acts of violence and terror are met by punishments of a prime-val character.' More than one Home Counties after-dinner conversation revolved around the idea of 'teaching the unions a lesson'. The need, in this view, was for some real leadership to rally the demoralized and lick the dissidents into shape.

By the middle of the decade, the situation had become serious enough for new kinds of middle-class politics to emerge. Heath was a discredited figure after his failure to deal with the miners, and so a number of the more adventurous were persuaded to give up on the Tory Party and strike out on their own. The new organizations ranged from single-issue pressure groups to umbrella coalitions, for example Sir Walter Walker's Civil Assistance, a private militia which claimed 100,000 members. Several were dominated by fanatics or cranks, but others proved quite successful at campaigning. Agitation on issues like the rates and estate duty produced thousands of letters and several large petitions, an avalanche of protests to newspaper editors and MPs. In 1975, the extent of activity was large enough to provoke a *Times* leader. There were signs, the newspaper concluded, of a 'middle-class revolt'.

The thing that prevented this happening, as will have become obvious by now, was the arrival of Mrs Thatcher. The middle class as a whole did not take instantly to the new leader, though she was always judged superior to Heath. Nevertheless, over time, middle-class anxieties certainly diminished. Thatcher emphasized the traditional and praised middle-class values, indeed declared herself willing to run the country on such precepts. She might be occasionally confused – and confusing – but she was obviously 'one of us' and this was appealing. Gradually, the middle class was flattered back into the Conservative fold. At the 1979 election, both parties in this relationship received their full rewards.

Given this history, it is easy to see why many middle-class people's memories of the 1970s gradually became entangled with, and then shaped by, the Tory version. The middle class felt it had been to the edge of the abyss during the decade and was deeply traumatized by the experience. The taste of fear and insecurity lingered on. Thatcher and her colleagues knew what this was all about and above all explained it. Over time, recollection and myth gradually fused to form a new 'truth'. Britain *had* been collapsing in the 1970s; Labour and the unions *were* to blame; and

Thatcher *was* the saviour. This is the version which still holds sway in some quarters today. In the late 1990s, it is surely high time to end such self-deception.

CHAPTER VIII

MIRACLE OR MIRAGE?: THE THATCHER YEARS 1979–1997

PAUL HIRST

When Mrs Thatcher became Conservative leader in 1975 she was widely seen as doomed to failure, so stridently right wing as to be unelectable. How did she not only get elected but go on to become Britain's longest-serving Prime Minister of the twentieth century? Her achievements are bitterly contested. Abroad she is seen as a world leader, comparable to Churchill, who restored Britain's reputation. This is particularly so in the USA and Russia, but opinions in Europe are far more divided, ranging from the grudging admiration of François Mitterrand to the active dislike of Helmut Kohl. In Britain opinion is sharply divided between those who revere her as Britain's saviour from the disasters of the 1970s and those who see her as setting about destroying everything they value.

Viewing a decade in terms of one person may seem unbalanced. Yet Mrs Thatcher did dominate the 1980s. She became unchallenged master of the Conservative Party, and the governments she led controlled and shaped Britain in a torrent of change without parallel. British institutions were transformed. The question we will return to is whether the changes were on balance for better or worse. The Major years will also be examined in order to assess her legacy and its consequences.

Mrs Thatcher enjoyed the benefits of Labour's meltdown, but she played the 1979 election cleverly and moved towards the middle ground. Her pitch to the British people was surprisingly mild, and she even quoted St Francis of Assisi to present herself as a peacemaker in a time of strife. The Tory campaign promised higher wage earners and skilled workers an end to restrictive incomes policies. Skilled workers were particularly incensed by the erosion of differentials brought about under the social contract. They switched decisively to the Conservatives – twice as many in key marginal areas voting Tory as Labour. Areas like the West Midlands and the industrial South-East therefore went to the Tories. Mrs Thatcher offered trade unionists a deal: she would restore free collective bargaining within fair industrial relations laws that curbed excessive union power. She also committed herself to honour the recently appointed Clegg Commission's awards on public sector pay, even though they would clearly be highly inflationary. Council house sales were a prominent and very popular policy, but large-scale privatizations were not proposed.

Most voters were not economists and so the Tories' espousal of a new hard-line monetarism passed them by. This doctrine was supposed to result in policies that killed inflation and restored full employment and growth. If voters wanted those things badly, as they did, then the Tories seemed to offer effective economic management without the rigidities and controls of Labour policy. If voters had paid any attention to the detail, they would have been none the wiser about the arcane notions emanating from the University of Chicago for controlling inflation by restricting the money supply.[1]

The Conservatives had a majority of 43, enough to govern without serious impediment from the opposition. Mrs Thatcher needed it because she and her vanguard had hijacked a party whose instincts were pragmatist and centrist. She faced a Cabinet composed of Tory grandees, many of whom despised her. The backbenches were still full of One-Nation worthies and paternalist knights from the shires. Mrs Thatcher had become a hard-nosed economic liberal who really believed people should fend for themselves and that the successful should not be cramped by the weak. This was alien to Conservative tradition.

The first Thatcher government was something unique in modern British history: a party led by a clique of intellectuals with a strong commitment to a radical ideology. Mrs Thatcher was not just a conviction politician, she really thought she had the ideas to back up her beliefs. Her confidence and that of those around her was staggering. Without it, and without the confusion and disarray of her opponents, she could never have dominated party and country and survived her first term. Her regime was born out of study groups, earnestly reading and underlining key texts like Friedrich Hayek's *The Road to Serfdom*.[2] Gradually, with much sound and fury, Mrs Thatcher prevailed over her sceptical grandees like Carrington, Gilmour, Prior and Pym – driving them out or bringing them to heel.[3] Party and civil service were remodelled on the logic of picking those who were 'one of us', willing to do the leader's bidding. Thus began a process of fusion between party and state that is fatal for honest government and that laid the foundation for the sleaze of the Major era.

The intellectuals made a mess of it. Milton Friedman's highly contentious monetarist doctrines were converted into the rigid controls of the Medium-Term Financial Strategy (MTFS). This policy aimed to restrict the growth of the money supply in order to control inflation, setting targets for different categories of money ($M1$, $M2$, $M3$ and so on), and also to reduce the budgetary deficit over a four-year period. In 1979 the economy was plunging into recession, and the MTFS gave it a further push. Output and employment plummeted: between 1979 and 1982 unemployment rose from 1.2 to 3 million, while industrial output fell by an average of 11 per cent (at its worst it fell by some 20 per cent). High interest rates (rising to 15.7 per cent in 1980) and the effects of North Sea oil coming on stream led to a rapid rise in the exchange rate (it rose 4.2 per cent in 1979 and 10.1 per cent in 1980). This devastated British manufacturing exports, driving firm after firm to the wall in sectors like engineering and textiles. Sterling reached a peak of $2.45 in October 1981.[4]

Much of British industry was uncompetitive by comparison with its foreign rivals. British productivity was low by comparison with German, Japan and the USA. Government policies emphasized this weakness by ruling out competition on price and by making investment prohibitively expensive. The combination of high interest rates, a high exchange rate and high inflation (prices rose 18 per cent in 1980, 11.9 per cent in 1981 and 8.8 per cent in 1982) destroyed many otherwise viable firms. About 25 per cent of manufacturing capacity was lost during this period. The government justified this as competitive pressure weeding out the inefficient. However, much more capacity would have been lost had not the government pragmatically continued to support the 'lame ducks' taken under the public wing in the 1970s, such as British Leyland and Rolls-Royce.

Exchange controls were abandoned and restrictions on consumer credit relaxed. In the long run this would render the restrictive monetary policies of the MTFS ineffective, because capital could be exported and imported at will, and because the supply of credit money could be controlled only by savage and deflationary rises in interest rates. These liberalizing moves laid the foundations for the subsequent credit-fuelled consumer boom of the mid-1980s. Had the restrictive monetary policies of the early years persisted, Britain's economy would have moved towards collapse. This was avoided by a relaxation of the money-supply limits and by a falling exchange rate. Mrs Thatcher was saved by her friend President Reagan. In 1981 the Federal Reserve Board in the US acted to halt the slide in the dollar, and thus gratuitously reduced the value of sterling. By 1982 some recovery was evident in the UK, with inflation and interest rates beginning to fall.

The recession of 1979–82 led to a marked split between North and South. Company failures concentrated in the old industrial areas in the North and the Midlands. Much of Southern England survived the shake-out relatively unscathed. The South's economy was far more centred on services, which had suffered relatively less than manufacturing. This was partly because services were either more competitive or actually benefited from high interest and exchange rates (like the financial sector). It was also because non-financial services were not internationally traded to the same extent as manufacturing and did not find the exchange rate so much of a constraint. The result was a radical difference of experience and a growing sense of two nations, one based on leafy Southern suburbs and the other on blighted Northern industrial wastelands. This showed up in subsequent elections: the North and the Celtic fringe voting Labour, the prosperous regions of England voting Tory. Fortunately for Mrs Thatcher, the South was both populous and contained more of the key marginals. Labour piled up huge majorities in its Northern and Celtic safe seats.

Thus when Mrs Thatcher called an election in 1983 she had the advantage of a modest recovery. She was also lucky to be the victor of the Falklands War in 1982. Here she survived perhaps the worst crisis of her first term more by luck than by judgement, only just getting through the tense Saturday night when the invasion was debated in the House of Commons. British policy had sent all the wrong signals to the Argentinians and expenditure cuts were about to cripple the fleet. Britain's armed services did what they do best; they fought an improvised colonial war with relatively small forces on both sides. Even so, it was a close-run thing. Many ships survived only because the Argentinians had bought a job-lot of old bombs on the cheap. Again, Mrs Thatcher's special relationship with Ronald Reagan stood her in good stead. American help was central in the form of access to high-level classified intelligence and fresh supplies of missiles flown directly to Ascension Island when British stocks ran out.

Perhaps neither the recovery nor the Falklands would have counted for much had Mrs Thatcher faced a credible dominant opposition party. During her first administration Labour had torn itself apart and rendered itself unelectable. The rise of Bennite leftism led to civil war within the party. Labour collapsed at the grass roots and became easy prey to ultra-leftist entryists and unrepresentative activists. The left was committed to several extremely unpopular policies: to extensive nationalizations, to anti-nuclear unilateralism, and to import controls that stemmed partly from economic dogma and partly from visceral hostility to Europe. Some pragmatic party members led by the Gang of Four (Roy Jenkins, David Owen, William Rodgers and Shirley Williams) left to form the new Social Democratic Party (SDP). The pragmatists who remained were thus made ineffectual by the hysteria and the sheer nastiness of the left. The left behaved as if it were carrying out a revolution, but it was an inward-looking revolution. Obsessed by the enemy within, they failed to campaign effectively against the Conservatives. Labour spoke only to itself and to its own hard-core constituencies. Cowed and cornered by the left, the party elected the ineffectual Michael Foot as its leader, rather than the dynamic and effective Denis Healey. Healey barely contained the challenge of Tony Benn, tribune of the left, for the post of deputy leader.

In the election Foot fought a campaign well suited to the 1880s, speaking to the faithful in Labour clubs across the country. The opposition was split. Labour was lucky to see off the challenge of the SDP/Liberal Alliance for second place. Alliance support peaked too soon and Labour enjoyed the advantage of solid regional bastions of support, whereas the SDP vote was spread more evenly across the country. Labour gained far more seats than the Alliance, but Mrs Thatcher won a majority of 144 on 42.4 per cent of the vote. The election hardly showed that Mrs Thatcher enjoyed genuine majority support for her policies, quite the contrary, but the electoral system gave her the means to carry them out without check.

The election was, however, a decisive defeat for the Bennite left, who had dictated a manifesto aptly called 'the longest suicide note in history'. In the aftermath Neil Kinnock was elected party leader and he began the long, slow and painful process of rebuilding the party as a credible alternative government. Slowly the left was marginalized, Trotskyite infiltrating 'entryists' into local Labour parties were expelled, and the most electorally damaging policies dropped. Even so the process was by no means complete in 1987 and finally had to await Tony Blair.

The first Thatcher government had begun with four key priorities: to cut inflation to zero if possible; to contain and then reverse the growth in public expenditure, thereby preventing the 'crowding out' of private consumption and investment by the state; to deregulate the economy, and in particular the financial system; and to curb trade union power. Compared to what was to follow, the changes the government was able to achieve in socioeconomic institutions were relatively modest. The Tories had mixed success in meeting their key objectives.

By 1983 inflation had been reduced to 4.6 per cent, but at the price of a massive recession. On taxation and expenditure the record was equally mixed. Geoffrey Howe as Chancellor of the Exchequer reduced the top rate of tax from 83 per cent to 60 per cent and the basic rate from 33 per cent to 30 per cent in 1979. Thereafter, little could be achieved because of the soaring costs of unemployment benefit. National Insurance contributions and other taxes were raised. Local authority spending was curtailed by imposing caps on local rating powers. The control of council spending, which had risen dramatically in the 1960s and 1970s, was a central element in cutting overall government spending. Thus Geoffrey Howe started the gradual process of the virtually complete centralization of local government finances under Treasury and Department of the Environment (DoE) control. A succession of acts reduced the scope of trade union power. Secondary picketing was outlawed and workers were limited to striking against their own direct employer. The liability of unions at law for their actions was increased. Individuals were given rights against their unions, and unions were required to ballot in advance before strikes rather than hold mass meetings with a show of hands.

Some of those objectives were widely supported by the general public. Ordinary workers had become subject to income tax only in the 1960s. Cutting direct taxes was thus a policy that went down well at the bottom of the earnings scale as well as at the top. By 1979 unions had become unpopular even with their own members. Many ordinary unionists felt that they were bullied into action by mass pressure and that the activists, who orchestrated it, were out of touch. In early 1979 opinion polls showed that some two-thirds of the population and a majority of union members were in favour of the pay norms imposed by the Callaghan government. Pay policy was nevertheless broken by undisciplined unions and radical shop stewards, while TUC bosses and the government seemed powerless. Thus the first wave of union reforms were accepted as necessary. Inflation was a real problem for most people. The 1970s had been a struggle for the employed to keep their wages up. Many weak groups of workers suffered, and claimants and pensioners were hard hit.

Mrs Thatcher had failed to roll back the state. Public expenditure remained stubbornly resistant, because cuts were swamped by rising costs from unemployment (in 1980 government expenditure was 43.2 per cent of GDP, in 1995 it was 42.5 per cent). The privatization programme of the first term was distinctly modest. The first complete privatization flotation was the specialist medical services group Amersham International in 1982. This set a precedent by being grossly undervalued on sale, with purchasers of the shares making a large windfall profit. The government's holdings in firms like British Petroleum, British Aerospace and Cable and Wireless were sold off in tranches throughout the 1980s. Privatization revenues were used simply to boost current spending, also setting a precedent. Neither North Sea oil revenues nor privatization receipts were used for major capital projects or for industrial modernization. In that sense all the Conservative administrations of the 1980s and 1990s threw away two once-and-for-all bonuses on current consumption, and this in a country with low levels of public and private investment by international standards.

Council house sales were successful and popular. Something like one million homes were sold off; many were well-built semis in good repair on attractive estates. They were forcibly sold against the wishes of local authorities, for whom these older houses were solid revenue earners, since their capital costs were mostly already paid off. Local authorities were bad at managing their housing stock and often very unpopular with tenants for niggardly restrictions and delays with repairs. Tenants bought enthusiastically, since in the main they were offered an under-priced asset on very favourable terms. Privatization made sense; if receipts could be ploughed back into new public housing starts then existing tenants who bought and future tenants were both catered for. Mrs Thatcher had an aversion to local authority housing, however, and councils (whether Tory or Labour) were forced to add receipts from sales to their reserves. During the 1980s public housing completions fell to a mere trickle, less than 10 per cent of their post-war peak.

The second Thatcher administration gave a higher priority to privatization and financial deregulation. An active wave of selling disposed of British Airways, British Gas, British Shipbuilders, British Leyland and Rolls-Royce. Most of those flotations were popular with the general public, offering instant windfall gains. At its worst, government policy appeared to be a get-rich-quick bribe of selling the nation its own assets at knock-down prices, exemplified by the British Gas advertising campaign 'Tell Sid'. Some of these major privatizations were sensible and successful. After all, most of the firms in the manufacturing and commercial services sectors that had been nationalized were taken into the public sector for non-ideological reasons, simply because they were in danger of going bankrupt. Public ownership had helped them to survive. The question raised by privatization was thus not one of principle, but whether the state got a good return. The answer seemed to be no, for having rescued the private sector in the first place, the government sold assets back to it at less than their full value.

The second term also saw a determined attempt to deregulate the capital markets. In 1986 'Big Bang' deregulated the City and opened up trading to a wider range of financial institutions, including foreign banks. The earlier abolition of exchange controls and the financial liberalization of the mid-1980s exposed the country to international capital flows in a way unseen since the 1920s. In 1983 the balance of trade in manufactured goods moved into deficit for the first time. Since it became the 'workshop of the world' in the early nineteenth century, Britain had always exported far more manufactured goods than it imported. In the 1960s it still had a large surplus (about £40 billion at current prices). However, 'metal bashing' was now out of favour in government circles. Britain's advantage was seen to lie in services and particularly in financial services. Provided the UK could attract foreign capital, the current balance of trade was of no consequence.

In the second term household consumption rose rapidly, driven upwards by a wave of easy credit. All pretence of controlling the supply of credit money through the MTFS had been abandoned. A fevered consumption boom developed in the South. House prices rocketed. Many workers found the value of their houses appreciating faster than their annual incomes. It was thus possible to borrow to meet current consumption on such rapidly inflating assets. Average earnings had risen consistently above inflation throughout the 1980s; in 1986 the difference reached a peak when prices rose by 3.4 per cent and earnings by 7.9 per cent. Unemployment was low in successful districts; skills shortages were leading to tight labour markets and in turn driving up wages. Rising house prices put a ring fence around this regional boom, denying the unemployed from the North any chance of entry.

Thus when Mrs Thatcher called her third general election in 1987 the notion that she had engineered an economic miracle was generally accepted in the media and widely believed abroad.

That industrial output was lower than in 1973 was of no matter, nor was the fact that the boom was unsustainable. Inflation was picking up and household indebtedness reaching dangerous levels.

In 1983 Mrs Thatcher had General Galtieri's scalp on her belt and in 1987 she had Arthur Scargill's. The miners' strike of 1984– 5 had turned into a virtual military operation. The police were in effect centralized and thousands of them drafted from all over the country to confront the miners in their key northern pits. Orgreave Colliery at times looked like a medieval Samurai battle filmed by Kurosawa. Civil liberties took a battering. The police set up road blocks and at their discretion forbade people to travel. The strike was a mess. Scargill's autocratic manner made it almost certain that the National Union of Miners would lose. The miners in the key Midlands coalfields next to the big power stations split under the leadership of Ray Lynk and formed the Union of Democratic Mineworkers (UDM). Scargill had also forced a strike at a time when the Coal Board, with government support, had built up huge coal reserves. The strike was a closer-run thing than it looked, and it divided the country. Even though it was the wrong strike at the wrong time, many people supported the miners and helped them with money and food. Their prolonged resistance ended in defeat, but the miners returned to work in a dignified manner. Nevertheless, it showed once more the spectre of union power to suburban Southerners and Mrs Thatcher could pose as their protector against industrial disruption.

The 1987 election saw Labour fight a more effective campaign and its policies were less suicidal than in 1983. Nevertheless, the election simply confirmed the Conservative position in the polls and they were returned with a landslide victory, 101 seats on 42.3 per cent of the vote. The logic of a split opposition vote in a first-past-the-post system once again told in favour of the Tories. But the election was decisive in one sense, as it showed Labour as the dominant opposition party. Labour had been lucky to halt a surge by the Alliance, which had benefited from the bad publicity surrounding leftist candidates like Peter Tatchell and Deirdre

Wood imposed by narrow groups of constituency activists. The 1987 defeat led to the break-up of the SDP and the merger of its majority with the Liberals to form the Liberal Democrats. David Owen led the rump into the political wilderness.

Mrs Thatcher was emboldened by her third victory. She allowed her Chancellor, Nigel Lawson, to offer a give-away budget in 1988. He reduced the top rate of income tax from 60 per cent to 40 per cent and the standard rate to 25 per cent. Lawson's hubris over-stoked a consumption boom that was about to get out of control. Inflation rose to 7.8 per cent in 1989 and 9.5 per cent in 1990. The second half of the 1980s also showed a steady decline in Britain's external payments position, with a trade deficit of over £20 billion in 1989. Mrs Thatcher had committed herself to a single market in Europe by the end of 1992 and passed the Single European Act in 1986. She was perhaps unaware, as an economic liberal, that creating open markets would require a major erosion of British sovereignty. Lawson had begun the strategy of tracking the Deutschmark, letting the pound appreciate against it with the eventual objective of entering the European Monetary System (EMS).

After 1987 the privatization agenda was renewed in earnest again, this time involving British Steel, the water industry and the distribution part of the electricity industry. Mrs Thatcher had also been determined to reform the rating system and had included a one-line proposal in the 1987 manifesto. Thus began the process that led to the hated poll tax and her eventual downfall. During this period a determined attempt was to be made to reform the education system, and to wrest control from local authorities and the teaching profession. The 1988 Education Act imposed a baroque and unworkable national curriculum on state schools. Subsequently it would have to be slimmed down and revised. Mrs Thatcher talked about getting the state off people's backs. But whether it was deciding in the tiniest detail what was taught in classrooms or how much local voters could spend on local services, the state seemed firmly in control. Indeed, government intervention was proliferating. Privatization actually bred regulation, as the utilities could not simply be let loose on the public as unchecked monopolies. An alphabet soup of regulatory bodies developed covering each of the major industries – OFTEL, OFGAS, OFWAT and so on.

The Tories had entered power in 1979 committed to demolishing the corporate state and getting rid of quangos. To some extent they did this, running down the machinery of co-operation between industry, labour and the state built up since the 1950s. They excluded unions from influence, even abolishing bodies like the National Economic Development Office. They took no interest in promoting dialogue between the major social interests to co-ordinate commitments in economic policy. This was anathema to the new free-market philosophy. The underlying assumption here was that markets work because of competition between firms and individuals, and thus institutionalized co-operation is a threat to the allocative efficiency of markets. Corporatism was also challenged by the Tories as government by unelected bodies, which threatened Parliamentary sovereignty. However, the government soon found this type of rule irresistible, and quangos grew apace during the third term. Under Mrs Thatcher's successor, John Major, their role accelerated to the point where they controlled one-third of central government expenditure and offered a vast field of patronage to be filled by the right kind of people.[5]

The poll tax grew into a monster behind the scenes during the third term. Nobody had the courage to kill the Prime Minister's pet project and most ministers tried to avoid involvement, with the exception of the ideologically driven Nicholas Ridley and the eager-to-please Kenneth Baker. When it was introduced in England in 1990 it had a predictable effect. It was grossly unfair and regressive, and it forced the poor to part with money they could ill afford. Widespread non-payment in Scotland, where the tax had been introduced first in 1989, should have prepared the government for what would happen, but ministers seemed surprised by the ferocity of the riots and the scale of evasion. It reduced the country to chaos, and undermined the rule of law by criminalizing the feckless and helpless. The public turned against Mrs Thatcher in a way they had not done since the 1980–1 period. This was not helped by her increasingly autocratic and regal manner. She was evidently out of touch with the public and did not seem to care. Many Conservatives came to fear that she was an electoral liability. Her Euroscepticism had already begun to be internally divisive. She had started the battle over Europe that was to reduce the party to impotence in the 1990s. She consistently opposed her own Chancellor, Nigel Lawson, over Europe and monetary policy, undermining him from the sidelines by using Professor Alan Walters as an alternative economic adviser.

This led to a leadership challenge. Thatcher's fall was entirely due to fear on the part of backbenchers that she would bring them down with her. The problem was that she had no natural successor. Her autocratic style had militated against preparing for this, and over the years she had merely promoted a series of nonentities as the 'coming man'. They had all vanished without trace, apart from the latest one – John Major. Established figures were dismissed because the party was so ridden by factional strife. Douglas Hurd was ruled out for what would have been an astonishing reason in any previous Conservative administration, that he had been to Eton and his manners were too patrician. Michael Heseltine was widely hated for his disloyalty and he could command the support of no more than a couple of members of the Cabinet. John Major emerged as the man who divided the party the least. He had Mrs Thatcher's favour and yet he appeared to offer a more emollient and less dictatorial style. Major won the leadership election, after Mrs Thatcher withdrew having failed to win a convincing endorsement.

Major's rise was meteoric. He had occupied two of the major offices of state, Foreign Secretary and Chancellor of the Exchequer, in the year previous to his appointment as Prime Minister. In one sense the fact that he had risen rapidly and had little experience was an advantage; he had no track record and thus did not attract enemies in the fraught internal conflicts of the party. As Chancellor in October 1990 he had persuaded Mrs Thatcher to abandon her long-standing opposition to EMS entry. At one level her resistance was rational. Britain entered into the Exchange Rate Mechanism of the System at the target rate of 2.95 DM +/− 6 per cent, but this was at a time when Britain's inflation rate was three times that of Germany. Major saw this as a great coup, not least because it took the wind out of the Labour Party's sails. ERM membership was a central plank of Labour's economic policy and its panacea against inflation. This short-term triumph was to sow the seeds of his own disaster.

During 1991 the Major government revised the poll tax to remove its most obnoxious features. To householders it came to appear suspiciously like the rates, and they might have wondered why its introduction and revision had cost the country several wasted billions. The central priority was to get inflation down, but the overheating boom of 1988–90 took a lot to kill. The government relentlessly put up interest rates, which rose to nearly 15 per cent in 1990, in a desperate attempt to control the growth of credit. The inflation rate fell in 1991, but by then the boom had turned into a rapidly accelerating recession. The 1980s miracle had well and truly faded. The housing market collapsed. Over a million people owed more on their houses than they were worth. Output fell and unemployment began to rise again towards 3 million. This time misery was more equally shared. In the early 1980s the South had escaped the worst of the recession, but now its over-heating service-sector economy was hardest hit. The suburbs found out that unemployment was not just for Northern manual workers.

In these circumstances Major held on to the bitter end in 1992 before calling the election. To widespread surprise, even among Cabinet ministers, the Tories were returned with a majority of twenty and 43 per cent of the vote against Labour's 35 per cent. That the Conservatives had a modest majority on a proportion of the vote that had previously yielded a margin of 144 seats showed the effect of a dominant opposition party and one that performed better in the marginals than it did overall. Floating voters seem to have been turned by the fear factor: in a deepening recession they wanted competent economic management and were unwilling to put in an untried Labour administration. They also seem to have been impressed by Conservative threats of massive Labour tax rises, by the fear that Labour constitutional-reform proposals would undermine the union with Scotland, and by the merciless pillorying of Neil Kinnock in the tabloid press.

Major won apparently against all the odds. For the first time a Conservative administration returned to face the economic mess it had created – unlike 1964 and 1974. Major immediately destroyed the Tories' reputation for competence in economic management. The unsustainability of Britain's position in the ERM had now become glaringly apparent. Britain had to devalue or face an even greater collapse of output and employment. Suddenly, the markets woke up and began to desert sterling. Speculators like George Soros ended the misery by forcing the issue. Major and his Chancellor, Norman Lamont, dithered. They refused an orderly devaluation within the ERM and expended Britain's currency reserves against a titanic wave of selling that ended on Black Wednesday in September with Britain leaving the ERM and devaluing by some 20 per cent. Some £5 billion were wasted in this defence of the indefensible that made Wilson's temporizing in 1966–7 look mild by comparison.

As if this were not enough, Michael Heseltine had decided to shut down the greater part of Britain's coal industry. A privatized electricity industry could not be made to buy coal as the nation-alized Central Electricity Generating Board had. Even the loyal UDM pits were to be shut, to the horror of Ray Lynk, who thought the Conservatives owed him one. A wave of revulsion swept Britain, even among many Tories. Demonstrating miners were waved to by affluent shoppers in London's West End. The government backtracked, only to implement most of the plan and to sell the remainder of the industry to a private company for a song.

Many thought Major's administration would be more centrist and less Thatcherite. They were wrong. Things Mrs Thatcher would never have contemplated doing were done almost in a fit of absent-mindedness. This was Thatcherism on autopilot. The NHS was reorganized to create an 'internal market', leading to widespread complaints of burgeoning bureaucracy and inequality, as fundholding general practitioners in direct control of their own budgets seemed to be able to get a better deal for their patients than non-fundholding colleagues. Education was subject to cease-less and restless change: the reduction of the power of local education authorities by giving schools powers of management, the introduction of national testing and performance league tables, the revision of the training of schoolteachers, and the imposition of a system of national inspection conducted by yet another quango, OFSTED, which was extremely unpopular with tea-chers.

Privatization continued, as the logic of boosting current spend-ing by selling capital assets became unavoidable in a period of severe pressure on public finances. Unlikely candidates like British Railways and the nuclear power industry were brought forward. Under Michael Howard, the Home Secretary, a sustained attack on civil liberties and on rehabilitative penal policy was conducted until the day the election was called in 1997. Act after act restricted rights of free assembly, gave the police draconian powers to control ravers and travellers, abolished the right to silence (a centuries-old protection against self-incrimination, widely seen by lawyers as a core part of a fair adversarial system), and obliged the courts to impose fixed sentences for certain crimes. Howard's admin-istrative decisions reduced penal policy to chaos: he drove up the prison population to unprecedented levels and reduced prison regimes to the brutal warehousing of inmates with no provision for training or reform.

The fourth Tory term was dominated by three issues that the

party managers would have wished to avoid: taxation, Europe and 'sleaze'. On none of these issues was the government in control, and each could be said to have led in equal measure to its demise. Mr Major won the 1992 election by promising to cut taxes 'year on year', and instilling fear that Labour would cost the average family £1,000 more in tax. The government knew before the election that there was a massive hole (some £25 billion) in its revenue and spending plans. After the election it introduced a series of tax rises; particularly hated was VAT at 8 per cent on domestic heating. Along with the fiasco of Black Wednesday this undermined the government's credibility and its reputation for economic competence.

Major entered the election in 1992 apparently having put Europe behind him. The Maastricht Treaty was seen by the Tories as a triumph. Major had circumvented a break with Britain's EU partners and avoided using the veto to hold up progress to greater integration. Britain evaded being in a minority of one by signing a different treaty from other states. Two crucial opt-outs were negotiated by Major. The UK, alone of the twelve signatories, was exempt from the provisions of the Social Chapter on working conditions and rights. Britain also reserved its position on whether to join a single currency in 1999. The apparent success at Maastricht evaporated after the election. Major became a prisoner of the Eurosceptic right, who became ever more strident and undisciplined in their opposition to monetary union and, in many cases, to the EU itself. As the fourth term developed the Conservatives increasingly seemed an utterly divided party led by a man without authority, a Prime Minister who could survive only by trimming to appease the warring factions. Even the staging of a leadership election in 1995 had little effect in restoring the Prime Minister's authority. Although Major won by a substantial margin against a former member of his Cabinet, John Redwood, the divisions resurfaced within a matter of weeks.

'Sleaze' built up slowly through the 1990s. The UK is not a grossly corrupt country, but it is one with a strong distaste for corruption. Corruption is not new: the Liberal administration of 1906–14 had its share of scandals (notably the Marconi Affair); the last years of Macmillan's government were marked by an aura of moral decay and the seediness of the Profumo affair; Wilson was hardly stainless as he shamelessly honoured the shady characters he gathered around him. The point is that the institutions and the people in them had changed under the impact of Mrs Thatcher's rule. On the Tory side fewer MPs were independently wealthy grandees with Eton, Oxford and the Guards backgrounds. Most were professional politicians from modest families who expected to live from politics, and live well. Over the eighteen years of Conservative government the connection between big business, professional lobbying firms and government had become ever more systematic. MPs and their wives commonly became directors and consultants for major firms. Prominent Tories found lucrative posts as officials and members of governing bodies in the new quangocracy. MPs asked questions for their backers and got paid for it. Ministers leaving office joined the boards of companies they had been instrumental in privatizing. The Tory Party began to resemble the old *Nomenklatura* of the Soviet Union, an official class of party members for whom the highest offices were reserved. As the scandals like 'cash for questions' surfaced, the principal effect was on the traditional Tory voter. These people had voted for the Conservatives because they saw them as upright and honourable, capable of governing in the national interest. They saw Labour as untrustworthy and in hock to the unions. 'Sleaze' damaged the Tories at their core, and made it easier for people to abandon the habits of a lifetime and either abstain or even, against recent experience, switch directly from Conservative to Labour.

It was this crude kind of corruption, rather than the intricacies of the Westland Affair in Mrs Thatcher's second term or the Arms for Iraq Affair in the 1990s, which damaged the Tories with ordinary voters. For political insiders and commentators, however, the Scott inquiry about Iraq and the Nolan inquiry into parliamentary standards revealed how far the traditional standards and procedures essential to Britain's political system had simply ceased to apply. An unwritten constitution can work only if politicians honour its conventions far more often than they break them. An unwritten constitution in the hands of unprincipled scoundrels is no protection at all. The biggest danger to good government now seemed to be that the narrowest forms of politics had subsumed policy – decisions were made to wrongfoot the opposition or to gain a small media advantage. Michael Howard clearly made policy in order to push Labour into opposing him, so that it could be presented as 'soft on crime'. A good deal of education policy seems to have been made in the same way, such as Major's promise to introduce a grammar school into every town. Mrs Thatcher was ideologically driven and frequently prejudiced, but she was obsessive about taking policy-making seriously and believed that it should address real problems. Where governing, electioneering and managing the media get mixed up, the political system has moved well beyond Harold Wilson's dictum that 'A week is a long time in politics,' and it becomes a matter only of fixing the Six O'Clock News.

If the Conservatives had lost their way and become a discredited and divided party, they had the bad luck to find the opposition transformed. Unfair as the tabloid media may have been to Neil Kinnock, voters instinctively distrusted him in numbers that were too great to ignore. His defeat in 1992 led to his immediate resignation and his replacement by John Smith. Smith worked hard to make the party electable without abandoning its core values. He tried to reduce the perception of Labour as a party in hock to trade union bosses by abolishing the bloc vote and establishing the democratic principle of one member one vote. John Smith died suddenly of a heart attack in 1994 and was replaced by Tony Blair. Blair pushed forward the process of 'modernization' at breakneck speed, ditching the party's founding Clause Four, which stated the socialist objective of introducing common ownership of the means of production, distribution and exchange. Blair decided that the break with the past should be signalled by calling the party 'New Labour'. This antagonized many traditional supporters, as did the steady process of policy revision, but it also attracted thousands of new members.

The Blair diagnosis was that a contented majority was satisfied with the main lines of the Thatcher revolution, but that the population could be persuaded to accept a government committed to greater fairness, one that was less exclusively committed to favouring the rich. These were modest aims, but Blair and his circle were well aware that elections in the UK are decided by floating voters in marginal constituencies. Such people do not have strong political loyalties and tend to vote for the party they perceive will do the best for them and their families. They tend to be afraid of radical change and averse to high taxes. Hence the modest reforms within tight spending limits proposed in the Labour manifesto.

The 1997 election led to a Conservative defeat that was unprecedented in modern times. The Labour landslide exceeded even the Liberal victory of 1906. Labour won 418 seats to the Conservatives' 165. The Conservatives lost many hitherto rock-solid seats, like Wimbledon, and also key figures in the contest to succeed John Major, such as Michael Portillo and Malcolm Rifkind. Yet this catastrophic defeat followed an ultra-cautious Labour campaign. Labour insiders seem never to have believed that such a victory was possible, and were discounting it even as it occurred. A 10.5 per cent swing from Conservatives to Labour is unheard of; yet one should remember that a majority of all voters still supported other parties than the winner. Labour's share of the vote was 44 per cent, just 1 per cent more than the Conservatives got in 1992. This was clearly a vote *against* the Conservatives. The proportion of the electorate voting fell by 7 per cent as against 1992, indicating that many disillusioned Conservatives stayed at home. Massive swings of 14–18 per cent in both Tory marginals and some of the safe seats showed active

Liberal–Labour tactical voting but also a large protest vote by Tories rejecting their own party.

Superficially, Labour's victory looked like a political earthquake. Labour appeared to be in an unassailable position to govern as it wished. Yet the leadership had committed the party in explicit election pledges not to tax and spend, and to very modest objectives in economic and social policy. Underneath the rhetoric of national renewal was a profoundly cautious agenda that accepted most of the Conservatives' changes in the previous eighteen years. This was not 1945, more like 1951, when the Tories won but accepted most of the post-1945 Labour reforms. Only in one area were Labour's proposed changes radical, that of constitutional reform. If Labour realized its agenda for devolution, reform of the House of Lords, a bill of rights, freedom of information and a referendum on proportional representation, it would be the biggest shake-up since the Reform Act of 1832. The paradox is that a party whose every instinct is to govern cautiously is also committed to reshape the political system. If it succeeds in doing so, especially if proportional representation is introduced, no British government will ever be able to rule in the autocratic way Mrs Thatcher's did. Proportional representation would virtually rule out majorities on the scale of 1983 and 1987, or of Blair's in 1997. Whatever the outcome of Labour's period in office, the eighteen years of Conservative dominance inaugurated by Mrs Thatcher's victory in 1979 were at an end.

How can we assess the legacy of nearly two decades of Conservative rule and that of Mrs Thatcher in particular? One way is to consider her own goals and how far she met them. Another is to examine the state of the country and its ability to survive as an advanced industrial power. Mrs Thatcher sought to raise the level of economic performance by improving the efficiency of markets and removing obstacles to their working, like the trade union powers. She removed union influence to the point where the UN's International Labour Organization regards Britain as out of step among advanced economies and seriously deficient in the protection of workers' rights. Not unexpectedly, the Conservatives are robust in their response to such comment. They claim that the industrial relations climate and flexible labour markets have made the UK the prime location for foreign inward investment in the EU. However, it should be pointed out that the UK exports more capital than it receives in foreign direct investment, and that Ireland, with a very different labour relations regime and with corporatist consultation, has also been very successful at attracting investment.

Conservative policies did not raise overall growth rates above those achieved in the 1950s and 1960s; indeed, during the Thatcher years growth was no better than it had been in the 1970s. From April 1957 to March 1968 GDP grew at 3.3 per cent; between March 1968 and February 1979 it grew at 2.4 per cent; and between February 1979 and January 1990 it grew at 2 per cent.[6] Some economists, like Nick Crafts, argue that looking backwards is meaningless.[7] Britain is now growing faster relative to its European neighbours than it did earlier. The reason is that their growth rates have slowed, while the UK's have returned to trend. Yet Britain's fitful growth, severe recessions followed by periods of recovery, does not mean much if output is merely restored to previous levels – Britain was close to the bottom of the Organization for Economic Co-operation and Development league table of growth of manufacturing output in 1979–88.[8] Output grew less rapidly in manufacturing in the Thatcher years (0.9 per cent) than it had in the 1970s (1.1 per cent) and during 1957–68 (3.7 per cent).[9] Moreover, Britain experienced a deteriorating external position during these years, in contrast to substantial French and German trade surpluses. France and Germany have both suffered lower growth since the 1980s, but it would be wholly partisan to ascribe this to inflexible labour markets and high levels of welfare spending. Both countries have stuck to policies that sacrificed growth and employment to the goal of low inflation. Also both have maintained their position within the narrow band of the ERM, in France's case with great difficulty and sacrifice. In other words both countries have consistently followed the Bundesbank's version of monetarism since the early 1980s. The UK in contrast has followed highly inconsistent economic policies, allowing inflationary growth in the mid-1980s, and benefiting from the forced devaluation of 1992. Thus it may be argued that it is the financial rectitude of France and Germany that is responsible for much of their unemployment, rather than labour-market rigidities or high levels of welfare. Indeed, Franco-German levels of welfare have cushioned their societies against the full effects of their restrictive macroeconomic policies.

On productivity, economists debate the issue hotly. Did the UK experience a revolution as it cast off the overmanning and restrictive practices of the past? Did productivity improve because managers acquired the 'power to manage' as a result of Mrs Thatcher's policies? Or did bankruptcies and the scrapping of a great many plants allow the survivors to work closer to capacity themselves (for example, by working more shifts) and thus use existing plants more efficiently?[10] The answer is by no means clear, but one thing is obvious: productivity was not driven up by new investment in more up-to-date processes. Investment fell rapidly after 1979, grew again from 1983 to 1990, and then fell drastically from 1990 through to 1995.

On balance, one might conclude that there was a great deal of economic dislocation for a very modest amount of renewal. Moreover, the changes divided the country sharply into haves and have-nots. Inequality has grown to Victorian dimensions.[11] The UK was beaten only by New Zealand in the extent to which incomes have become more unequal since the 1970s. There is a vast burden of unemployment and underemployment – 25 per cent of men of working age are 'economically inactive' and 19 per cent of households below retirement age have no members who are economically active. General government expenditure is now higher as a percentage GDP than it was in 1970 (42.5 per cent against 37.3 per cent), but a higher proportion is made up of benefits for those not in work, with the consequence that the proportion of GDP spent on other public services like education is now lower than it was in the 1970s.

Mrs Thatcher's aim was to make Britain an individualistic enterprise society. Yet there is very little evidence that the British have become individualistic in terms of values. The successive reports of the authoritative British Social Attitudes survey show a population wedded to institutions like the NHS, sceptical about the behaviour of the corporate sector, committed to good public services, and generally unThatcherite. The top 0.5 per cent of income earners (those with incomes of £100,000 a year and over) have every reason to be enthusiastic about the Thatcher years, and it is among the elites that one finds the staunchest and most strident pro-Tory views, followed by the old (the Conservative Party's average age for members is sixty-two). This is hardly the changing of hearts and minds that Mrs Thatcher imagined. Even the skilled and white-collar workers who voted Tory have been following a tradition of family-centred individualism established in the 1950s. Basildon did not begin to vote with its wallet only after Mrs Thatcher came along. Such voters expect parties to deliver, and too many in this sector have been made redundant or suffered negative equity on their houses to see the Tory years as an unalloyed benefit.

Mrs Thatcher claimed that she would roll back the state and give people control over their own affairs through market choices. This must be her most unequivocal failure. The state is if anything more intrusive now than it was in the 1970s. It is also far more centralized and less accountable. Local government has been replaced by central government or by unelected bodies like quangos. Elected officials have been replaced by managers. Spending powers and performance targets have been centralized in huge 'super ministries' like the Department for Education and Employment. Parliament has less control over the increasingly numerous and complex bills driven through it. Institutions that operated at arm's length like the BBC or the universities have been subjected to direct pressures and greater indirect controls.

Civil liberties have been curtailed. The extent to which such developments have raised concern can be seen in the works produced by Conservative insiders like Ferdinand Mount or Simon Jenkins. The latter's *Accountable to None: The Tory Nationalisation of Britain* argues that, far from promoting an open and liberal society, on Hayekian lines, the Tories have produced a centralized bureaucratic state.[12] Compared to the 1970s, central government control over services and spending is far greater and benefits fewer people.

Abroad Mrs Thatcher is often seen as a hero of the Second Cold War, the 'Iron Lady' who helped President Reagan to face down and destroy the Communist 'evil empire'. Many British people also supported her as a 'strong' leader, and disliked Major as weak. Britain's role in 1980s foreign policy issues was marginal. The Falklands War altered little, since the islands were so peripheral. The UK may have been useful to the USA when it was most isolated in gung-ho action, like the bombing of Libya in 1986. In the end, however, it was the superpowers which mattered; Mrs Thatcher was not invited to the Gorbachev–Reagan summit in Reykjavik. Moreover, while Labour unilateralism was futile and politically damaging, Mrs Thatcher's enthusiasm for nuclear weapons was excessive. She saddled Britain with the costs of the Trident missile at a time when nuclear arsenals were being reduced and the Cold War was ending. The expenditure on Trident could have modernized the UK's rail network and the London Underground. A strong leader in a weak country ultimately amounts to little, and Britain reverted to type under Major. A country that tries to punch above its weight for too long will eventually find its weakness exposed.

The long-term legacy of the Conservative governments of the 1970s and 1980s is difficult to assess. The shattering defeat of 1997 is obviously an emphatic public rejection of the Major years. Even so, many discontented voters across the political spectrum still praise 'Maggie' and lament the weakness of her successor. Tony Blair went out of his way to endorse certain aspects of the

Thatcher revolution and declare them permanent. History may be less generous to her. It is likely that in twenty years' time few will talk of 'miracles'. The judgement may be that she wasted Britain's greatest asset in the twentieth century, North Sea oil. Not only did she fail to modernize British industry, the years of her reign marked the UK's fall from being one of the wealthiest countries in the EU to being in danger of being overtaken by Spain.

Britain now faces a fundamental choice, whether to enter fully into the European project or to withdraw to the periphery. It is unlikely that the states at the core will either abandon the further integration of Europe or allow Britain to hinder it much longer. The UK can hardly prosper if it marginalizes itself in relation to the region of the world that takes the majority of its exports. Mrs Thatcher helped to create the Eurosceptic monster and it has divided and defeated the Tory Party. Yet it may have grown too big to be contained. Europhobia and xenophobia are expanding far beyond the Little Englander circles of the Tory Party. The danger is that Labour may trim before this wind of public opinion and turn more Eurosceptic for short-term political advantage. Mrs Thatcher's real political legacy would then be that Britain became an inward-looking and provincial country. English nationalism and economic modernization are incompatible. Mrs Thatcher wanted modernization, on her terms, and failed to achieve it, but she succeeded all too well in promoting a nationalism that can lead only to backwardness. Let us hope she failed in that too.

NOTES

PREFACE

1 This phrase was coined by Peter Hennessy. See Peter Hennessy, 'The Attlee Governments, 1945–1951' in Peter Hennessy and Anthony Seldon (eds), *Ruling Performance: British Governments from Attlee to Thatcher* (Oxford, 1987), p. 50.

CHAPTER I: 'HUNGER ... IS A VERY GOOD THING':
BRITAIN IN THE 1930S

1 Norman Tebbit, *Upwardly Mobile* (London, 1988), pp. 2–3.

2 W. D. Rubinstein, *Wealth and Inequality in Britain* (London, 1986).

3 On health, especially, see Helen Jones, *Health and Society in Twentieth-Century Britain* (London, 1994) and Charles Webster, 'Health, Welfare and Unemployment', *Past and Present*, 109, November 1985, pp. 204–30.

4 R. E. Catterall, 'Electrical Engineering', in N. Buxton and D. H. Aldcroft (eds), *British Industry Between the Wars: Instability and Industrial Development, 1919–1939* (London, 1979), pp. 260–6.

5 Stephen Humphries, *Hooligans or Rebels? An Oral History of Working-Class Childhood and Youth, 1889–1939* (Oxford, 1981), p. 60.

6 John Hilton, *Rich Man, Poor Man* (London, 1944), pp. 11–12. Much of this section relies on this interesting work.

7 Angela Lambert, *1939: The Last Season of Peace* (London, 1989);

Alan A. Jackson, *The Middle Classes, 1900–1950* (Nairn, 1991).

8 On the economy I have relied on Sean Glynn and Alan Booth, *Modern Britain: An Economic and Social History* (London, 1996), and Ross McKibbin, 'Class and Conventional Wisdom: The Conservative Party and the "Public" in Inter-war Britain', in his *The Ideologies of Class: Social Relations in Britain, 1880–1950* (Oxford, 1990).

9 Keith Middlemas and John Barnes, *Baldwin: A Biography* (London, 1969), p. 735.

10 John Burns (1858–1943), Socialist, Lib–Lab MP and Cabinet Minister. Ernest Bevin (1881–1951), General Secretary of the Transport and General Workers' Union and Foreign Secretary in the 1945–51 Labour government. Mass-Observation was a research organization set up by Tom Harrison and Charles Madge in 1937 to study the lives of the British people.

CHAPTER II: THE GOOD WAR: 1939–1945

1 I would like to thank Lindsay Abbot and Alec Macdonald for their comments on this chapter.

2 Margaret Thatcher, *The Path to Power* (London, 1995), pp. 28–31, 43–52.

3 Quoted in Paul Addison, *The Road to 1945* (London, 1975), p. 72.

4 See 'The Lion and the Unicorn', in Sonia Orwell and Ian Angus (eds), *The Collected Essays, Journalism and Letters of George Orwell*, vol. 2 (Harmondsworth, 1970), pp. 74–134.

5 Evan Durbin, *What Have We to Defend?* (London, 1942), p. 81.

6 Quoted in Addison, *1945*, p. 72.

7 Eric Heffer, *Never a Yes Man* (London, 1991), p. 24.

8 Jennie Lee, *This Great Journey* (London, 1963), p. 195.

9 Text of speech to the Fabian Society, 8 June 1943, Herbert Morrison news cuttings, Labour Party Archive, Manchester.

10 MF/M1, Election Material – Devonport 1945–65, Michael Foot papers, Labour Party Archive, Manchester.

CHAPTER III: CHURCHILL AND THE PRICE OF VICTORY: 1939–1945

1 John Ramsden, ' "That Will Depend on Who Writes the History": Winston Churchill as His Own Historian', an inaugural lecture at Queen Mary and Westfield College, University of London, 1996.

2 Andrew Roberts, *Eminent Churchillians* (London, 1994), p. 186.

3 Maurice Cowling, 'Why We Should Not Have Gone to War', *Sunday Telegraph*, 20 August 1989, p. 17.

4 *Sydney Morning Herald*, 8 October 1987.

5 Alan Clark, 'A Reputation Ripe for Revision', *The Times*, 2 January 1993.

6 John Charmley, *Churchill: The End of Glory* (London, 1993), p. 649.

7 Malcolm MacDonald, *Titans and Others* (London, 1972), p. 96.

8 Stephen Roskill, *Churchill and the Admirals* (London, 1977), p. 277.

9 John Colville, *The Fringes of Power: Downing Street Diaries, 1939–1955* (London, 1985), pp. 228–9, entry for 21 August 1940.

10 John Ramsden, *The Age of Churchill and Eden, 1940–1957* (London, 1996), pp. 40–1.

11 Winston S. Churchill, *The Second World War*, vol. 6: *Triumph and Tragedy* (London, 1954), p. 652, 'Programme for July 1945'.

CHAPTER IV: RECONSTRUCTING BRITAIN: LABOUR IN POWER 1945–1951

1 *Economic Survey for 1947*, Parliamentary Papers 1946/7, vol. XIX, para. 66.

2 John Kent, *British Imperial Strategy and the Origins of the Cold War* (Leicester, 1994), p. 142.

3 *Report of the Commissioner of Police for the Metropolis 1948*, Parliamentary Papers 1948/9, vol. XIX, appendix.

4 Alix Kilroy, *Public Servant, Private Woman* (London, 1988), pp. 249–50.

5 *Seventh Report from the Select Committee on the Estimates*, 'The Administration of the NHS', Parliamentary Papers 1948/9, vol. VII.

6 Jim Fyrth (ed.), *Labour's High Noon: The Government and the Economy, 1945–51* (London, 1993).

7 Correlli Barnett, *The Lost Victory: British Dreams, British Realities, 1945–1950* (London, 1995).

CHAPTER V: 'NEVER-NEVER LAND':
BRITAIN UNDER THE CONSERVATIVES 1951–1964

1 John Charmley, *A History of Conservative Politics, 1900–1996* (London, 1996), p. 142.
2 Public Record Office, CP (52) 202 FS, 'British Overseas Obligations', 18 June 1953, quoted in Henry Pelling, *Churchill's Peacetime Ministry, 1951–55* (London, 1997), p. 58.
3 David Butler, 'Voting Behaviour and Its Study in Britain', *British Journal of Sociology*, VI(2), June 1955, p. 102.
4 See Walter Bagehot, *The English Constitution* (1867; C. A. Watts & Co. edn, 1964), pp. 82–3.
5 A. S. C. Ross, 'U and Non-U: An Essay in Sociological Linguistics', *Encounter*, 26, November 1955, pp. 11–20; also Nancy Mitford, 'The English Aristocracy', *Encounter*, 24, September 1955, pp. 5–12.
6 Lindsay Anderson, 'Get Out and Push', *Encounter*, 50, November 1957, pp. 14–22.
7 Denis Potter, *The Changing Forest: Life in the Forest of Dean Today* (London, 1962; Minerva edn, 1996), p. 87.
8 See Malcolm Muggeridge, 'The Queen and I: A Memoir and Some Reflections', *Encounter*, 94, July 1961, pp. 17–23; Henry Fairlie, 'An Anatomy of Hysteria', *Spectator*, 8 November 1957. See also Ben Pimlott, *The Queen: A Biography of Elizabeth II* (London, 1996), pp. 276–88.
9 F. S. L. Lyons, *Ireland Since the Famine* (London, 1973), p. 754.
10 Public Record Office, PREM 11. 3325, 'Memorandum by the Prime Minister', 29 December 1960–3 January 1961; see also Harold Macmillan, *Pointing the Way, 1959–1961* (London, 1972), pp. 323–6.
11 Hugh Thomas, 'The Establishment and Society' in Hugh Thomas (ed.), *The Establishment* (London, 1959), p. 18.

CHAPTER VI: THE WILSON YEARS: 1964–1970

1 Janet Morgan (ed.), *The Backbench Diaries of Richard Crossman* (London, 1981), p. 973.

2 Callaghan memorandum on July 1966 crisis, 12 August 1997 (Callaghan Papers).

3 Public Records Office, CAB 129/119, note by Secretary of the Cabinet, 16 December 1964.

4 *Economist*, 23 July 1966.

5 Interview with Sir Alec Cairncross, 14 January 1995.

6 Edmund Dell, *The Chancellors* (London, 1996), pp. 350ff.

7 Lyndon B. Johnson Presidential papers, Austin, Texas, NSF country file, box 216: background paper, February 1968.

8 Clive Ponting, *Breach of Promise: Labour in Power, 1964–70* (London, 1988), p. 226.

9 Public Record Office, PREM 8/1405, Sir Oliver Franks to Attlee, 15 July 1950.

10 Tony Benn, *Out of the Wilderness: Diaries, 1963–67* (London, 1987), p. 496.

11 Susan Crosland, *Tony Crosland* (London, 1982), p. 148.

12 *Parliamentary Debates*, 5th ser., vol. 776, 947ff. (27 January 1969).

13 Peter Jenkins, *The Battle of Downing Street* (London, 1970), p. 153.

14 *New Statesman*, 26 June 1970.

15 See Charles Kindleberger, 'Why Did the Golden Age Last So Long?', in Frances Cairncross (ed.), *Changing Perceptions of Economic Policy* (London, 1981), pp. 15–33. He takes the 'Golden Age' as going up to 1973.

16 Ben Pimlott, *Harold Wilson* (London, 1992), p. 567.

CHAPTER VII: 'YOU'VE NEVER HAD IT SO BAD'?: BRITAIN IN THE 1970S

1 The following paragraphs necessarily summarize heavily. Readers who desire a fuller account should consult Kenneth O. Morgan's excellent *The People's Peace: British History, 1945–1989* (Oxford, 1990).

2 *New Society*, 3 August 1978.

3 *Economist*, 3 February 1979.

4 *Personnel Management*, 11(2), February 1979.

5 Margaret Thatcher, *Speeches to the Conservative Party Conferences, 1975–1988* (London, 1989), p. 109.

6 Ann Barr and Peter York, *The Official Sloane Ranger Handbook* (London, 1982), p. 13.

CHAPTER VIII: MIRACLE OR MIRAGE?: THE THATCHER YEARS
1979–1997

1 Keith Smith, *The British Economic Crisis* (Harmondsworth, 1984), chs 6 and 7, gives an accessible account of monetarism.

2 Published in London, in 1944.

3 Ian Gilmour, *Inside Right* (London, 1978) for the one-nation world view and *Dancing with Dogma* (London, 1992) for a Tory critique of Thatcherism.

4 N. M. Healey (ed.), *Britain's Economic Miracle* (London, 1993) is an accessible collection assessing Britain's economic performance in the 1980s.

5 Stuart Weir and Wendy Hall, *Ego Trip: Extra-governmental organisations in the United Kingdom and Their Accountability* (London, 1994) surveys the 'quango state'.

6 Ken Coutts, Wynne Godley, Bob Rowthorn and Genarro Zezza, *Britain's Economic Problems and Policies in the 1990s* (London, 1990), p. 7.

7 *Prospect*, April 1997, pp. 16–18.

8 Healey, *Britain's Economic Miracle*, p. 100, fig. 5.2.

9 Coutts et al., p. 11.

10 D. H. Blackaby and L. C. Hunt, 'An Assessment of Britain's Productivity Record in the 1980s: Has There Been a Miracle?' in Healey, *Britain's Economic Miracle*, pp. 109–26.

11 Commission on Social Justice, *The Justice Gap* (London, 1993).

12 Simon Jenkins, *Accountable to None* (London, 1995) and Ferdinand Mount, *The British Constitution Now* (London, 1992).

FURTHER READING

CHAPTER I: 'HUNGER ... IS A VERY GOOD THING':
BRITAIN IN THE 1930S

Walter Greenwood, *Love on the Dole* (Harmondsworth, 1969).

Mass-Observation, *Britain* (Cresset Library edn, 1986).

Scott Newton, *Profits of Peace: The Political Economy of Anglo-German Appeasement* (Oxford, 1996).

George Orwell, *The Road to Wigan Pier* (Harmondsworth, 1962).

J. B. Priestley, *English Journey* (Harmondsworth, 1987).

Andrew Thorpe, *Britain in the 1930s* (Oxford, 1992).

CHAPTER II: THE GOOD WAR: 1939–1945

Paul Addison, *The Road to 1945* (London, 1975).

Angus Calder, *The People's War* (London, 1969).

Steven Fielding, Peter Thompson and Nick Tiratsoo, *'England Arise!': The Labour Party and Popular Politics in the 1940s* (Manchester, 1995).

Kevin Jefferys, *The Churchill Coalition and Wartime Politics* (Manchester, 1991).

Harold L. Smith (ed.), *War and Social Change* (Manchester, 1986).

CHAPTER III: CHURCHILL AND THE PRICE
OF VICTORY: 1939–1945

Paul Addison, *Churchill on the Home Front, 1900–1955* (1992).

Tuvia Ben-Moshe, *Churchill: Strategy and History* (1992).

John Charmley, *Churchill: The End of Glory* (1993).

Basil Liddell Hart, 'The Military Strategist', in A. J. P. Taylor and others, *Churchill: Four Faces and the Man* (1969).

John Keegan, 'Churchill's Strategy', in Robert Blake and W. R. Louis (eds), *Churchill* (1993).

John Ramsden, *The Age of Churchill and Eden, 1940–1957* (1995).

CHAPTER IV: RECONSTRUCTING BRITAIN:
LABOUR IN POWER 1945–1951

Sir Alec Cairncross, *Years of Recovery: British Economic Policy, 1945–51* (London, 1986).

Steven Fielding, Peter Thompson and Nick Tiratsoo, *'England Arise!': The Labour Party and Popular Politics in the 1940s* (Manchester, 1995).

Martin Francis, *Ideas and Politics under Labour, 1945–51* (Manchester, 1997).

Peter Hennessy, *Never Again: Britain, 1945–51* (London, 1992).

Kenneth O. Morgan, *Labour in Power, 1945–51* (Oxford, 1984).

Jim Tomlinson, *Democratic Socialism and Economic Policy: The Attlee Years* (Cambridge, 1997).

CHAPTER V: 'NEVER-NEVER LAND':
BRITAIN UNDER THE CONSERVATIVES 1951–1964

Tony Benn, *Years of Hope: Diaries, Letters and Papers, 1940–62*, ed. Ruth Winstone (London, 1994).

Terry Gourvish and Alan O'Day (eds), *Britain Since 1945* (London, 1991).

Robert Holland, *The Pursuit of Greatness: Britain and the World Role, 1900–1970* (London, 1991).

James Obelkevich, 'Consumption', in Peter Catterall and James Obelkevich, *Understanding Post-War British Society* (London, 1994), pp. 141–54.

Denis Potter, *The Changing Forest: Life in the Forest of Dean Today* (London, 1962; Minerva edn, 1996).

Gordon T. Stewart, 'Tenzing's Two Wrist-Watches: The Conquest of

Everest and Late Imperial Culture in Britain', *Past and Present*, 149, November 1995, pp. 170–97.

CHAPTER VI: THE WILSON YEARS: 1964–1970

Sir Alec Cairncross, *Managing the Economy in the 1960s* (London, 1996).

Richard Coopey, Steven Fielding and Nick Tiratsoo (eds), *The Wilson Governments, 1964–1970* (London, 1993).

Edmund Dell, *The Chancellors: A History of the Chancellors of the Exchequer, 1945–1990* (London, 1996).

Denis Healey, *The Time of My Life* (London, 1989).

Robert Hewison, *Too Much: Art and Society in the Sixties, 1960–75* (London, 1986).

Roy Jenkins, *A Life at the Centre* (London, 1991).

Kenneth O. Morgan, *Callaghan: A Life* (Oxford, 1997).

Ben Pimlott, *Harold Wilson* (London, 1992).

Philip Ziegler, *Wilson: The Authorised Life* (London, 1993).

CHAPTER VII: 'YOU'VE NEVER HAD IT SO BAD'?: BRITAIN IN THE 1970S

Michael Artis and David Cobham (eds), *Labour's Economic Policies, 1974–1979* (Manchester, 1991).

Ian Bradley, *The English Middle Classes Are Alive and Kicking* (London, 1982).

Sir Alec Cairncross, *The British Economy Since 1945* (London, 1992).

Theo Nichols, *The British Worker Question* (London, 1986).

Robert Taylor, *The Fifth Estate: Britain's Unions in the Modern World* (London, 1978).

CHAPTER VIII: MIRACLE OR MIRAGE?: THE THATCHER YEARS 1979–1997

Andrew Gamble, *The Free Economy and the Strong State*, (London, 2nd edn, 1994).

Stuart Hall and Martin Jacques (eds), *The Politics of Thatcherism* (London, 1983).

Will Hutton, *The State We're In* (London, 1995).
Peter Jenkins, *Mrs Thatcher's Revolution* (London, 1987).
David Marquand, *The Unprincipled Society* (London, 1988).
Hugo Young, *One of Us* (London, 1989).

CONTRIBUTORS

1 Tony Mason was born in Gainsborough and for the last twenty-five years has taught social history at the University of Warwick.

2 Steven Fielding is a Lecturer in the Department of Politics and Contemporary History at Salford University. He studied at St John's College, Cambridge as well as the Centre for the Study of Social History, Warwick University, and is the author of a number of works on the Labour Party.

3 Paul Addison teaches history at the University of Edinburgh, where he is Director of the Centre for Second World War Studies. He is the author of *The Road to 1945: British Politics and the Second World War* (1975) and *Churchill on the Home Front, 1900–1945* (1992).

4 Jim Tomlinson is Professor of Economic History and Head of the Department of Government at Brunel University. He has published extensively on the economic history of twentieth-century Britain, most recently *Democratic Socialism and Economic Policy: The Attlee Years* (1997).

5 Dilwyn Porter is Reader in History at Worcester College of Higher Education and a Research Fellow at the Business History Unit, London School of Economics. He is the co-author, with Scott Newton, of *Modernization Frustrated: The Politics of Industrial Decline Since 1900* (1988) and has subsequently

published a number of articles and chapters on Britain since 1945.

6 Kenneth O. Morgan is Fellow of the British Academy, an Honorary Fellow of The Queen's College, Oxford, and a former Vice-Chancellor. His twenty-two books include *Keir Hardie* (1975), *Labour in Power* (1984), *Labour People* (1987), *The People's Peace, 1945–1990* (1992) and the official life of Lord Callaghan (September 1997).

7 Nick Tiratsoo is a Senior Research Fellow at the University of Luton and a Visiting Research Fellow at the Business History Unit, London School of Economics. He has published widely on the history of the Labour Party and is currently writing a study of post-war British management.

8 Paul Hirst is Professor of Social Theory at Birkbeck College, University of London. He is the author of numerous books, including *After Thatcher* (1989) and *From Statism to Pluralism* (1997). He is a member of the Executive of Charter 88 and of the *Political Quarterly* editorial board.

INDEX

abortion law, 150
Abrams, Mark, 121
Abse, Leo, 150
Accountable to None, 216
Addison, Paul, 25
agricultural workers, unemployment, 2
alcohol, postwar taxation, 95
Alliance, 196, 201
Altrincham, Lord (John Grigg), 116
Amersham International, 198
Anatomy of Britain, 130
Anderson, Lindsay, 113
Anglo-American Council on Productivity, 85
Ankle, Delsie, 122
appeasement, 17–18, 27, 29, 31, 68–9
aristocracy, lifestyle (1930s), 13, 14
armed forces: unfitness of applicants, 7; conscription, 19; RAF role, 19; wartime class distinctions, 36; Northern Ireland, 155; Falklands War, 195
arms industry, 16
Armstrong, William, 136, 138
Army Bureau of Current Affairs (ABCA), 70
Army Territorial Service, 39
arts: end of censorship, 149; drama and music, 150
Arts Council, 150
atomic bomb, Britain's first, 105
Attlee, Clement: wartime coalition, 29, 46, 61, 67; election (1945), 49, 50, 74; opinion of Churchill, 53; government, 58, 77, 86, 93, 99–101, 134, 146; election defeat (1951), 103; left-wing revolt, 111; successor, 124
Auden, W.H., 1
austerity, 87–9

Bagehot, Walter, 109
Baker, Kenneth, 203
balance of payments: postwar, 79, 84, 86–7, 89, 91; crisis (1951–2), 103–4; deficit (1959–60), 125–6; deficit (1964), 136; surplus (1969), 142; deficit (1973), 167, 168
Baldwin, Stanley, 16, 19, 31–2, 55, 160
Bank of England, nationalization, 80
bankruptcies, 193, 214
Barber, Anthony, 166, 167, 174
Barnett, Correlli, 26, 100
Battle of Britain, 30, 68
BBC, 109, 118, 215
Beamish, Sir Tufton, 57
Beatles, 132, 149, 157
Beaverbrook, Lord, 70
Ben-Moshe, Tuvia, 65
Benn, Tony: on 1950s, 103, 106; role in Wilson governments, 139, 169–70; EEC policy, 148; left- wing champion, 169, 195–6; reputation, 188; deputy leadership election, 196
Bevan, Aneurin, 67, 92–3, 111, 124, 134
Beveridge, Sir William, 43–5, 72, 134

Beveridge Report, 43–6, 72, 82

Bevin, Ernest: on poverty of desire, 23; wartime Minister of Labour, 30, 37, 38, 69, 70; postwar Foreign Secretary, 86–7, 105, 143

bicycles, 1, 5, 11

'Big Bang', 200

Birmingham Mail, 118

Black Wednesday, 206, 208

Blackett, Professor, 139

Blair, Tony, 197, 210–11, 212, 216–17

Blitz, 35–6

Bloom, John, 119

bombing, 16, 20, 35–6

Bond, Edward, 149

Booth, Charles, 3

Boothby, Robert, 28

Boyd Orr, J., 7

Bracken, Brendan, 70

Brandt, Willy, 149

Brideshead Revisited, 41–2

Bristol, poverty, 4

British Aerospace, 198

British Airways, 199

British Empire: British policy (1930s), 16, 17, 19–20, 58; British policy (wartime), 20, 56, 61–4, 75; British policy (postwar), 60; British policy (1950s and 1960s), 124–5, 130; *see also* Commonwealth

British Employers' Confederation, 45

British Expeditionary Force, 61

British Film Institute, 150

British Gas, 199

British Housewives League, 89

British Leyland, 194, 199

British Medical Association, 7

British Olympic Committee, 19

British Petroleum, 198

British Railways, 207

British Shipbuilders, 199

British Social Attitudes Survey, 215

British Steel, 202

Brogan, Colm, 27

Brown, George: leadership election (1963), 134; role in Wilson government, 135, 136, 138–9, 140, 142, 143, 148

budgets: Dalton's (1947), 85; Gaitskell's (1951), 134; Callaghan's (1964), 137, (1965), 137, (1966), 139, (1967), 141; Jenkins' (1968), 142; Barber's (1971), 166; Healey's (1975), 170; Howe's (1979), 197; Lawson's (1988), 202

building societies, 120

building trades (1930s), 4

Bundesbank, 214

burial insurance, 11

Burns, John, 23

Butler, R.A.: appeasement policy, 61–2, 64; wartime education role, 71; relationship with Churchill, 71, 73; Chancellor of Exchequer, 104, 107; party leadership question, 115

Butlin's holiday camps, 97

Butskellism, 107, 108

Butt, Ronald, 184

Cable and Wireless, 198

Cairncross, Alec, 136, 141, 161

Calder, Angus, 25

Callaghan, James: election campaign (1945), 49; on permissiveness, 132, 157; leadership election (1963), 134; Chancellor of Exchequer, 135–8, 141–2; US relations, 143; European policy, 148; Home Secretary, 150, 152, 155–8; opposition to Industrial Relations Bill, 159; Foreign Secretary, 169; leadership election (1976), 170; Prime Minister, 170–2, 174, 176, 198; election defeat (1979), 172, 173

Campaign for Nuclear Disarmament (CND), 124

Capital Gains Tax, 137

capital punishment, abolition, 150

Carnegie Trust, 9, 10

Carrington, Lord, 193

cars: (1930s), 5; (1950s), 112, 119, 122

Castle, Barbara, 134, 135, 158–9

Catering and Wages Bill (1943), 68

censorship, 149

Central Electricity Generating Board, 206

Central Office of Information, 85

Chamberlain, Neville: Prime Minister, 71; Munich agreement, 18; appeasement policy, 27–9, 55, 64; wartime administration, 34–5; succeeded by Churchill, 29, 54–5, 57; public opinion of, 31, 129; Cowling's view of, 59; War Cabinet, 61

Charles, Prince of Wales, 154

Charmley, John, 60

chemical industry, growth (1930s), 4

Chicago, University of, 192

child care, 96

Churchill, Randolph, 124

Churchill, Winston: on public works policy, 15; on Empire, 20, 56, 63; relationship with Conservative party, 54–5, 69–75; wartime role, 25, 29–30, 64–5, 71–3; question of peace with Germany, 61, 63; relationship with Labour in wartime coalition, 26–7, 30, 57, 67, 69–70, 72–3; on women's war work, 38; plans for peacetime, 42–3, 71; on Beveridge report, 45; election (1945), 49–50, 65–6, 73–6; election (1951), 103; government, 103, 104–6, 186; resignation, 111; reputation, 53–4, 59–61, 143, 191

Churchill's War, 59

cinema: (1930s), 5; wartime, 40; postwar, 97

Civil Assistance, 189

Clark, Alan, 60, 63

class differences: mortality rates (1930s), 8, 22; lifestyles (1930s), 12–14; wartime, 33–7; postwar, 91; U and non-U, 112–13

Clause Four, 134, 210

Clegg Commission, 192

Cliveden, 68

closed shop debate, 179–80

clothes: middle class (1930s), 13; New Look, 88–9

coal heating (1930s), 8–9

coal industry: unemployment, 2; wartime, 38; nationalization question, 70; nationalization, 80–1; coal shortages, 83; miners' strike (1971–72), 167, 180; miners' strike (1974), 168, 180; miners' strike (1984–85), 201; Heseltine's policy, 206–7

Cohn-Bendit, Daniel (Danny the Red), 156

Cold War, 80, 100, 216

Colleges of Advanced Technology, 150

Colville, John, 71

Commonwealth, 105, 144–8, *see also* British Empire

Communist Party, 22

Community Relations Commission, 152

comprehensive education, 151, 187

Confederation of British Industry (CBI), 138, 182

conscription, 19

consensus politics, 107, 108

Conservative Party: governments (1920s and 1930s), 14–16, 22; policies, 14–16; election (1935), 22; appeasement policy, 17–18, 27, 29, 31, 68–9; wartime coalition, 30, 32–3, 57; Beveridge report, 45; election (1945), 26, 48–50, 58, 66–7, 74–5; Churchill's status, 54–5, 69–75; anti-austerity policies, 89, 91; election (1951), 103; welfare state commitment, 107; leadership choice (1957), 115–16; leadership choice (1963), 131; election (1964), 131; trade union policy, 166; elections (1974), 168–9, 185; leadership election (1975), 182, 189; election (1979), 176, 18; Thatcher leadership, 192–3; election (1983), 195–6; Major leadership, 208; sleaze, 208–10; election (1997), 211–12, 216

consumption: (1930s), 4–5, 11; postwar, 80, 85, 87, 88; (1950s), 108, 112; 'never had it so good', 118–21; boom (1980s), 200, 202

Cook, Peter, 128

Cooper, Duff, 71

Coronation, 108–11

Corporation Tax, 137

corruption, 208–10

cotton industry, 85

council house sales, 192, 199

Cousins, Frank, 139, 139–40, 152

Coward, Noël, 40–1

Cowling, Maurice, 58–9

Crafts, Nick, 213

credit: restrictions (1952), 104; expansion (1950s), 119–20; restrictions lifted (1980s), 194; expansion (1980s), 200

cricket, 97
crime rate (1930s), 23
Cripps, Sir Stafford, 84, 136
Critchley, Julian, 128
Crook, County Durham, 2
Crosland, Anthony, 132, 135, 136, 148
Crossman, Richard, 134, 135
Crowther, Lord, 154

Daily Mail, 54
Daily Mirror, 69
Daily Telegraph, 45, 54
Dalton, Hugh, 69
dance-halls, 5
Davies, Harold, 144
de Gaulle, Charles, 128, 141, 148, 149
death rates (1930s), 6, 8
debt (1930s), 12
debutantes, 13
Decline and Fall of the Middle Class and How It Can Fight Back, 187
defence: rearmament (1930s), 16, 19; Korean War, 92–3, 99; atomic bomb, 105; US security role, 105; Macmillan policy, 123–5; commitments east of Suez, 138, 143, 147
deflation, 14, 142
Dell, Edmund, 142
denationalization, 103
Denning, Lord, 128
dental care: (1930s), 2–3, 6–7, 93; NHS, 93, 94
Depression, Great (1929–32), 14–15, 21, 51
deregulation, 197, 199, 200
devaluation: (1949), 90, 91; question of (1964), 136; (1967), 140–1, 206; Black Wednesday, 206
devolution, 161, 212
diet, 2–3
divorce laws, 150
dockworkers: unemployment, 2; strike (1967), 141; strike (1970), 165
dole, 21
Domestic Violence and Matrimonial Proceedings Act (1976), 175
Douglas-Home, Sir Alec, 56, 131, 133
drugs, 157

Dunkirk evacuation, 30, 31, 51, 61
Durbin, Evan, 31
Dutschke, Rudi, 156

Early Morning, 149
Economics Survey for 1947, 86
Economist, 107, 119, 140, 182
economy: deflation policy, 14; gold standard, 15; free trade, 15; US loans, 79, 84; currency controls, 84, 99; state control, 84–5; Sterling Area, 86; devaluation (1949), 90, 91; 1950s, 102–3; floating pound scheme, 104; stop- go, 127, 138; pressure on pound (1964), 136–7, (1966–67), 140–1; international aid package (1964), 137; Wilson government policy, 138; devaluation, 140–1; IMF loan, 170–1; Medium-Term Financial Strategy, 193, 194, 200; recession (1979–82), 193, 194, 205, 213; exchange controls abolition, 200; manufactured goods balance of trade, 200; recession (1990s), 205, 213; growth rate, 213–14; *see also* balance of payments, inflation, interest rates
Eden, Anthony, 20, 73, 105, 111, 113–15, 118
education: class differences (1930s), 9–10; grammar schools, 9, 10, 101, 151, 210; school building programme, 87, 100; free secondary, 94; skills improvement, 100–1; expenditure, 107, 108, 215; Northern Ireland, 122–3; new universities, 150; polytechnics, 151, 187; Open University, 151, 161; ending of 'eleven plus', 151; comprehensivism, 151; private schools, 151, 187; national curriculum, 202; school management, 207; performance league tables, 207; OFSTED, 207
Education Act (1944), 10, 71, 101
Education Act (1988), 202
Edward VIII, King, 23
Eisenhower, Dwight D., 106, 111
elections, *see* general elections
electrical engineering, growth (1930s), 4
electricity: consumption, 5, 9; postwar shutdowns, 83; nationalization, 90; privatization, 202, 206

Elizabeth, Queen (Queen Mother), 36
Elizabeth II, Queen, 108–9, 115
employment, full, 78, 96–7, 104, 142, *see also*
  unemployment
Encounter, 112, 117
engineering industry, 193
English and National Review, 116
English Constitution, The, 109
entertainment (1930s), 4–5, 11
Equal Pay Act (1970), 175
Establishment, The, 130
Europe: British role (1950s), 105;
  Eurosceptics, 208, 217; British role
  (1997), 217
European Economic Community (EEC),
  127, 141, 148–9, 167
European Free Trade Area, 137
European Monetary System (EMS), 202,
  205
European Union (EU), 208, 213
evacuation, wartime, 20, 34–5
Evans, Gwynfor, 153
evening classes, 100–1
Everest expedition (1953), 110
Ewing, Winifred, 154
exchange rate, 104, 193, 194
Exchange Rate Mechanism (ERM), 205,
  206
exports, 80, 85, 90–1, 98–9, 100, 193

Falklands, 148; War, 195, 216
family: size, 4; allowances, 96
Fascism: rise of, 16; in Britain, 22
Federation of British Industries, 45
feminism, 96
Financial Times, 119, 121, 178
fishermen, unemployment, 2
Fleming, Anne, 140
food: working-class diet (1930s), 2–3, 6;
  school dinners, 7; school milk, 7; poverty
  studies, 7
Foot, Michael, 26, 31, 49, 134, 170, 196
football, 97, 110–11, 160; pools, 11, 12
foreign policy: (1950s) 105–6; (1980s), 216
France: Suez (1956), 114; economy, 213–14
Francis of Assisi, St, 192
Franks, Oliver, 144

Fremantle, Sir F., 7
Friedman, Milton, 193
friendly societies, 5
Future of Socialism, 132

Gaitskell, Hugh, 92, 107, 124, 128, 134,
  148
Galbraith, John Kenneth, 143
Gallup, 121, 129, 176
Galtieri, General, 201
gambling, 12
Gandhi, Mahatma, 63
gas, nationalization, 90
gender, wartime division of labour, 38–9; *see
  also* women
general elections: (1935), 22–3; (1945), 26,
  48–50, 53, 58, 66–7, 74–5, 77; (1950), 90,
  91–2; (1951), 103, 106; (1955), 106, 111–
  12; (1959), 106, 119, 121, 125, 127;
  (1964), 131, 133; (1966), 133; (1970), 133,
  160, 164; (February 1974), 168–9, 185;
  (October 1974), 169, 185; (1979), 26, 173,
  184, 186, 191–2; (1983), 26, 195–6;
  (1987), 200, 201–2; (1992), 205–6, 208;
  (1997), 211–12, 216; *see also* voting
General Strike, 54
Gentle Sex, The, 39
George VI, King, 29, 36
Germany: health and fitness, 7; war threat,
  16, 17; British appeasement policy, 17–
  18, 27; economy, 127, 213–14
Gilmour, Ian, 193
gold standard, 15
Gorbachev, Mikhail, 216
Gordon Walker, Patrick, 133
Government of India Act (1935), 20
grammar schools, 9, 10, 101, 151, 210
gramophones, 5, 11
Greenwood, Arthur, 61
Grigg, John, *see* Altrincham
Guevara, Che, 157
Guilty Men, 31–2

Halifax, Lord, 29–30, 61, 62, 64
Hardie, Keir, 161
Hayek, F.A., 47, 50, 193
Hayhoe, Barney, 183

Healey, Denis: Minister of Defence, 135; US relations, 143; European policy, 148; Chancellor of Exchequer, 169–72; deputy leadership election, 196

health: dental care (1930s), 2–3, 6–7; health care (1930s), 5–6, 93; NHS creation, 81; private practice, 81; health centres, 87; postwar standard, 91

Heath, Edward: European policy, 127; race relations, 152; party leadership, 158, 189; personality and background, 158, 165; election (1970), 158, 160; government, 165–9, 186; elections (1974), 168–9, 185

Heathcoat Amory, Derick, 119

Heffer, Eric, 36

Heseltine, Michael, 55, 204, 206

Hillary, Edmund, 110

Hilton, John, 11, 12

Himmler, Heinrich, 59

hire-purchase, 5, 11, 112, 119–20

Hitler, Adolf, 17, 18, 25, 27–31, 56, 58–60, 62–5

holidays, 97

homosexuality, law reform, 150

Hong Kong, 147

Hornby, Derrick, 182

Hospital Saturday Funds, 11

hospitals: (1930s), 5; nationalization, 81; building programme, 87, 100

Houghton, Douglas, 159

House of Lords, 212

housing: building (1930s), 4; overcrowding, 8; regional and class differences (1930s), 8; election issue (1945), 72, 78, 82–3; postwar shortage, 49, 82–3; postwar legislation, 83; postwar building, 83, 87, 94–5, 100; new- town schemes, 95; Macmillan's policy, 107–8; expenditure, 108; home ownership, 120, 187; property boom (1970s), 167; council house sales, 192, 199; rising prices (1980s), 200; negative equity, 205

Howard, Michael, 207, 210

Howe, Geoffrey, 197

Hunt, John, 110

Hunt, Lord, 155

Hurd, Douglas, 204

Hutber, Patrick, 187, 188

immigration legislation: (1962), 118; (1968), 152

Impact of Hitler, The, 58–9

import: controls (1952), 104; surcharge (1964), 137

Import Duties Act (1932), 15

In Place of Strife, 159

In Which We Serve, 40–1

income tax: (1930s), 4; wartime, 57; postwar, 95; (1970), 165; (1979), 197; (1988), 202

incomes policy: (1948–50), 98; public sector 'pay pause', 126; Heath's, 167; Callaghan's 5 per cent policy (1978), 172, 198; Conservative manifesto (1979), 192

Independent, 164

India, independence, 63, 100

individualism, 215

Indo-China war, 111

Industrial Relations Act (1971), 166

Industrial Relations Bill (1969), 159

infant mortality, 6, 22, 33

inflation: postwar, 84; (1960s), 142; (1970s), 163, 165, 175, 198; (1980s), 193, 194, 197, 200, 202; (1990s), 205

insurance: burial, 11; unemployment, 21; social, *see* national insurance

interest rates, 15, 137, 193, 194, 205

International Labour Organization (ILO), 212

International Monetary Fund (IMF), 141, 170–1, 172

investment: postwar, 80, 85, 87, 91, 98, 100; (1950s), 108; (1970s), 167; (1980s), 214; (1990s), 214

Iraq arms affair, 209

Ireland, *see* Irish Republic, Northern Ireland

Irish Republic, 156

iron and steel industry: nationalization, 90; supplies, 98; steel denationalization, 103

Irving, David, 59–60

Isherwood, Christopher, 3

Italy: health and fitness, 7; war threat, 16; Abyssinia, 17

ITN, 118

Ivanov, Yevgeny, 128

Jacobson, Dan, 117
Japan: British relations, 16, 19; Manchuria, 17
Jarrow, 68
Jay, Douglas, 47, 136, 138, 148
Jay, Peter, 138
Jenkins, Roy: Home Secretary, 132, 135, 149; Chancellor of Exchequer, 135, 142, 148, 158; European policy, 140, 148; Industrial Relations Bill attitude, 159; SDP, 196
Jenkins, Simon, 216
Jews, 18, 36, 63
Johnson, Lyndon B., 133, 137, 143, 144
Johnson, Paul, 160, 179
Jones, Jack, 158, 172
Joseph, Sir Keith, 184
Journey Together, 41

Kagan, Joe, 133
Kaldor, Nicky, 136, 139
Kaunda, Kenneth, 146
Keegan, John, 65
Keeler, Christine, 128
Kennedy, John F., 125, 133
Keynes, John Maynard, 14
Khrushchev, Nikita, 123
Kilbrandon, Lord, 154
King, Martin Luther, 154
Kinnock, Neil, 196, 206, 210
Kirby, J., 7
Kohl, Helmut, 191
Korean War, 92, 99, 111

Labour Party: administrations (1920s and 1930s), 14, 22; election (1935), 22–3; wartime coalition, 29–30, 42–3, 57, 67–8, 72; Beveridge report, 45–6; election (1945), 26, 48–50, 75, 77, 78; Attlee government programme, 77–8; election (1951), 103, 104; left-wing revolt (1955), 111; nuclear policy, 111, 124, 216; attitude to royal prerogative, 115–16; election (1959), 121; European policy, 148; leadership election (1963), 134; election (1964), 131, 133; election (1966), 133; election (1970), 133, 160–1, 164;

membership (1970), 161; relationship with trade unions, 161, 187, 210; election (1974), 168–9; leadership election (1976), 170; Lib-Lab pact, 171, 172; SDP split, 196; Foot leadership election, 196; election (1983), 26, 195–6; Kinnock leadership, 196–7, 210; election (1992), 206, 208; Blair leadership, 210–11; New Labour, 211; election (1997), 211–12, 216
Lady Chatterley's Lover, 129, 149
Lamont, Norman, 206
Lancaster, Osbert, 188
Latey Commission, 157
law and order: crime rate (1930s), 23; student unrest (1960s), 156–7; legislation (1990s), 207, 210
Lawson, Nigel, 202, 204
League of Nations, 17
Leary, Timothy, 157
Lee, Jennie, 37, 135, 151
Lee Kuan Yew, 147
leisure, 97
Let Us Face the Future, 48
Letwin, Shirley Robin, 185
Lewin, Ronald, 65
Lewis, Saunders, 153
Liberal Democrats, 202
Liberal Party: election (1906), 211; Marconi Affair, 209; First World War, 55–6; Orpington victory, 126; election (1974), 168; Lib-Lab pact, 171, 172; Liberal Alliance, 196; Liberal Democrats, 202
Liddell Hart, Basil, 65
Life and Death of Colonel Blimp, The, 69
Listener, 109
Lloyd, Selwyn, 104–5, 114, 126
Lloyd George, David, 14, 154
local authorities: health care, 6, 81; compulsory purchase powers, 66; housing, 83, 108, 199; education, 151, 202, 207; control of spending, 197; council house sales, 199; replaced by central government, 215
Longford, Lord, 135
Low (cartoonist), 110
Lynk, Ray, 201, 206

Lynn, Vera, 25
Lyons, F.S.L., 122

Maastricht Treaty, 208
McDougall, Donald, 136
McGonigle, Dr G.C.M., 7
Macmillan, Harold: housing policy, 107–8; party leadership, 115; government, 118, 123–31, 186; immigration legislation, 118; image, 123; defence policy, 123–5; foreign policy, 144; 'night of the long knives', 126; public sector pay pause, 126–7; European policy, 127–8; Profumo affair, 128–9, 209; resignation, 129–30; successor, 131
McNamara, Robert, 125, 143
Maginot Line, 28
mail-order sales, 119
Major, John, 191, 193, 203–8, 210–11, 216
Manchester Guardian, 110
Marconi Affair, 209
Markham, Violet, 109
Marshall Aid, 89, 100
Mass-Observation, 23
maternal mortality, 6
Maudling, Reginald, 136
Medium-Term Financial Strategy (MTFS), 193, 194, 200
Merrill, Robert, 143
Messina Conference (1955), 127
Methven, Sir John, 182
middle class: lifestyle (1930s), 13–14; wartime effects, 57; NHS benefits, 94, 95; youth protest, 156–7; Tory militancy (1970s), 187–9
Miles, Bernard, 40
Miller, Max, 162
Mills, John, 40
miners' strikes: (1971–72), 167, 180; (1974), 168, 180; (1984–85), 201
Mitford, Nancy, 112–13
Mitterrand, François, 191
modernization, 97–9, 100, 131, 138
Monckton, Walter, 104
Monday Club, 184
monetarism, 192, 193
Morrison, Herbert, 46–8

mortality rates (1930s), 6, 7–8, 22; wartime, 33
mortgages, 120
Mosley, Oswald, 14, 63
motor industry, growth (1930s), 4, see also cars
motorbikes, 1, 5
Mount, Ferdinand, 216
Mr Churchill's Declaration of Policy to the Electors, 73
Muggeridge, Malcolm, 113, 116
Munich agreement, 18, 20, 55, 73
Mussolini, Benito, 61, 62, 63

Nasser, Gamal Abdel, 113–14
National Assistance, 94
National Assistance Act (1948), 82
National Coal Board, 80, 167, 168, 201
National Economic Development Office, 203
National Health Service (NHS), creation, 44, 81, 87; funding, 81, 92; standards of health care, 93–4; expenditure (1950s), 108; reorganization, 207; public opinion, 215
National Health Service Act (1946), 73, 87
National Industrial Relations Court, 166, 167
National Insurance: Beveridge Report, 43–4, 82; creation of system, 81–2; flat-rate contributions, 44, 82, 95; benefit levels, 82; women, 96; contributions raised, 197
National Insurance Act (1946), 73, 81–2
National Lottery, 12
National Plan, 139
National Theatre Company, 150
National Unemployed Workers' Movement (NUWM), 21, 22
National Union of Miners, 201
nationalization: postwar Labour programme, 49, 77–8, 90, 91, 97, 99; Churchill's attitude, 70; left-wing Labour proposals (1970s), 169; see also denationalization
NATO, creation, 143
New Look, 88
New Society, 176

New Statesman, 109, 160
Nixon, Richard M., 144
Nolan inquiry, 209–10
Norgay, Tenzing, 110
North Sea oil, 171–2, 193, 198, 217
Northern Ireland: Coronation celebrations, 109; position of Catholics, 122–3; civil rights campaign, 154–5, 156; Callaghan's policy, 155, 158, 161; Bloody Sunday, 156
Norton Villiers Triumph, 170
Notting Hill riots, 116–17
nuclear power industry, privatization, 207
Nuclear Test Ban Treaty (1963), 129
nuclear weapons: atomic bomb, 105; Korean War, 111; Labour policy, 111, 124, 134; Britain's independent nuclear deterrent, 124–5, 143; CND, 124; Test Ban Treaty, 129; Thatcher policy, 216
nurseries, 96

OFGAS, 203
OFSTED, 207
OFTEL, 203
OFWAT, 203
oil: embargo (1967), 141; price shock (1973), 168, 174; North Sea, 171–2, 193, 198, 217
Olympic Games, 19
Open University, 151, 161
opinion polls: wartime, 44, 69; (1950s), 118, 120–1; (1960s), 129; (1970), 160; (1976–78), 176; trade union members, 178–9; (1979), 198; British Social Attitudes, 215
Organization for Economic Co- operation and Development (OECD), 213
Orpington by-election (1962), 126
Orwell, George, 31
Owen, David, 196, 202

Paisley, Ian, 155
Parker, Hugh, 181
pawn shops, 12
pensions, 82, 198
permissiveness, 132, 149, 157
petrol rationing, 88
Physical Training and Recreation Act, 7
picketing, 197

Picture Post, 2, 42
Plaid Cymru, 153, *see also* Welsh Nationalists
planning, 77, 78, 84–5, 138–9
Polaris, 125, 156
police, 201, 207
politics, interest in, 23, 106–7
poll tax, 202, 203–4, 205
polytechnics, 151, 187
Portillo, Michael, 211
Post Office Savings Bank, 11
Potter, Dennis, 115
pottery workers, unemployment, 2
poverty, 3, 21, 97
Powell, Enoch, 152–3
Prices and Incomes Board, 165
Prior, James, 193
prisons, 207
Private Eye, 135, 188
privatization, 192, 198–9, 202–3
productivity, 85, 98–9, 193–4, 214
Profumo, John, 128–9, 209
proportional representation, 212
Prytz, Bjorn, 62
public expenditure: (1970s), 158, 175; (1980s), 197, 198
public houses, 5
public sector: pay, 126, 192; employment, 142
Punch, 18, 188
Pym, Francis, 193

quangos, 203, 209
Quant, Mary, 149
queuing, 88

race relations: wartime, 36, 39–40; Notting Hill riots, 116–17; (1950s), 117–18; immigration legislation (1962), 118; discrimination, 122; Wilson era, 134, 149–51; East African Asians, 152; Commonwealth immigrants Bill (1968), 152; violence, 153; racial equality legislation, 175
Race Relations Board, 152
radio (1930s), 4–5
rationing, 33, 57, 84, 88, 103–4
Reagan, Ronald, 194, 195, 216

rearmament: (1930s), 16, 19; Korean War, 92–3, 99

recession: (1979–82), 193, 194, 205, 213; (1990s), 205, 213

redundancy legislation, 175

Redwood, John, 208

refrigerators, 112, 119, 122

regional differences: unemployment (1930s), 2, 14, 21; new industries (1930s), 4; mortality rates (1930s), 6, 7–8; government policy (1930s), 15–16; political allegiances, (1930s), 22; political allegiances (1950), 91; political allegiances (1979), 192; recession (1979–82), 194–5; unemployment (1980s), 200; unemployment (1990s), 205

Rent Act (1957), 108

Reynaud, Pierre, 61

Rhodesia, 145–7

Rice-Davies, Mandy, 128

Richardson, Jo, 175

Ridley, Nicholas, 203

Rifkind, Malcolm, 211

Right Approach to the Economy, The, 183

road-haulage, denationalization, 103

Road to Serfdom, The, 47, 193

Robbins Report, 150

Rodgers, William, 196

Rolls-Royce, 166, 194, 199

Rome, Treaty of, 127

Rommel, Erwin, 42, 57

Roosevelt, Franklin D., 56, 133

Roskill, Stephen, 65

Ross, Alan, 112, 113

Ross, Willie, 132

Rostow, Walt, 144

Rowntree, Seebohm, 3, 97

Royal Air Force, 19, 30

Royal Navy, 28, 41, 125

Royal Ulster Constabulary (RUC), 109, 155

salaries (1930s), 4

Salisbury, Lord, 115

Sampson, Anthony, 130

Saturday Evening Post, 116

savings (1930s), 5, 11–12

Scandal 63, 129

Scanlon, Hugh, 152

Scargill, Arthur, 188, 201

Scarman, Lord, 155

Schmidt, Helmut, 149

school: dinners, 7; milk, 7; leaving age, 9; building programme, 87; curriculum, 202; management, 207; inspection, 207; *see also* education

Scotland: nationalism, 153–4, 160; poll tax, 203; devolution, 161, 212

Scott inquiry, 209

Scottish Daily News, 170

Scottish Insurance Corporation, 122

Scottish Nationalists, 153–4, 160

seamen's strikes: (1966), 139; (1976), 170

Second World War, 25, 50

secondary modern schools, 101

Selective Employment Tax, 139

self-employed, unemployment (1930s), 2

Sex Discrimination Act (1975), 175

Shanks, Michael, 130

Shinwell, Emmanuel, 67, 83

shipbuilding industry: unemployment, 2; wartime, 38

shopping facilities, 96

Shore, Peter, 139

Silkin, Lewis, 66

Silverman, Sydney, 150

Simpson, Wallis, 23

Single European Act, 202

Six-Day War (1967), 141

Skybolt, 125, 128

sleaze, 193, 208–10

slum-clearance, 8, 108

Smith, Ian, 145–6

Smith, John, 210

Social Chapter, 208

social contract, 174

Social Democratic Party (SDP), 196, 202

Social Insurance and Allied Services, 43, 72

social services, expenditure (1950s), 107

socialism, 57, 78, 99, 132, 134, 185

Socialist Commentary, 121

Soros, George, 206

South Africa, Wilson policy, 134, 145

sovereignty, 202

Soviet Union (USSR): British policy

towards, 17, 19, 56; Nazi pact, 19;
Stalingrad (1942), 42; Conservative policy
towards, 56; control of Eastern Europe,
75; Hungary invasion, 114
Spanish Civil War, 18
Special Areas Act (1934), 15
spectacles, 93–4
Spectator, 185
sport, football pools, 11, 12
Stagnant Society, The, 130
Stalin, Joseph, 56, 106
state, role of, 215–16
Steel, David, 150
steel industry: nationalization, 90;
denationalization, 103
Sterling Area, 86
Stewart, Michael, 139, 144
Stone, Norman, 173
strikes: General (1926), 54; seamen (1966),
139; dockworkers (1967), 141; (1970s),
163–4, 180–2; dock (1970), 165; miners
(1971–72), 167, 180; miners (1974), 168,
180; seamen (1976), 170; winter of
discontent, 172–3, 182, 183; British
experience, 180–1; causation, 181;
picketing, 197; ballots, 197; miners
(1984–85), 201
Suez crisis (1956), 113–15, 118, 124, 143
sugar: consumption (1930s), 4; 'Mr Cube'
campaign, 91
summit meetings, 106, 111
Sunday Telegraph, 187
Sunday Times, 129
Sydney Morning Herald, 59

Tatchell, Peter, 201
Tate and Lyle, 91
Taverner, Jane, 9
taxation: income tax (1930s), 4; import
duties (1930s), 15; wartime, 33, 57; NHS
funding, 81; welfare funding, 95; income
tax (postwar), 95; Capital Gains Tax, 137;
Corporation Tax, 137; Selective
Employment Tax, 139; income tax (1970),
165; Labour policy, 187; (1979), 197;
Thatcher policy, 197; income tax
reduction (1988), 202; Major government

rises, 208
Taylor, A.J.P., 26, 53
Taylor, Robert, 178
Tebbit, Norman, 1–2
technical schools, 9, 10, 101
technology, 134, 138, 139
telephone, 13
television sets, 112, 119, 122
textile industry: unemployment (1930s), 2;
man-made fibres (1930s), 4; (1980s), 193
Thatcher, Margaret: on wartime
government, 26–7; on Beveridge, 44;
leadership election (1975), 182–3;
industrial relations policy, 183–4, 197–8;
election (1979), 184–5, 186, 191–2;
saviour of middle class, 189–90;
governments, 191–204, 210, 211, 212;
monetary policies, 193–4; Westland
Affair, 209; election (1983), 195–6;
privatization, 198–200, 202; deregulation
of capital markets, 200; miners' strike,
201; election (1987), 201–2; role of state,
202–3, 215; poll tax, 203–4; leadership
election (1990), 55, 204; successor, 207;
comparison with Wilson, 162; legacy,
212–17; influence, 173, 211, 216–17;
reputation, 191
Thomas, George, 132, 154
Thomas, Hugh, 130
Times, The, 20, 60, 117, 120, 122, 189
tobacco: consumption (1930s), 4, 11;
taxation (postwar), 95
Town and Country Planning Act, 66
Trade Disputes Act (1927), 70
trade unions: wartime conditions, 37–8;
postwar government relations, 98;
nationalization policy, 99; membership,
104, 178–9; Industrial Relations Bill, 159;
relationship with Labour Party, 161, 187,
210; strikes (1970s), 163; Conservative
Party policy, 166, 183; Industrial
Relations Act (1971), 166; registration,
166; wage restraint policy, 170, 172, 177;
pay bargaining role (1970s), 177;
leadership, 177–9; closed shops, 179;
Thatcher policy, 183–4, 192, 197, 212; pay
policy, 198; exclusion from influence, 203

Trades Union Congress (TUC), 70, 138, 159, 170, 172, 177, 198

Trident missiles, 216

Tynged yr Iaith, 153

U and non-U, 112–13, 130

unemployment: (1930s), 1–3, 6, 14–16, 21, 97; wartime, 37–8; Beveridge report, 44; benefits, 44, 45; election issue (1945), 72, 78; Labour government policy, 77; 1950s level, 112; 1970s rise, 165; Heath's policy, 174; rise (1980s), 193, 197; benefit costs, 197; regional (1980s), 200; in South (1990s), 205; expenditure on, 214–15

unemployment insurance, 21

Union of Democratic Mineworkers (UDM), 201, 206

unions, *see* trade unions

United States of America (USA): wartime involvement, 42; Conservative policy towards, 56, 64; loan, 79, 84, 99; British dependence on, 75, 86–7, 99–100, 137–4, 143–4; Marshall Aid, 89, 100, 143; Korean War, 92, 111; 'special relationship', 100, 114, 125, 142–4; security role, 105, 125, 138, 143; British aid package (1964), 137; Vietnam, 138, 140, 143–4; Federal Reserve Board, 194

universities, 150–1, 156–7, 215

upper class, 13, 112

Upper Clyde Shipbuilders, 166

USSR, *see* Soviet Union

VAT on domestic heating, 208

Vietnam: Wilson policy, 134, 140, 143–4; US expectations, 138; youth protest, 156

voting: regional differences, 22, 91; turnout in general elections, 106–7; extension of franchise, 106, 157; split opposition vote, 201; proportional representation, 212

wages: (1930s), 4, 21; wartime, 37; TUC restraint policy, 170, 172; *see also* incomes policy

Wales: nationalism, 140, 153, 160; devolution, 161, 212

Walker, Sir Walter, 189

Walker-Heneage-Vivian, Rhoda, 13

Wall Street Journal, 163

Walsall by-election (1976), 170

Walters, Alan, 204

washing machines, 112, 119, 122

water industry, privatization, 202

Waugh, Evelyn, 41–2

wealth, distribution of, 11, 169

welfare: benefits (1930s), 4, 21; Beveridge report, 43–7; Labour government programme (1945), 77

welfare state: election issue (1945), 72, 78; legislation, 82; Attlee government's record, 100

Welsh National Opera, 150

Welsh Nationalists, 140, 153, 160

West Indies, wartime immigrants, 40

Westland Affair, 209

Westminster, Statute of (1931), 20

Whitehouse, Mary, 149

Wigg, George, 128, 134

Wilde, Oscar, 150

Williams, Marcia, 134

Williams, Shirley, 196

Wilson, Harold: 'bonfire of controls', 89, 103; leadership election (1963), 128; election (1964), 131, 133; governments (1964–70), 132–62, 174; personality and style, 132–4, 162, 210; cabinet, 135; economic policies, 136–9; US relations, 137–8, 143–4; election (1966), 139; sterling crisis, 140–2, 206; defence policy, 143; Commonwealth policy, 144–8; European policy, 148–9; libertarianism, 149–50; education policy, 150–1; race relations, 151–3; Scottish and Welsh nationalism, 153–4; Northern Ireland policy, 154–6; industrial relations policy, 158–9; election (1970), 160, 164; elections (1974), 168–9; government (1974–75), 169–70; retirement, 170; honours list, 209

Wodehouse, P.G., 188

women: unemployment (1930s), 2; health (1930s), 6–7; wartime work, 38–9; responses to postwar rationing, 88–9; welfare state effects, 95–6; employment (postwar), 96; rights legislation, 175

Women's Institutes, 15
Women's Land Army, 40
Wood, Deirdre, 201–2
Wood, Sir Kingsley, 45
Wootton Committee, 157
working class: lifestyle (1930s), 12; taxation (postwar), 95; affluence (1950s), 121;

response to Suez, 115, 130

Yalta agreement, 56
Yom Kippur War (1973), 168
York, poverty, 3, 97
Yorke, Peter, 187–8
young people: (1950s), 106; (1960s), 156–7

750
850
+e
―――
1100